Charity, Challenge, and Change

**Recent Titles in
Contributions in Women's Studies**

CHARITY, CHALLENGE, AND CHANGE

Religious Dimensions of the Mid-Nineteenth-Century Women's Movement in Germany

Catherine M. Prelinger

Contributions in Women's Studies, Number 75

GREENWOOD PRESS
New York • Westport, Connecticut • London

Library of Congress Cataloging-in-Publication Data

Prelinger, Catherine M.
   Charity, challenge, and change.

   (Contributions in women's studies, ISSN 0147–104X ;
no. 75)
   Bibliography: p.
   Includes index.
   1. Feminism—Germany—History—19th century.
2. Feminism—Religious aspects—History—19th century.
3. Women—Education—Germany—History—19th century.
4. Voluntarism—Germany—History—19th century.
5. Church charities—Germany—History—19th century.
6. Germany—Church history—19th century. I. Title.
II. Series.
HQ1626.P74 1987   305.4′2′0943   86–19432
ISBN 0–313–25401–X (lib. bdg. : alk. paper)

Library of Congress Catalog Card Number: 86–19432
ISBN: 0–313–25401–X
ISSN: 0147–104X

First published in 1987

Greenwood Press, Inc.
88 Post Road West, Westport, Connecticut 06881

Printed in the United States of America

The paper used in this book complies with the
Permanent Paper Standard issued by the National
Information Standards Organization (Z39.48–1984).

10 9 8 7 6 5 4 3 2 1

Copyright Acknowledgment

Chapter 2: Benevolent Visiting: Feminized Philanthropy in the Service of Or-
thodoxy, is a revised and expanded version of an earlier essay, "Prelude to
Consciousness: Amalie Sieveking and the Female Association for the Care of
the Poor and Sick," which appeared in *German Women in the Nineteenth Century:
A Social History*, edited by John C. Fout, Holmes & Meier Publishers, Inc., New
York, N.Y., 1984.

For
Ernst

Contents

Preface

This book had its genesis in my long-standing interest in the radical religious movements of the 1840s in Germany and the relationship of those religious movements with the women's movement of the period. From a political perspective, the women's movement was a facet of the revolution in Germany of 1848–49, particularly in its late and radical period. From a religious perspective, the women's movement was a phase in the older and broader development of voluntary and professional roles for women in philanthrophy and related enterprises, one shaped and influenced by the premises of contemporary religious radicalism, and one that has not been previously analyzed.[1] By religious radicalism I have in mind primarily the ideas and institutions associated with German-Catholicism and related independent congregations that aimed at an assimilation of Protestants, Catholics, and Jews in acknowledging the immanence of God. The feminist agenda of the religious radicals was very specific, at least as it was voiced by its most prominent spokesperson: it summoned women to enter the field of charity and to transform it into one of social reform, to feminize and deconfessionalize early childhood education, and to secularize and expand women's higher education so that women could accomplish these goals. Changes in the nature of the family and woman's place in it were obviously implicit.

This agenda, I argue, was formulated in response to two historic circumstances peculiar to the German situation. One was the long denial of public roles for women within the tradition of German Protestantism, as well as the unavailability of similar roles for Catholic women—conditions which were reinforced by German secular culture. The other was the energetic and very effective entrance of conservative women into the philanthropic arena under the inspiration of the Protestant Awakening. The 1848 revolution and the concomitant women's movement created the opportunity for religious radicals to appeal to a broader constituency; because of an ambivalence toward political activity by women, feminists of the period found their agenda enormously appealing. It also, however, threatened the hegemony of orthodox women in the newly feminized areas of charity: benevolent visiting, children's welfare and early childhood education, and nursing. The intensity and quality of their opposition articulated particularly in the person of their major female leader Amalie Sieveking, a member of the Hamburg patriciate, reveals a sense of vulnerability derived from the relative novelty of Protestant female philanthropy. Sieveking and her peers responded to the post-revolutionary reaction by emphasizing the compatibility of their efforts with the old order. Representatives of reaction within the church and the state in turn marshalled their resources to extinguish religious as well as political manifestations of feminism. They did this partly by outright repression, but also partly by trying to divert the appeal of feminist initiatives into the support and expansion of alternative channels of service for women, building on the experience of charitable institutions earlier in the century. In this sense, the women's movement of the revolution had a permanent, albeit unintended, effect on the development of women's philanthropy in Germany.

The discussion opens with a historical account of the exclusion of women from public roles in the churches, the secular reinforcement of this tradition, and its reversal in the nineteenth century under ecclesiastical auspices. It goes on to examine the nature of the challenge initiated by orthodox women to create a charitable realm for themselves as volunteers. Here I seek to identify both what was innovative in this initiative as well as what ultimately permitted the ready cooperation with reaction. Earlier scholars, looking at the Female Association for the Care of the Poor and Sick, the institution that introduced the Protestant female laity to philanthropic activity, have failed to recognize the extent to which the organization was a national one, one that extended to many cities besides Hamburg. The association itself has been considered a monument to the life of Amalie Sieveking, an exceptional woman in a line of male philanthropists. I try to claim the association as a legacy for the history of women, one with an ambivalent relationship to the history of feminism.

The central concern of this study is an analysis of the feminist agenda originating among the women sympathizers of the German-Catholic—or free—congregation in Hamburg, the ultimate nationalization of this agenda, and the effort at a collaborative alliance between religious and political feminism. I myself have discussed the women's college in Hamburg (*Hamburger Hochschule fuer das weibliche Geschlecht*) in an earlier article but I did not at that time appreciate the nature of the network of which the college was only a segment.[2] At its height, this network included kindergartens, primary schools, and a great variety of charitable activities. These projects fell victim to the reaction; for this reason the lives and aspirations of their members are little known to us. An overview of the reaction which concludes the study illuminates the process by which orthodox charities tried to coopt the appeal of the revolutionary movement. It also suggests that loss of independence was the price orthodox women and their organizations paid for their collaboration.

Looking at mid-nineteenth-century feminism from the perspective of its religious orientation raises some longer-range interpretive questions. One relates to the apparent conservativism of the bourgeois women's movement at the end of the century. This movement claimed roots in the revolutionary period. Through the leadership of Louise Otto, whose career as a journalist and social novelist bridged both eras, the two movements were linked. In his *Feminist Movement in Germany 1894–1933*, Richard J. Evans, the most prolific writer on nineteenth-century German feminism whether in German or English, amply if not always sympathetically demonstrates the commingling of moral and political goals which late-nineteenth-century bourgeois feminism conspicuously displayed. He contrasts this quality with what he believes was a more purely political commitment by the movement in its initial phase.[3] The material presented here from my research suggests that religion penetrated politics from the start, that in fact religion predominated because it seemed to offer a more viable strategy for addressing the distinctive concerns of women. Barbara Greven-Aschoff's beautifully articulated book, *Die buergerliche Frauenbewegung in Deutschland 1894–1933*, supercedes Evans' work.[4] She argues that precisely the distinctive ethical and educational concerns of bourgeois feminism, anchored as they were in the social diversity of imperial and Weimar Germany, precluded uniform political action within the existing party structure. This was a structure from which women were largely excluded as well as one to which many of them felt morally superior. Greven-Aschoff nevertheless locates the roots of bourgeois feminism in the natural rights ideology that informed the political revolution of 1848. The religious radicalism that so many progressive women of the revolutionary period embraced, however, seems to me a more plausible explanation of the link between the earlier and later women's movements.

The evidence of this book should also add to the continuing dialogue about "woman's nature." A number of German feminist historians have illuminated the devastating effect on working-class and middle-class women alike of the emergence of the bourgeois family and the concomitant philosophic distinction between the nature of the sexes. A theoretical discourse creating the ground for the concept of woman's nature developed as early as the final decades of the eighteenth century. What is commonly overlooked is that women collaborated in creating this concept. Feminists of the mid-century elaborated an ideology of woman's nature in their belief that it would legitimate a sphere beyond the reach of both traditional religion and patriarchal control. Whatever the merits or illusions of this stance, it is one that must be examined both as a facet of religious sectarianism and as a feminist strategy in the 1840s. Within the context of inter-confessional charity the concept of woman's nature appeared as an alternative to, not a reinforcement of, Christianity, and it was invoked by women who considered the patriarchal family with its Christian ethos far more constraining than the bourgeois family. The tyranny of woman's nature, so poignantly documented in the scholarship of Ute Gerhard, Barbara Duden, and Karin Hausen,[5] must be viewed against the tyranny of orthodoxy that women themselves were trying to dislodge.

The cultivation of a female consciousness, one embracing the ethos of motherhood within the doctrine of woman's nature on the part of German women, resonates with the much more vibrant development of women's roles in the United States. Mary Ryan's "empire of mothers" and Nancy F. Cott's *The Bonds of Womanhood* capture the emotional texture of American domesticity, which allowed women a virtual hegemony in the home and ultimately extended to charity and church.[6] German women never even approached this dubious exercise of power.

Autonomy in the domestic sphere ultimately eluded them. Their admission to the public sphere as philanthropists and educators was increasingly circumscribed by the imposition of male control and the priorities of state and church. "Spiritual Motherhood," as Ann Taylor Allen has described the Froebel revival in imperial Germany, was intended to regenerate society by introducing order and community to working-class children under the auspices of middle-class women. In their role as social purveyors of nurture and discipline, however, these women acted as agents of society. They neither created a new social agenda nor could their activity translate into familial power. A companion piece by James Albisetti suggests the constancy of bourgeois women in the cause of higher education for women. Their often stubborn persistence reflected the unyielding attitude of a state determined to resist demands long since met in the United States through the seven sister colleges.[7] The concept of national feminism, which Amy Hackett has examined, ultimately permitted German women to work for the attainment of suffrage. Uneasy with the doctrine of "rights," the bourgeois women's movement equated the social services they rendered with the military service required of men, service which presumably entitled men to vote.[8] American women demanded the vote as a right. To American women, the function of the state was one of service to its constituents; the reverse was true for German women. The concept of female service, indeed sacrifice, that was embedded in the German suffrage campaign acted to legitimate a permanent division of relationships to the state along gender lines. This book focuses on the earlier, less familiar mid-century period where some of the proclivities of German feminism had their origin, but where guidance from the work of other scholars is minimal. I have not systematically compared or contrasted American and British experience but some comparisons are inevitable and others will suggest themselves to the reader.

Of necessity the scope of this book is limited. When I first started my research, my task was largely one of discovery and reclamation. The first two volumes of Louise Otto's *Frauen-Zeitung* were available only in the German Democratic Republic. Since then, that newspaper has been photocopied in full and published in excerpts.[9] Ruth-Ellen B. Joeres has published a fine selection of Otto's writings incorporated in a biographical essay; Maria Wagner and Stanley Zucker respectively have made the work of Mathilde Franziska Anneke and Kathinka Zitz-Halein accessible to a wide audience.[10] War damage accounts for the occasionally modest yield of some of my own archival visits; more serious is the absence of archival material from Breslau and Koenigsberg, to which I had no access.

The nature of material available to the student of women in mid-century Germany shapes the issues one can address. A singular advantage I have found in looking at this period from the perspective of religion is the clarity with which women's issues, such as marriage, divorce, child-bearing and rearing, and friendship, emerge. This approach has also uncovered a significant number of unfamiliar women whose centrality to mid-nineteenth-century feminism can now be established. Within the quasi-religious organizations these women founded, their distinctive styles of leadership and association are highly visible. The great fluidity of class boundaries among them also becomes apparent. For while the bourgeois women's movement of the later century certainly had its antecedents here, neither in composition nor attitude can the earlier movement be adequately encompassed in the term "bourgeois." The discourse of the period, particularly its controversy, was transacted very largely in religious terms, by men as well as women.

Among the women I have investigated there was no firm dichotomy between personal and public lives; because ethical values permeated their thinking, personal and public fell along a single continuum. Richard Evans argues that feminists of the nineteenth century sacrificed what he calls "personal fulfillment" in the service of a greater cause. His argument is a logical corollary to his restrictive definition of "feminist" as a person committed to "the doctrine of equal rights for women, based on a theory of the equality of the sexes."[11] My own understanding of the meaning cannot improve on the statement by Marion A. Kaplan:

> To appreciate women as an active force in history, feminism ought not to be defined merely as an attempt to gain suffrage or legal equality; students of history must look for women's achievements and appraise their lives in a far broader context. Furthermore, an understanding of the variety of ideas and methods with which women tried to gain more control over the making of their own history suggests to us that feminism is a process rather than an ideology. While recognizable over time, it assumes different forms and expresses different historical goals.[12]

There are two other definitional points I should address briefly. I have used the term "progressive," particularly with respect to women, in the most general and inclusive sense of the word, much as conventional histories of the period adopt the concept "party of movement" when neither "liberal" nor "radical" is quite accurate. I have also used the term "inter-confessional"; the American equivalent might be "inter-denominational." Europeans are rightly sensitive to the term "denomination," which has no equivalent on the continent; the commitment to a confession is what distinguishes a religious affiliation.

In the course of my work on this book, I have incurred many debts. To the German Academic Exchange Service (DAAD), the American Philosophical Society, and the National Endowment for the Humanities, I am grateful for stipends which supported my research. To Dr. Kurt Sieveking I am obliged for permission to use the papers of Amalie Sieveking in the Hamburg Staatsarchiv. Successive archivists in Hamburg, particularly Drs. Plog and Schneider, were exceedingly helpful with materials on the wider circle of Hamburg women. The administrator as well as the Friends of the Pestalozzi-Froebel Verband were supportive and generous during my Berlin stay in 1978; so were the librarians at the library of the Inner Mission. I am also grateful to Sr. Ruth Felgentreff of the Fachbuecherei fuer Frauendiakonie in Kaiserswerth.

Janet W. James and Joan W. Scott gave careful and suggestive readings to this manuscript in an earlier form. Their critique was invaluable. So were comments from Amy Hackett, Jean H. Quataert, and Stanley Zucker. I owe a more diffuse debt to my friends and sister historians in the Berkshire Conference of Women Historians. Both at our annual meetings and at the large conferences on the history of women, this group has been a perpetual source of stimulation, support, and colleagiality to me. To the Research Associates and Visiting Lecturers in Women's Studies at the Harvard Divinity School, 1982–83, of which I was privileged to be a member, I want to express a similar indebtedness.

I am grateful to Alice Christensen for typing the first draft of this book as well as for her patience. To Ernst Prelinger I am indebted for a great many things, but his assistance with word processing and printing deserves particular thanks.

NOTES

1. For example, Christoph Sachsse and Florian Tennstedt, *Geschichte der Armenfuersorge in Deutschland vom Spaetmittelalter bis zum Ersten Weltkrieg* (Stuttgart, Berlin, Cologne, Mainz: W. Kohlhammer, 1980), pp. 233–35, deals with the subject only tangentially in the later century.

2. Catherine M. Prelinger, "Religious Dissent, Women's Rights and the Hamburger Hochschule fuer das weibliche Geschlecht in Mid-Nineteenth-Century Germany," *Church History* 45 (1976): 42–55.

3. Richard J. Evans, *The Feminist Movement in Germany 1894–1933* (London and Beverly Hills: SAGE Publications, 1976).

4. Barbara Greven-Aschoff, *Die buergerliche Frauenbewegung in Deutschland 1894–1933* (Goettingen: Vanderhoeck und Rupprecht, 1981).

5. Ute Gerhard, *Verhaeltnissse und Verhinderungen: Frauenarbeit, Familie und Rechte der Frauen im 19. Jahrhundert. Mit Dokumenten* (Frankfurt a.M.: Suhrkamp Verlag, 1978); Barbara Duden, "Das schoene Eigentum. Zur Herausbildung des buergerlichen Frauenbildes an der Wende vom 18. zum 19. Jahrhundert," *Kursbuch* 47 (March 1977): 125–42;

Karin Hausen, "Family and Role-Division: The Polarisation of Sexual Stereotypes in the Nineteenth Century—An Aspect of the Dissociation of Work and Family Life," *The German Family. Essays on the Social History of the Family in Nineteenth- and Twentieth-Century Germany*, ed. Richard J. Evans and W. R. Lee (London: Croom Helm; Totowa, N.J.: Barnes and Noble, 1981), pp. 51–83.

6. Mary P. Ryan, *The Empire of the Mother: American Writing about Domesticity 1830–1860* (New York: Institute for Research in History and Haworth Press, 1982); Nancy F. Cott, *The Bonds of Womanhood: "Woman's Sphere" in New England, 1780–1835* (New Haven and London: Yale University Press, 1977); Ann Douglas, *The Feminization of American Culture* (New York: Alfred A. Knopf, 1977).

7. Ann Taylor Allen, "Spiritual Motherhood: German Feminists and the Kindergarten Movement, 1848–1911," *History of Education Quarterly* 22 (Fall 1982): 319–39; James Albisetti, "Could Separate be Equal? Helene Lange and Women's Education in Imperial Germany," ibid., pp. 301–18.

8. Amy K. Hackett, "The German Women's Movement and Suffrage, 1890–1914. A Study of National Feminism," *Modern European Social History*, ed. Robert J. Bezucha (Lexington, Mass., Toronto, London: D. C. Heath, 1971): 354–86. *See also* Greven-Aschoff, *Die buergerliche Frauenbewegung* cited above.

9. Ute Gerhard, Elisabeth Hannover-Drueck, Romina Schmitter, eds., *"Dem Reich der Freiheit werb' ich Buergerinnen." Die Frauenzeitung von Louise Otto* (Frankfurt a.M.: Syndikat, 1979).

10. Ruth-Ellen Boetcher Joeres, ed., *Die Anfaenge der deutschen Frauenbewegung: Louise Otto-Peters* (Frankfurt a.M.: Fischer Taschenbuchverlag, 1983); idem, "Louise Otto and her Journals: A Chapter in Nineteenth-Century German Feminism," *Internationales Archiv fuer Sozialgeschichte der deutschen Literatur* 4 (1979): 100–129; Maria Wagner, ed., *Mathilde Franziska Anneke in Selbstzeugnissen und Dokumenten* (Frankfurt a.M.: Fischer Taschenbuch Verlag, 1980); Stanley Zucker, "Female Political Opposition in Pre-1848 Germany. The Role of Kathinka Zitz-Halein," *German Women in the Nineteenth Century: A Social History*, ed. John C. Fout (New York and London: Holmes and Meier, 1984), pp. 133–50.

11. Evans, "Women's History: The Limits of Reclamation," *Social History* 5 (May 1980): 276; idem, *The Feminists. Women's Emancipation Movements in Europe, America and Australasia 1840–1920* (London: Croom Helm; New York: Barnes and Noble, 1977), p. 39.

12. Marion A. Kaplan, *The Jewish Feminist Movement in Germany. The Campaigns of the Juedischer Frauenbund, 1904–1938* (Westport, Conn. and London: Greenwood Press, 1979), p. 7.

Abbreviations

ARCHIVES

FlAr	Fachbuecherei fuer Frauendiakonie und Fliednerarchiv
GlAr Krlsr	Generallandesarchiv Karlsruhe
H HstAr W	Hessisches Hauptstaatsarchiv Wiesbaden
PFVAr	Pestalozzi-Froebel Verband Archiv
StAr D	Staatsarchiv Dresden
StAr Dmst	Staatsarchiv Darmstadt
StAr Hlbg	Stadtarchiv Heidelberg
StAr Hmbg	Staatsarchiv Hamburg
StAr Mainz	Stadtarchiv Mainz

PUBLICATIONS, ORGANIZATIONS, AND COLLECTIONS

AKZ	*Allgemeine Kirchen-Zeitung*
AuKF	*Der Armen- und Krankenfreund. Eine Zeitschrift fuer die Diakonie der evangelischen Kirche*
BAKZ	*Berliner Allgemeine Kirchenzeitung*
FCL	*Fuer christkatholisches Leben. Materialien zur Geschichte der christkatholischen Kirche*

FVUA, [1.-8.] Jahres-Bericht	*[Erster- Achter] Jahres-Bericht des Frauen-Vereins zur Unterstuetzung der Armenpflege*
FZ	*Frauen-Zeitung; Frauen-Zeitung fuer die hoeheren weiblichen Interessen*
Nls AWS	Schriftlicher Nachlass von Amalie Wilhelmine Sieveking
Nls EW	Emilie Wuestenfelds Nachlass
WVAK, [1.–25.] Bericht	*[Erster-Fuenfundzwanzigster] Bericht ueber die Leistungen des weiblichen Vereins fuer Armen- und Krankenpflege*
ZVHG	*Zeitschrift des Vereins fuer Hamburgische Geschichte*

Charity, Challenge, and Change

CHAPTER 1

Protestant Philanthropy: A Male Preserve Admits Women

"This voluntary effort of Christian women is one of the most distinctive evidences of social regeneration of our times,"[1] proclaimed the clergyman Johann Hinrich Wichern in 1847; as founder of the Inner Mission, Wichern became the most prominent leader of Protestant charity in Germany. The same year, Louise Otto wrote for the radical *News of the Saxon Fatherland* (*Saechsische Vaterlandsblaetter*): "It is above all the religious movement to which we are indebted for the rapid advance of female participation in the issues of the times."[2] Otto was already launched on the career of social advocacy that made her a principal feminist of the German revolution of 1848. The two contemporaries agreed on virtually nothing—Otto called the Rauhe Haus, Wichern's home for delinquent boys, the *graue Haus*, the gray house—but their agreement that a new era commenced with the entrance of women into the public sphere as religious activists suggests that some historic course had been altered.

The exclusion of women from public roles in the church was well entrenched. The widespread collaboration of women in Christian charity as it had so richly unfolded in the Catholic countries of western Europe had no counterpart in Protestant— or even Catholic—Germany. This deficit persisted into the early nineteenth century, distinguishing Germany from, for instance, England where women exercised substantial power in public charity by their presence and their wealth. The degree of novelty surrounding the assimilation of Protestant women into German charitable enterprise can perhaps best be measured by reference to the King of Prussia, Frederick William IV, and his initial reluctance to staff Bethanien, the hospital he founded in Berlin in 1845, with nursing deaconesses. He proposed instead to revive the Order of the Swan, a benevolent male foundation of the Reformation![3] An explanation must be sought in the original character of German Protestantism as well as in the more recent religious and secular past.

THE LUTHERAN TRADITION

Women's emergence in charity after their long absence developed within an ecclesiastical and political context modified by a series of social and demographic upheavals, no one of which alone accounts for the change. Women's experience occasionally shared the generality of historic experience; more often it was distinctively determined by gender. The absence of a tradition of female philanthropy was intrinsic to the very nature of Lutheranism. Martin Luther (1483–1546) himself cast out the role of good works from the process of Christian redemption and placed the entire burden of salvation on the faith of the individual believer who, in turn, was deemed without merit until God extended the gift of faith through grace. The repudiation of celibacy on Luther's part and the subsequent dissolution of celibate orders eliminated the very institutions where the charitable dimension of Christianity had been practiced. With respect both to good works and to celibacy, Luther was at least evenhanded in his attitude toward female and male believers.

Gender distinctions assumed a distinctive importance in the impact of Luther's concept of the centrality of the family. The significance of marriage and the family to Luther's system of belief can hardly be exaggerated. The doctrine of the priesthood of all believers and the emphasis upon Scripture, which Luther's translation made available to the laity, constituted an essential modification of the role of the visible church and meant that the family became the focus of many functions previously identified with the church. The educative responsibility of the family was paramount, particularly in the initial stages of the Reformation, as a vehicle for enacting change and a means of implementing the Lutheran vernacular in religious practice. The mother, no less than the father, assumed an obligation to read and interpret the Scriptures within the family and to instruct its members in the catechism. Education for Luther largely preempted the role of charity as the principal mode of Christian activity. Where the differentiation between genders and the subjection of woman to man found its particular expression in Lutheranism was in the institution of clerical marriage. For Luther's insistence on the marriage of the clergy was intended not only to eradicate the ideal of celibacy but to serve a didactic function for marriages in general. There is a whole literature on the wife of the pastor. She was viewed both as a partner and as an obedient subordinate to her spouse in his Christian calling. To her fell the multitudinous tasks of parochial charity but the less important ones: she might visit the sick of the parish but her husband administered the eucharist to the dying. The earliest speculations about restoring the scriptural office of deaconess in the nineteenth-century German state church commonly used the pastor's wife as a model for what the deaconess might be expected to do.[4] The clerical marriage came to absorb the function of charity to itself and in this sense acted as a deterrent to serious charity by lay women at the same time that it served as their model. But the model offered was that of the wife assisting the husband in his vocation, whatever that might be, not of the woman carrying out charitable functions in the community.

There was also another very fundamental deterrent to female activity within Luther's theology. That was the central position of the Word of God enunciated in church by the male clergy. The enhancement of preaching severely reduced the role of women not only in charity but in all visible and public aspects of congregational life.[5]

The Reformation churches perpetuated these aspects of Luther's work; they also assumed the character of bureaucratic subordination to the state. The doctrine of *cuius regio eius religio* that extended the religion of the ruler to his subjects also transferred significant power over ecclesiastical affairs to the reigning princes, particularly the Protestant princes who owed no allegiance to the papacy. The property and endowments formerly held by Catholic foundations—those institutions once responsible for the administration of a multitude of charitable and educative functions—were absorbed by secular authorities. These resources, where they were not dissipated altogether, became the basis for the secular—particularly municipal—administration of poor relief. Shaped by Luther's own mistrust of charity, this enterprise focused on the elimination of begging. The secession of the Lutheran church from the work of charity carried with it important implications for the role of women. What is more, the contract between church and state was so securely drawn already in Luther's own time that the emergence of a tradition of sectarianism was never a serious possibility in Germany. The spontaneous development of religious alternatives so familiar to British and American experience, alternatives which commonly enhanced the possibility of Christian service for women, was unknown. The Thirty Years War and the growth of despotism in the German states precluded as well the appearance of private initiatives.[6]

By contrast, the advent of Protestantism stimulated a vigorous charitable response in the European Catholic church of the Counter-Reformation. Within the inherited framework women themselves, like the Daughters of Charity and the Ursulines, created ingenious forms of community and distinctive varieties of service. There were virtually no repercussions of these developments in Catholic Germany. A couple of contemplative orders of Sisters of Elizabeth (*Elisabethinerinnen*) survived the Reformation but efforts to install societies of St. Vincent (*Vinzentinerinnen*) were thwarted.[7] As far as foundations were concerned, the Thirty Years War completed the task of the Reformation. Sisters of Charity (*Barmherzige Schwestern*) became the generic name in Germany for all congregations of Catholic women organized around nursing services; their advent was postponed until the nineteenth century.

OTHER GERMAN TRADITIONS

Within German Protestantism the Reformed Church promoted a tradition that differed from Luther's. Its constituents included several vigorous congregations on the lower Rhine and the allegiance of a number of royal houses. Principal among these were the Hohenzollerns of Prussia, although their activities on behalf of the Reformed faith were limited by the very traditionalist Lutheran commitment of their domains. Like Calvinism elsewhere, the Reformed Church in Germany nurtured an activist Christianity; the presbyterial-synodal form of its church polity guaranteed access by the laity to church governance. For a period in the early seventeenth century, women of one of the lower Rhine congregations even ministered to other women in a capacity identified with the scriptural diaconate.[8]

Pietism in the eighteenth century introduced a new spirit into German Christianity. The overriding preoccupation of Pietism was with the problem of sin and individual salvation. The focus was personal experience in religion and the direct, unmediated interaction of the believer with God. Hence the moral quality of life assumed an importance that overshadowed liturgical and doctrinal considerations and worship adopted forms that were spontaneous and non-traditional. Allied to the new humanitarianism of the Enlightenment, the Pietist spirit with its emphasis on practical Christianity provided a strong incentive to philanthropy and to mission. Two of the great philanthropic enterprises of the eighteenth century owed their origins to Pietism: Francke's orphanage at Halle and the municipal poor relief organization in Hamburg organized by Kaspar von Voght (1752–1839). Neither institution offered any role to women, however. At the Pietist community of Herrnhut which the Count von Zinzendorf (1700–1760) sponsored on his estates, originally as a refuge for persecuted Moravians, life itself became an act of worship. Zinzendorf welcomed members of all confessions into his community, Catholics as well as Lutherans and members of the Reformed Church. For this reason, Pietism always represented a separatist threat to the contemporary established churches. Confessional egalitarianism and class egalitarianism at Herrnhut were enlarged to embrace gender egalitarianism as well; the opportunities for practical Christian service implicit in Pietism were extended to include women.[9] The disciplined communal life required of single women at Herrnhut and the custom of arranging marriages by lot, however, meant that the Herrnhut experience did not create a very usable model for women of subsequent generations.

The German Enlightenment produced one vibrant defense of women's public participation: Theodor Gottlieb von Hippel's *On the Civic Improvement of Women* (*Ueber die buergerliche Verbesserung der Weiber*) which appeared in the same year as Mary Wollstonecraft's defense of women's rights (1792). Hippel criticized the constitutions of the French Republic for excluding women from civic rights and called for the full integration of women into public life by means of equal education. He ascribed women's apparent intellectual limitations solely to the inadequacies of their education. Among the Romantics, the institution of the salon, notably in Berlin, created an arena for the exercise of both intellectual and personal emancipation on the part of women such as Rahel Varnhagen (1772–1833) and Bettina von Arnim (1785–1859). The quality of their commitment to creativity and autonomy both in their ideas and in the styles of their lives was unequalled in any other decade of the century.[10] Jewish women played a prominent role in the life of the salon, anticipating the integration of Jews and Christians in the women's movement in the mid-century.

Otherwise public activity by women whether in the guise of charity or not received essentially no legitimation from secular sources. Through most of the early modern period the roles of women as well as those of men had been understood in terms of status and by reference to social and economic function. Karin Hausen has demonstrated a significant change in the language of encyclopedias and handbooks at the close of the eighteenth century.[11] Sex roles were no longer formulated in functional terms; they were anchored rather in nature.

The character or disposition of the sexes assumed the quality of natural endowments. The attributes of women and of men were discussed in the vocabulary of biology and destiny. Fueled by the Enlightenment, a general determination to decode the rational plan of nature penetrated discussion and definitions of the sexes. To decipher the different natural destinies and distinctive talents of the two sexes according to the preordained plan of the universe was the aim. Johann Gottlieb Fichte's examination of natural law (*Grundlage des Naturrechts nach Prinzipien der Wissenschaftslehre*) (1796) created the basis for the ideology of woman's nature that dominated the nineteenth century. It supported differentiation of women's and men's rights and diluted the threat of women's emancipation implicit in the natural rights doctrine of the French Revolution. Fichte ascribed passivity to woman's nature; for women, love and surrender corresponded to the requirements of nature and reason, and consequently demanded the relinquishment of civic personhood and property ownership in marriage. The husband "is his wife's natural representative in the state, and in society as a whole. This is her relationship to society, her public relationship."[12]

THE AWAKENING AND THE WAR OF LIBERATION

The crisis of the Napoleonic invasion invoked a different agenda: Pietism entered the ecclesiastical mainstream. Germany was gripped by the religious Awakening, which swept much of Europe, England, and the United States as well. In Germany, though, it was identified with patriotic resistance to the French. The combined task of defying French cultural domination by renewing the quality of religious life and at the same time specifically resisting the political oppression associated with the French occupation is exemplified in the person of Friedrich Daniel Schleiermacher (1768–1834), Germany's greatest theologian since Luther. Schleiermacher redefined religion in such a way as to permit its integration with modern secular values while at the same time preserving a distinctive and Protestant character. He did so by addressing the human condition directly and referred his listeners to their own feelings and consciousness. He defined religion as "a surrender, a submission to be moved by the whole."[13]

Schleiermacher reached the zenith of his preaching career after Prussia's military defeat at the battle of Jena in 1806. During the occupation of the country by French troops political gatherings were outlawed. The clergy became the spokesmen of national revival, the sermon, the rallying cry of resistance. The War of Liberation (1812–13) was undertaken in the name of

religion and the offensive against Napoleon was interpreted as
the mandate of God. The Minister of Worship wrote at the time:
"We are witnessing God's miracles.... This is the beginning of
a new era."[14]

Women responded to the sense of national emergency and
moral commitment with a variety of collective initiatives. They
organized themselves to care for the injured and founded associations to look after the abandoned victims of battle. By their
personal example, women of the Prussian royal family exiled in
Koenigsberg established a valuable precedent. As soon as the
national emergency abated in 1815, women's organizations disbanded, but the War of Liberation created a legacy that radical
as well as conservative women invoked in later generations.[15]

The charitable involvement of Protestant women, where it
existed at all, receded to the level of auxiliary and parish societies
for specific purposes; their duration and geographic range was
dictated by the task at hand. Schleiermacher himself seems to
have modified his mandate to women. In his *Catechism of Reason
for Gentlewomen* (*Katechismus der Vernunft fuer Edle Frauen*) of 1798
he challenged women to live not in order to obey but "to be and
to become," "to loose the fetters of ignorance," and to reach for
"independence," but in his sermons on marriage twenty years
later he retreated to the theme of obedience and subordination.[16]

REACTION

The liberation of Germany ended not only the participation
of women in public concerns, it also confounded the promise of
political reform nurtured in the years of occupation. Austrian
chancellor Metternich, architect of the peace settlement at the
Congress of Vienna, boasted: "I hope with the help of God to
strike down the German revolution as I have defeated the Con-
queror of Europe."[17] In the thwarted hopes for national unification and constitutional government the seeds of the revolution
of 1848 were sown. The articulated goals of the revolution, the
so-called March demands such as the abolition of feudal obligations, freedom of the press, and the right of association,
reflected at a political level frustrations that originated in the
Metternichean settlement. Metternich maintained order

through a system of rigid censorship and elaborate espionage which extended into the universities.

The promise of military and political reorganization in the Prussian state during the Stein-Hardenberg era gradually eroded. An opponent of the constitutional and national aspirations aroused during the Napoleonic wars, Metternich successfully guaranteed both external and internal security to the old dynasties through the German Confederation, which consisted of the hereditary lands of the Hapsburg Empire centered in Austria, the kingdom of Prussia, four other kingdoms, eighteen duchies, a number of princedoms, and four free city-states.

From the perspective of the religious confessions, what was significant in the Vienna settlement lay in the altered territorial jurisdictions of the restored dynasties. Boundaries of the post–Vienna peace congress no longer embraced populations of the same religious confession as they previously had. The reorganization of political territories in 1815 left only two predominantly Catholic states: Austria and Bavaria. Large numbers of Catholics in the Rhineland became citizens of Protestant Prussia, joining those in Silesia, annexed during the last century. Wuerttemberg and Baden as well as the Protestant states of the North lost their former religious homogeneity. The Vienna settlement thereby destroyed a situation in which the Protestant prince served as head of the church because he was its foremost member; his authority henceforth became an attribute of his secular sovereignty and therefore absolute.[18]

The monarchs who ruled Prussia after the war, Frederick William III (1797–1840) and Frederick William IV, on the throne from 1840–61, unlike Frederick the Great were deeply religious men. They took advantage of their newly acquired power to intervene directly in church affairs, both Catholic and Protestant, a strategy practiced with varying success by the other dynasts as well. The early nineteenth century witnessed the vigorous exercise of secular authority in religion and a reversal of what had been the eighteenth century practice of indifferent toleration.

The Catholic church suffered particularly as a consequence of the peace settlement. Already in 1803 the church was disestablished within the Holy Roman Empire of the German Nation, an act which led to the enforced sale of vast quantities of church territory—96,700 square kilometers according to one account[19] —to the dissolution of orders and foundations, and to a reorganization of the church administration. With the complete demise of the empire under Napoleon in 1806 the autonomous ecclesiastical states disappeared as did offices such as the electoral prince bishoprics. The settlement of Vienna restored neither the property of the church nor the sovereignty of the ecclesiastical territories. But while financial depredations and structural upheaval threatened the very basis of the church's existence, Catholicism entered an era of great intellectual vigor and spiritual regeneration. The religious fervor of the war period stimulated a number of conversions. Catholic scholarship and Catholic propaganda flourished, extending the influence of the church as far north as Protestant Hamburg where members of the intelligentsia and the ruling elite were profoundly moved by the Catholic revival. Vienna and Munich were the centers of spiritual renewal in the South; Mainz, in close association with the church of Alsace, assumed the leadership of Catholicism in the West.[20]

The unprecedented and vigorous expansion of women's charitable orders into Germany from France was an important dimension of the Catholic renascence. Strasbourg in Alsace became the seat of the renewal of Sisters of Charity. They reintroduced their rule, and established a training center and hospital whose vitality made it the model of female religious life for Germany and the source of mounting demands for the sisters' services. Under the terms of the post-revolutionary settlement, the territorial and secular rulers alone were in a position to implement the restoration of Catholic charitable services and as a consequence many of them looked to Strasbourg as a source of trained personnel. The process was a slow one. The administration at Strasbourg insisted on retaining control of sisters in the field; in Catholic cities incorporated by Protestant states the requirements of the order were further complicated by confessional difference. As late as 1847 the Bishop at Mainz complained that there existed in his entire diocese only one cloister of any kind.[21]

PROTESTANT-CATHOLIC RIVALRY IN THE RHINELAND

In the Prussian Rhineland and Westphalia the issue of women religious was immersed in the more general animosity between Prussian statism and Catholic militancy, a struggle which took on a strident tone. In an effort to insure the assimilation of the newly acquired provinces the Prussian government reserved all of the important civic appointments, notably the offices of *Ober-praesidenten* and *Regierungspraesidenten*. Secular surveillance over church affairs was intrusive in matters concerning the training of clergy, the reintroduction of orders, and the application of canon law. The antagonism between the Prussian state and the Catholic church finally erupted over the issue of mixed marriage and the contradictions between canon and secular law. Canon law required that the partners of a mixed marriage promise to educate their children as Catholics. Prussian civil law required that children adhere to the religion of the parent of their own gender. Marriage between Prussian officers and local Rhenish women offered the occasion of the dispute: Frederick William III considered undignified the possibility that sons of his bureaucrats might be raised as Catholics. Droste-Vischering adhered to the strict interpretation of canon law and when, as Archbishop of Cologne, he refused to modify his position, Prussian authorities had him arrested in 1837 and incarcerated in a fortress.[22]

This tyrannical act occasioned the dramatic reaffirmation of ultramontanism in the Rhineland. In a number of unanticipated ways the resulting resurgence of Catholicism was consequential for women's lives. The campaign to introduce an office for women in the Protestant church represented one response to Catholic militancy. A very different kind of response was the appearance of the German-Catholic movement, the dissident sect to which Louise Otto ascribed so much importance when she spoke of the introduction of women to the public sphere. The dissidents organized originally to protest the pilgrimage to Trier in 1844 and the exhibition of a relic there, the Holy Coat, purportedly worn by Jesus on the eve of the crucifixion. The pilgrimage was designed to celebrate the accession of Wilhelm

Arnoldi to the bishopric at Trier and the conclusion of an agreement with the Prussian state that settled a number of outstanding
issues, among them mixed marriages. The assumption of power
by Frederick William IV, a Pietist and romantic, brought with it
a decided shift in the nature of Prussian religious policy, one no
less intrusive but one motivated by a different ideological intent.
Protestants were no less victims of statism than were Catholics.
Collaboration among the two Protestant traditions extended beyond the exigencies of the war years. In Prussia and in most of
the other German states the tercentenary of the Reformation in
1817 was celebrated by the formal unification of the Lutheran
and Reformed churches in the new united state church, the
Evangelical Church. Unlike some of the other states where the
union was implemented by synods and congregations, Frederick
William III considered it his personal mission to enforce confessional unification in Prussia and imposed a liturgy, the *Agende*,
which he himself drafted. The ensuing strife established the tone
of acrimony and ecclesiastical litigiousness that extended to the
revolution and colored what might have been political debates
with religious overtones. The impetus to create alternative forms
of religious service and the pastoral network to implement them
emerged from this controversy; so did the reaffirmation of charity as a variety of alternate Christianity.[23]

The new united church created an appointed bureaucracy of
provincial consistories and superintendents who supervised local
clergy and their congregations as "prefects of the government."
Only those men whose creed, political views, associations, and
activities seemed to support the official position could expect
preferment. Many new theological graduates got no parishes at
all. A Scottish visitor to Prussia in 1835 said that there were 262
candidates for every single parish living in the Evangelical
Church. The surplus of clerical candidates as a social phenomenon impinged on the condition of women in important ways.
Many of the candidates became tutors or teachers while they
waited for more congenial employment, or they directed the
private upper schools for girls. They contributed heavily to the
confessional character of these schools,[24] which, combined with
the lack of a substantial curriculum, alienated many of their
students and created the spokeswomen of the 1840s. Fanny Le-

wald (1811–1889), the prolific feminist novelist, recalled her anguish as a school girl, whose academic performance was always excellent, when a visiting dignitary representing church and state remarked: "Well now, your head would have been better sitting on the shoulders of a boy!" Lewald observed that without realizing it, "that excellent man had touched one of my secret wounds, for a long while already I had envied all boys because they were boys and could study."[25]

Church attendance among Protestants declined during this period. There were obviously factors other than coercion from the state that loosened church ties. Preachers of the Awakening, for instance, blamed the introduction of machinery in various forms of production that required Sunday work. To the intelligentsia, German classicism itself assumed the character of a religion and church attendance for them was increasingly irrelevant. Nevertheless contemporaries believed that there was a connection between dwindling church attendance and ecclesiastical rigidity in the churches of the Protestant establishment.[26]

ALTERNATE EXPRESSIONS OF PIETY

Lay piety at the same time did not decline. It found expression outside the confines of the church. One collection of house devotions, for instance, Heinrich Zschokke's *Stunden der Andacht* or *Hours of Devotion*, a book for household use, was reprinted annually from 1816 until 1842. Infused by the spirit of the Enlightenment, this volume eulogized the values of personal morality, friendship, domesticity, and the love of nature.[27]

Very different in tone were the private devotions associated with the Pommeranian Awakening and the leadership of Adolf von Thadden-Trieglaff (1796–1882) in the 1820s and 1830s, supported by Frederick William IV when he was still Crown Prince of Prussia. Pietism here was joined with Lutheran orthodoxy and carried the explicit intent of providing an alternative to the state church services.[28] The non-confessional quality of eighteenth-century Pietism had vanished. With it disappeared as well the class-free and gender-free spirit. For as Wangemann, a visiting clergyman, observed: "A number of distinguished women moved among the guests and asked for nothing more in compensation for their hospitality than to have a protective screen set for them in the rear of the session from where they could attend the proceedings unobserved." Although the conventicles have been associated with the feminization of religion, men, not women, dominated them.[29]

Like the conventicles where private worship took the place of church services, Protestant activism also functioned as a form of discontent with the state churches. In Wuerttemberg, for instance, the ecumenical Pietist tradition of the eighteenth century survived. Lutherans joined forces with Calvinists as far afield as Switzerland in missionary activities under the auspices of the Basel Mission Society. They cultivated close contact with English non-conformity in the work of distributing Bibles and tracts. Similar proselytizing activities made their appearance in the valley of the Wupper River as one aspect of the resistance of the Reformed Church to the United Church of Prussia. These commitments were also integrally connected with a resurgence of Prussian charity.

The rescue house (*Rettungshaus*) constituted the charitable innovation of the period, one associated with a number of the most prominent male philanthropists. These establishments were designed to shelter and educate abandoned or delinquent children; many of them started in response to the wartime phenomenon of homeless children. Theoretically the new charities might have produced opportunities for women; one of their founders believed that destitute children should be exposed to the guidance of both sexes since they were deprived of their natural families. But in fact the emphasis of the new philanthropy was heavily pedagogical—education was identified with the redeeming love of God—so that the patriarchal potential within the system was constantly reinforced. The culmination of this development was reached at the Rauhe Haus, the institution founded in Hamburg by Johann Hinrich Wichern (1808–1881), which anticipated the Inner Mission. To serve as personnel for his establishment, as well as for other institutions in the field, Wichern founded an entire order of lay brothers. Ironically it was during the same decade that two major initiatives were undertaken that finally ended the male monopoly of Protestant charity, one in the Rhineland and the other in the North.[30] In the light of the pervasiveness of patriarchy in both the structure and the attitudes of contemporary life, the successful introduction of women into the Protestant charitable system suggests that we need to look at the impact of forces external to the institutional development of philanthropy.

CHANGES IN THE GERMAN FAMILY STRUCTURE

The inclusion of women in charitable activity was in fact implemented by the concomitant change in the structure of the German family in process during the early part of the century: the breakdown of the traditional patriarchal household and its slow replacement by the bourgeois family. As the German historian Otto Brunner has insisted, the concept of "family" is a relatively new one. Until the beginning of the nineteenth century the concept of the household (*das ganze Haus*) was common usage. It was only replaced when the function of domestic economy and the notion of house servants subject to the master's rule disappeared from the understanding of family. Family came to represent a private domestic institution detached from productive activity, consisting solely of a man, his wife, and their children. This change occurred at different rates and at different times and places. The household while it prevailed was the basic social unit in town as well as in the countryside. Virtually all occupations were organized within a household context. Production and consumption merged and no distinction was recognized between domestic and occupational functions. Functions were divided along lines of gender; the father presided over the entire operation. There were no separate spheres; his wife served as his helpmeet and, particularly in his absence, might act on his behalf.[31]

Civil law reinforced a father's dominion over his household. In the Prussian Civil Code (*Allgemeines Landrecht*) of 1794, a body of law that served as a model for other German states as well, marital provisions of the statute made a man guardian over his wife and, while local law controlled the actual administration of her property, normally this property was transferred to the husband. She could not sign any legal agreement or enter into any

contract without his consent. A father exercised absolute jurisdiction over his children, particularly over daughters who, as
single women even in their forties, had no rights in civil law.
The divorce provisions of the law reflected a functional, pragmatic view of marriage. Childless couples were permitted to divorce by mutual consent. Others, including couples with
children, for reasons of insurmountable personal aversion. Divorce was also permitted to both sides on grounds of infidelity.
Frederick the Great whose legacy inspired Prussian Code was
responsible for these provisions, provisions certainly contrary to
Christian views of marriage. He was convinced that only well-
suited couples would continue to procreate and produce the
children needed to fill the ranks of the Prussian army. The
relative ease of divorce coupled with provisions to insure a father's guardianship over his children extended well into nineteenth-century Germany, even as the nature of the family itself
changed.[32]

The period that this study embraces coincides with the transformation of the household and the emergence of the bourgeois
family (*buergerliche Familie*). Social production was increasingly
located outside the household and separated from domestic
activities while the home assumed an increasingly private character. This is the epoch of Biedermeier portraiture: the exag-
geratedly sentimental portrayal in both graphic and literary
representation of the nuclear family in its living room and children's nursery. The wife and mother was relegated to the con-
finement of her home; contrary to the practice of earlier
generations, she, and no longer the husband, could be defined
exclusively in terms of family. The emergent system not only
reduced the productive role of the woman—in the wealthier
classes she was absolved from the responsibility of everything
but the oversight of the domestic household and obliged to live
a life of leisure—but the increasing insistence on marriage as
woman's natural destiny deprived single women of the most
minimal basis for a meaningful existence. Servants in the traditional household were young people of the same class as the
household they entered; servants in the bourgeois family were
usually young peasant women seeking work in town because the
rural economy could no longer support them. Single gentle-

women hoped for employment as companions or governesses, positions that characteristically carried with them a loss of social status. The prescription of marriage and domesticity meant that the kind of intellectual activity that flourished briefly under female leadership in the Berlin salons at the turn of the century, for instance, had no subsequent German successors.[33]

Historians cite a variety of causes for the demise of the household and the emergence of the bourgeois family with its characteristic separation of occupation from domesticity. Capitalism ultimately was the major transforming force; in certain industries—weaving, for example—capitalist practices were grafted onto the household economy without at first reducing the participation of women in the productive process. For Germany the dramatic population increase during the early decades of the nineteenth century—more than 33 percent or from about twenty-nine million to about forty million inhabitants in the years 1815 to 1845—destabilized the household economy by overburdening rural production. During the years of French domination competition from British manufactured goods was contained by the Continental System; peasant families could supplement their income from cottage industry. Peace introduced a flood of factory goods to Germany. Declining opportunities in turn precipitated the urban migrations and foreign emigration characteristic of this period.[34]

Recent research emphasizes the gradualness of the modernization process in Germany and the resiliency of traditional institutions and attitudes. On the eve of the 1848 revolution 70 percent of the entire German population still lived on the land. Of those who lived in towns—four million, for example, in Prussia—most were small town residents; only 994,500 Prussians lived in the thirteen cities of over 30,000 inhabitants in a total population of some fifteen and a half million. The town resident was characteristically an artisan. In Saxony between 60 and 70 percent of the population was engaged in manufacturing. Much of this was spinning and weaving, which, notwithstanding the appearance of textile factories, remained predominantly a household industry, albeit conducted within the putting-out system. There were pockets of industry elsewhere, for instance in Hessen-Darmstadt, but little of it was mechanized.[35]

Traditional patterns prevailed well into the century; family size remained typically five to six persons; late marriage persisted, meaning that women characteristically married between the ages of twenty-seven and thirty-two, men, between twenty-nine and thirty-three. Infant mortality continued to be high and women's mortality, even discounting death as a result of childbirth, remained significantly higher than men's. By one estimate for the years 1810–1839, 134 women aged fifteen to forty-nine died for every 100 men in the same cohort.[36] The traditional family was resistant to change even under circumstance of urban and bureaucratic pressure. One dramatic change, of course, was the increase in illegitimate births. A frequent source was the rise in companionate marriages which had not been legitimated by law. German communities during the first decades of the century increasingly restricted the right of legal residency as well as that of marriage to those of specified financial resources. Legitimacy of marriage as well as of residency was beyond the reach of many working people. Single rural women employed as domestic servants in towns apart from their parents were vulnerable both to their employers and to promises of marriage by their peers which did not materialize.[37]

WOMEN ENTER THE PROTESTANT
CHARITABLE ESTABLISHMENT

The introduction of women into the German Protestant charitable enterprise reflects the erosion of the contemporary family structure. The women first caught up in the development of Protestant charity came from two polarities of familial change: displaced rural women of peasant or artisan background on the one hand and women from the ruling class made idle by growing wealth and the availability of servants on the other. Leadership for this innovation was provided from separate sources by two distinctive individuals, Theodor Fliedner (1800–1862), a pastor of the Prussian Evangelical Church at Kaiserswerth in the Rhine province outside of Duesseldorf, and Amalie Sieveking (1794–1859), a female member of the patriciate in the city-republic of Hamburg. Working independently and occasionally at cross purposes, Fliedner became known as "Restorer of the Apostolic

Office of Deaconess," and Sieveking as the "spiritual mother" of benevolent visiting by women in Germany.[38] Fliedner understood his work as an extension of his vocation as clergyman while Sieveking and her affiliates outside of Hamburg operated deliberately on the basis of independent, voluntary initiative. In this respect, the coalition of women's associations that she founded served as an immediate precedent for the initiative of her subsequent opponents: women committed to the possibility of interconfessional charity in its many ramifications who welcomed the revolution as an opportunity to implement their ideas.

The spirit that sustained the Protestant female diaconate locates the diaconate among those institutions and practices designed by the Prussian bureaucracy to contain the Catholic renascence in the Rhine province. As Fliedner, the director, complained to the British Quaker philanthropist Elizabeth Fry (1780–1845), the Sisters of Charity were like a "flood everywhere . . . in Protestant countries and hospitals . . . where they endeavor artfully to place their church in the best possible light to make proselytes of the sick and poor."[39] Fliedner's conduct suggests that the female diaconate, like other charitable and conventicle enterprises of the period, was also intended to supplement the deficient spirituality of Frederick William III's united church. Fliedner was a vocal opponent of the king's liturgy, the *Agende*, and he enjoyed many contacts with the German and Swiss preachers of revival, the tractarians, and the British non-conformists. His wife, Friedericke Muenster (1800–1842), was a devout member of the Reformed communion whose commitment to practical Christian service was informed by an experience of personal conversion during the Awakening.[40]

The foundation of the female diaconate followed a trip Fliedner made to England in 1824. His initial reflections suggest that the significance of women ministering to women which Elizabeth Fry's work embodied escaped him at first, for he concluded that English women had shown up the deficiencies of German men.[41] The asylum for female penitents released from prison in which his wife, her closest girlhood friend, and he himself collaborated persuaded Fliedner that German Protestant philanthropy was seriously flawed by the absence of women.[42] A tract published in 1835 echoed his sentiments:

Dark error...excluded your sex from the redeeming work for the kingdom of Christ. Don't you exclude yourselves further through false and wrong-headed notions of propriety...but rather take hold,...for it is day and soon the night cometh.[43]

Pragmatic considerations shaped the early female diaconate. Fliedner had accurately anticipated the nature of the opposition to his initiative: questions surrounding the introduction of women into a male perserve, the Catholicizing overtones of a quasi-order, and the threat to the patriarchal family implied in the recruitment of women.[44] Fliedner hoped to court public tolerance by confining the work of the early deaconesses to hospitals where the need for improved care was universally recognized. German hospitals of the period, where they existed at all, belonged to the domain of poor relief, not medicine. Their conditions were deplorable. Conventional attendants, female and male, came from the most marginal segment of society and were objects of public contempt.

The community of women at Kaiserswerth, when it finally materialized, was not unlike a Catholic order in its autonomy from the parish structure of the church. In their appearance and in their obedience to a rule, deaconesses were segregated from the laity. Their training embraced practical as well as spiritual instruction. When they were in the field, in municipal or private institutions, they remained under the jurisdiction of Kaiserswerth, and the wage for their service went to the motherhouse. The five-year term of service was renewable; deaconesses were entitled to perpetual care if they retired in the diaconate.

Beyond an external resemblance to a Catholic foundation, however, the experiment at Kaiserswerth was distinctive. It incorporated the marital and parental hierarchy of the model Lutheran clerical family into its structure and reconstituted on an institutional scale its educative and charitable functions. Fliedner and his wife shared the administration of the diaconate, adopting the titles Father and Mother. The deaconesses called one another "Sister." The diaconate proved to be a versatile institution, simultaneously realizing both innovative and reactionary goals. It acted in support of the forces seeking to introduce women into public activity through the field of charity, reversing a 300-year tradition that had excluded women from a significant role in the church and its charities. At the same time the deaconess institution did nothing to threaten the patriarchal family. On the contrary, at a time when the material as well as ideological bases of the patriarchal family were eroding, the diaconate served to enhance its stature by imitating its form and legitimating its mechanisms. Municipal and ecclesiastical officers who administered poor houses and hospitals as well as families who required attendants for their sick conducted negotiations and correspondence directly with Fliedner much as negotiations with a household head for an apprentice or servant were conducted. Hence at the most critical level, the introduction of the diaconate required no change in societal attitudes whatever. Within a decade of its founding the institution recorded in its annual report a total of 101 deaconesses; fifty-six of them were in the field in eighteen hospitals, orphanages, rescue houses, or parish institutions. The institution was supported by voluntary contributions.[45]

The success of recruitment at Kaiserswerth was derived in a large measure from the coincidence of goals articulated by Fliedner and the needs of a precarious segment of German womanhood: young single women deprived of a secure existence by the contemporary strains in the traditional economy. Their struggle for survival, both material and spiritual, is recorded in the autobiographic statements they were required to submit as part of the admission procedure to the diaconate. These documents chronicle the familial circumstances as well as the conversion experiences of the candidates. Many of the women who originally applied to Fliedner belonged to the peasantry and worked as servants. The demographic revolution that overburdened the economy, increased the population by 38 percent in thirty years, set a previously stable population wandering, and dramatically elevated the rate of illegitimacy also stimulated enrollment at Kaiserswerth, for single women were the most vulnerable of all. The surrogate family and its imagery elaborated at Kaiserswerth clearly resonated with the needs of these women; so did the spiritual vocation offered by the office of deaconess.

The patriarchal family model which served both Fliedner's goals and the deaconesses' needs so well might have developed along very different lines had Fliedner's original candidate for the office of Superintendent accepted his invitation. The history of German women and the opportunities they developed through charitable enterprise would certainly have been a different one. Fliedner first offered the superintendency of the diaconate to Amalie Sieveking, the Hamburg philanthropist. Sieveking had earned a reputation as a "Christian heroine" when she took over the supervision of female cholera patients in the infirmary of St. Ericus during the epidemic of 1831. Her success as a volunteer against great odds encouraged her to expand her activity and to recruit members of her own class for a society of benevolent visitors. Sieveking was committed to the status of singlehood. She wrote of herself in connection with a later offer: "Actually I am too used to a certain independent development in my religious life and I would feel myself too easily restricted by the forms imposed on me by others." She was also opposed to uniting the functions of the church and state in the single office of the clergyman.[46]

Fliedner's self-perception increasingly embraced a sense of his status as an official of the state church, and his financial and administrative gifts were well suited to the spirit of efficient bureaucracy dominating the Prussian court. The office of deaconess was officially acknowledged within the state church and the institution of the diaconate was recognized legally as a corporate entity under the oversight of the Rhine-Westphalian province of the Prussian United Church. The statutes, under protracted negotiation with the previous monarch, were confirmed by the new incumbent in 1846.[47]

Sieveking declined the offer from Kaiserswerth, but it was an offer of great consequence for her and for German women in general. It endowed her with a self-consciousness of her role and of the uniqueness and pioneering importance of her own organization. It made it possible for her to distance herself from any Catholic model of female orders, the model she thought was perpetuated in Fliedner's work, one that she herself had long emulated. She was freed to pursue something altogether different. Subsequently she occasionally criticized Fliedner's policies as too monastic; she did so as much to differentiate herself from him and legitimate her own organization as to influence the diaconate. Sieveking ridiculed Fliedner's apparent reluctance to release deaconesses at the end of their terms of service for the purpose of getting married.[48] Sieveking's own commitment was increasingly to forms of charitable service distinct from the church under auspices separate from the church on the part of women unattached to the church except as laity, but infused with a spirit of Christianity. The concept of Christian service by lay women performed in the context of everyday life offered immensely wider opportunities than the female diaconate.

Fliedner himself ultimately devoted a major commitment of his own talents and resources to promoting this wider kind of service. After the onset of the revolution and the attendant women's movement, Fliedner shifted the focus of his endeavors from a contest with Catholicism to a contest with the forces of liberalism and women's emancipation. For the time being, however, the leadership of conservative innovation belonged to Sieveking.

NOTES

1. [Johann Hinrich Wichern], "Frauenvereine fuer Arme und Kranke," *Fliegende Blaetter aus dem Rauhen Haus zu Horn* 4 (1847): 228.

2. Quoted in Margrit Twellmann, *Die deutsche Frauenbewegung. Ihre Anfaenge und erste Entwicklung*, vol. 2, *Quellen 1843–1889* (Meisenheim am Glan: Anton Hain, 1972), p. 5.

3. "Das graue Haus und die innere Mission," *FZ* 2, no. 25 (22 June 1850): 3; F. K. Prochaska, "Women in English Philanthropy, 1790–1830," *International Review of Social History* 19 (1974): 426–45; Martin Gerhardt, *Theodor Fliedner. Ein Lebensbild*, 2 vols. (Duesseldorf-Kaiserswerth: Buchhandlung der Diakonissenanstalt, 1933–37), 2: 224–28.

4. Gerda Schaffenorth and Klaus Thraede, *"Freunde in Christus werden . . ." Die Beziehung von Mann und Frau als Frage an Theologie und Kirche* (Gelnhausen, Berlin: Burckhardthaus-Verlag, Stein/Mfr.: Laetare Verlag, 1977), pp. 256–71, a euphoric view of the family in Lutheranism; Marilyn Chapin Massey, *Feminine Soul: The Fate of an Ideal* (Boston: Beacon Press, 1985), pp. 43–48, is critical; Hermann Werdermann, *Die deutsche evangelische Pfarrfrau. Ihre Geschichte in vier Jahrhunderten* (Witten: Westdeutscher Lutherverlag, 1935), pp. 275–76; in poetic form, "Die evangelische Pfarrfrau," *AuKF* 3 (March-April 1851): 19–20; Gerhardt, *Theodor Fliedner*, 2: 19, 112.

5. Gerhard Uhlhorn, *Die christliche Liebestaetigkeit* (Stuttgart: Verlag von D. Gundert, 1895), p. 729.

6. Wilhelm Liese, *Geschichte der Caritas*, 2 vols. (Freiburg i.B.: Caritasverlag, 1922), 1: 240–51, 307–8.

7. Ruth P. Liebowitz, "Virgins in the Service of Christ: The Dispute over an Active Apostolate for Women during the Counter-Reformation," *Women of Spirit: Female Leadership in the Jewish and Christian Traditions*, ed. Rosemary R. Ruether and Eleanor McLaughlin (New York: Simon and Schuster, 1979), p. 133; Liese, *Geschichte der Caritas*, 1: 285, 322; Uhlhorn, *Christliche Liebesthaetigkeit*, p. 652.

8. Hajo Holborn, *A History of Modern Germany: The Reformation* (New York: Alfred A. Knopf, 1959), pp. 259–60; "Erneuerung des apostolischen Diakonissen-Amtes vor und nach der Reformation des 16. Jahrhunderts," *AuKF* 1, no. 4 (1849): 13–14; "Das Diakonissen-Amt in der reformierten Gemeinde zu Wesel in der Reformations-Zeit," ibid. 6 (May-June 1854): 4–9.

9. Robert M. Bigler, *The Politics of German Protestantism: The Rise of the Protestant Church Elite in Prussia, 1815–1848* (Berkeley, Los Angeles, and London: University of California Press, 1972), pp. 11–16; Rosemary R. Ruether and Catherine M. Prelinger, "Sectarian and Utopian Groups in Colonial and Revolutionary America," *Women and Religion in America*, vol. 2, *The Eighteenth Century*, ed. Ruether and Rosemary S. Keller (San Francisco: Harper and Row, 1983), pp. 260–315; F. Ernest Stoeffler, *German Pietism during the Eighteenth Century* (Leiden: E. J. Brill, 1973).

10. Ute Gerhard, *Verhaeltnisse und Verhinderungen. Frauenarbeit, Familie und Rechte der Frauen im 19. Jahrhundert. Mit Dokumenten* (Frankfurt a.M.: Suhrkamp Verlag, 1978), pp. 133–34; Renate Moehrmann, *Die andere Frau. Emanzipationsansaetze deutscher Schriftstellerinnen im Vorfeld der Achtundvierziger-Revolution* (Stuttgart: J. B. Metzler, 1977), pp. 25, 30–36.

11. Karin Hausen, "Family and Role-Division: The Polarisation of Sexual Stereotypes in the Nineteenth Century—An Aspect of the Dissociation of Work and Family Life," *The German Family: Essays on the Social History of the Family in Nineteenth- and Twentieth-Century Germany*, ed. Richard J. Evans and W. R. Lee (London: Croom Helm; Totowa, N.J.: Barnes and Noble, 1981), pp. 51–83.

12. Quoted in Gerhard, *Verhaeltnisse*, p. 147.

13. Quoted in Sydney E. Ahlstrom, "The Romantic Religious Revolution and the Dilemmas of Religious History," *Church History* 46 (1977): 156–57.

14. Quoted in Bigler, *Politics*, p. 30; also Friedrich Wilhelm Kantzenbach, *Geschichte des Protestantismus von 1789–1848* (Guetersloh: Guetersloher Verlagshaus, 1969), p. 127.

15. Eduard Freiherr von der Goltz, *Deutsche Frauenarbeit in der Kriegs-zeit*, 2d ed. (Leipzig: J. C. Hinrichs'sche Buchhandlung, 1915), pp. 36–37; "Eine freiwillige Krankenpflegerin in den Befreiungskriegen," *AuKF* 17 (1865): 77–78; Gerhardt, *Theodor Fliedner*, 2: 14; *Der Demokrat* [Mainz], no. 34 (17 May 1849), p. 153.

16. Friedrich Daniel Schleiermacher, *Katechismus der Vernunft fuer Edle Frauen* (Neustadt an der Haardt: Musen-Verlag, 1947), n.p., "Der Glaube II;" idem, "Predigten ueber den christlichen Hausstand: Ueber die Ehe," *Werke: Auswahl*, 4 vols., ed. Otto Braun and D. Joh. Bauer (Leipzig: Felix Meiner, [1910]), 3: 211, 245.

17. Quoted in John L. Snell, *The Democratic Movement in Germany, 1789–1914*, ed. and comp. by Hans A. Schmitt (Chapel Hill: University of North Carolina Press, 1980), p. 22.

18. Holborn, *History of Modern Germany: 1648–1840* (New York: Alfred A. Knopf, 1964), p. 487.

19. Edgar Alexander, "Church and Society in Germany: Social and Political Movements and Ideas in German and Austrian Catholicism, 1789–1950," *Church and Society: Catholic Social and Political Thought and Movements 1789–1950*, ed. Joseph N. Moody (New York: Arts Inc., 1953), p. 360.

20. Franz Schnabel, *Deutsche Geschichte im neunzehnten Jahrhundert*, vol. 4, *Die religioesen Kraefte*, 3d ed. (Freiburg i.B.: Verlag Herder, 1955), pp. 44–97; also Holborn, *History of Modern Germany: 1648–1840*, pp. 498–509.

21. Emil Clemens Scherer, *Die Kongregation der barmherzigen Schwestern von Strassburg: Ein Bild ihres Werdens und Wirkens von 1734 bis zur Gegenwart* (Saaralben/Lohringen: Colportage catholique, 1930), pp. 227–53.

22. Ronald J. Ross, *The Beleaguered Tower: The Dilemma of Political Catholicism in Wilhelmine Germany* (Notre Dame: University of Notre Dame Press, 1976), pp. 6–10; Schnabel, *Deutsche Geschichte*, 4: 106–64.

23. Schnabel, *Deutsche Geschichte*, 4: 320–54; Bigler, *Politics*, pp. 37–41, 160–63; Uhlhorn, *Christliche Liebestaetigkeit*, pp. 699–700.

24. Bigler, *Politics*, pp. 39–63; Leonore O'Boyle, "The Problem of an Excess of Educated Men in Western Europe, 1800–1850," *Journal of Modern History* 42 (1970): 481; Anthony J. LaVolpa, *Prussian School-teachers: Profession and Office, 1763–1848* (Chapel Hill: University of North Carolina Press, 1980), pp. 98–105.

25. Quoted from her autobiography in *Frauenemanzipation im deutschen Vormaerz. Texte und Dokumente*, ed. Renate Moehrmann (Stuttgart: Philip Reklam Jun., 1978), p. 14.

26. Joseph Edmund Joerg, *Geschichte des Protestantismus in seiner neues-*

ten Entwicklung (Freiburg i.B.: Herder'scher Verlag, 1858), pp. 52–59; Christian Tischhauser, *Geschichte der evangelischen Kirche in der ersten Haelfte des 19. Jahrhunderts* (Basel: R. Reich, 1900), pp. 532–35, 543–44, 565, 420; Johannes B. Kissling, *Der deutsche Protestantismus 1817–1917*, 2 vols. (Muenster: Aschendorffischer Verlag, 1917–18), 1: 172–73. There is a letter from Victoria Gervinus, wife of the historian, to the historian Friedrich Dahlmann in Anton Heinrich Springer, *Friedrich Christoph Dahlmann*, 2 vols. (Leipzig: S. Hirzel, 1870–71), 2: 186, presuming that the coldness of state Protestantism explains his lack of church participation. Official church statistics were not collected by sex until late in the century. The discrepancy between female and male communicants in Hamburg recorded in 1878, Gustav Ritter (Pastor zu St. Michaelis), *Kirchlich-Statistische Zusammenstellungen ueber die christlichen Stadt- und Land-Gemeinden Hamburgs*, 14. Jahrgang 1878 (Hamburg: Graefe, 1879), p. 4, was cause for alarm. Per 100 communicants there were sixty-seven women and thirty-three men, ibid., p. 12.

27. Schnabel, *Deutsche Geschichte*, 4: 371–73.

28. Bigler, *Politics*, pp. 140–43; Holborn, *History of Modern Germany: 1648–1849*, p. 494.

29. Hermann Wangemann, *Sieben Buecher preussischer Kirchengeschichte. Eine aktenmaessige Darstellung des Kampfes um die Lutherische Kirche im XIX. Jahrhundert*, 3 vols. (Berlin: W. Schultze, 1860), 3: 73, 77 for quotation; Schnabel, *Deutsche Geschichte*, 4: 383–99; Holborn, *History of Modern Germany: 1648–1840*, pp. 494–95; Uhlhorn, *Christliche Liebestaetigkeit*, pp. 704, 711.

30. Uhlhorn, *Christliche Liebestaetigkeit*, pp. 706–35; Schnabel, *Deutsche Geschichte*, 4: 408–9; William O. Shanahan, *German Protestants Face the Social Question* (Notre Dame: Notre Dame University Press, 1954), pp. 61–79.

31. Otto Brunner, "Das ganze Haus und die alteuropaeische Oekonomik," *Neue Wege der Verfassungs- und Sozialgeschichte* (Goettingen: Vandenhoeck und Rupprecht, 1956), pp. 40–45; Michael Mitterauer and Reinhard Sieder, *The European Family: Patriarchy to Partnership from the Middle Ages to the Present*, trans. Karla Oosterveen and Manfred Hoerzinger (Oxford: Basil Blackwell, 1982), pp. 5–44; Lutz K. Berkner, "The Stem Family and the Developmental Cycle of the Peasant Household: An Eighteenth-Century Austrian Example," *American Historical Review* 77 (1972): 411; Jean H. Quataert, "The Shaping of Women's Work in Manufacturing: Guilds, Households, and the State in Central Europe, 1648–1870," ibid., 90 (1985): 1122–48, however, emphasizes the tension between guild and household work.

32. Richard J. Evans, *The Feminist Movement in Germany 1894–1933* (London and Beverly Hills: SAGE Publications, 1976), pp. 12–13.

33. Ingeborg Weber-Kellermann, *Die deutsche Familie. Versuch einer Sozialgeschichte* (Frankfurt a.M.: Suhrkamp Taschenbuch Verlag, 1974), pp. 102–18; Rolf Engelsing, "Das haeusliche Personal in der Epoche der Industrialisierung," *Zur Sozialgeschichte deutscher Mittel- und Unterschichten*, 2d ed. (Goettingen: Vandenhoeck und Rupprecht, 1978), pp. 227–29; Gerhard, *Verhaeltnisse*, pp. 92–95.

34. Hans Medick, "The proto-industrial family economy: The structural function of household and family during the transition from peasant society to industrial capitalism," *Social History* 1 (1976): 298–301; Karl Obermann, "Die deutsche Bevoelkerungsstatistik und die Bevoelkerungsstruktur des Deutschen Bundes in den Jahren um 1815," *Bevoelkerungsgeschichte*, ed. Wolfgang Koellmann and Peter Marschalck (Cologne: Kiepenheuer und Witsch, 1972), pp. 195–96; Mack Walker, *Germany and the Emigration, 1816–1885* (Cambridge, Mass.: Harvard University Press, 1964), pp. 2–3; demographic and economic changes briefly summarized in Donald G. Rohr, *The Origins of Social Liberalism in Germany* (Chicago and London: University of Chicago Press, 1963), pp. 12–49.

35. Obermann, "Deutsche Bevoelkerungsstatistik," pp. 211, 199, 202, 204–5.

36. Robert Lee, "Family and 'Modernisation': The Peasant Family and Social Change in Nineteenth-Century Bavaria," *The German Family*, ed. Evans and Lee, pp. 88, 91, 94; Arthur E. Imhof, "Women, Family and Death: Excess Mortality of Women in Women of Child-Bearing Age in Four Communities in Nineteenth-Century Germany," ibid., p. 159.

37. Mack Walker, *German Home Towns: Community, State and General Estate, 1648–1871* (Ithaca, N.Y. and London: Cornell University Press, 1971), pp. 309–21, 334–40, on residential requirements; Louise A. Tilly, Joan W. Scott, and Miriam Cohen, "Women's Work and European Fertility Patterns," *Journal of Interdisciplinary History* 6 (1976): 447–76, who emphasize that no change in attitude can be documented, contrary to Edward Shorter, *The Making of the Modern Family* (New York: Basic Books, 1975).

38. Georg Fliedner, *Theodor Fliedner. Durch Gottes Gnade Erneurer des apostolischen Diakonnissen-Amtes in der evangelischen Kirche*, 3 vols. (Kaiserswerth: Buchhandlung der Diakonissenanstalt, 1908–12); *WVAK, 19. Bericht*, p. 30.

39. Fliedner to Elizabeth Fry, 2 Dec. 1839, FlAr.

40. Gerhardt, *Theodor Fliedner*, cited above, and Anna Sticker, *Friedericke Fliedner und die Anfaenge der Frauendiakonie. Ein Quellenbuch*, 2d ed. (Neukirchen-Vluyn: Buchhandlung des Erziehungsvereins, 1963), are the best biographies.

41. [T. Fliedner], "Kurze Geschichte der Entstehung der ersten evangelischen Liebes-Anstalt zu Kaiserswerth," *AuKF* 8 (Jan.-Feb. 1856): 4.
42. Gerhardt, *Theodor Fliedner*, 2: 32–33.
43. Quoted in ibid., p. 39.
44. See Catherine M. Prelinger, "The Nineteenth-Century Deaconessate in Germany: The Efficacy of a Family Model," *German Women in the Eighteenth and Nineteenth Centuries: A Social and Literary History*, ed. Ruth-Ellen B. Joeres and Mary Jo Maynes (Bloomington: Indiana University Press, 1986), pp. 215–29, with extensive references for what follows.
45. [T. Fliedner], *9. Jahresbericht ueber die Diakonissen-Anstalt zu Kaiserswerth am Rhein* (1845), pp. 2–3.
46. Martin Hieronymus Hudtwalcker, *Ein halbes Jahrhundert aus meiner Lebensgeschichte*, 3 vols. (Hamburg: Agentur des Rauhen Hauses, 1862–64), 3: 387; [Emma Poel], *Denkwuerdigkeiten aus dem Leben von Amalie Sieveking in deren Auftrage von einer Freundin derselben verfasst* (Hamburg: Agentur des Rauhen Hauses, 1860), pp. 48, 377, 285–86.
47. John R. Gillis, *The Prussian Bureaucracy in Crisis, 1814–1860: Origins of an Administrative Ethos* (Stanford, Calif.: Stanford University Press, 1971), esp. p. 44; Gerhardt, *Theodor Fliedner*, 2: 150–56.
48. Gerhardt, *Theodor Fliedner*, 2: 179–80; Sieveking to Eduard Sieveking, Jr., 7 Dec. 1849, Nls AWS, StAr Hmbg.

CHAPTER 2

Benevolent Visiting: Feminized Philanthropy in the Service of Orthodoxy

Amalie Sieveking made philanthropic activity available to women by a route altogether new to Germany at a time when organized charity had been monopolized by men, and she did so not simply to improve the quality of charity but to improve the quality of women's lives. As she indicated in a speech she delivered in Bremen in 1841, nearly a decade after she had founded the Female Association for the Care of the Poor and Sick (*Weiblicher Verein fuer Armen- und Krankenpflege*) in Hamburg:

I had two things in mind with the idea that I was trying to implement. For one I hoped that it would provide benefits for the poor and suffering. But that alone was not my intention. To me at least as important were the benefits which it seemed to promise my sisters who would join me in such work of charity. The highest interests of my sex were close to my heart.[1]

Women themselves, in other words, were the object of Sieveking's attention; her aim was the cultivation of an appropriate arena for their energies. To critics who charged that charitable activity would divert women from their domestic duties, Sieveking made this rejoinder:

I have long since expressed my own view that in a great many cases, namely those of the upper classes, household and other domestic responsibilities do not offer the female side of the family a sufficient arena for the sum of their energies.[2]

Sieveking was convinced that the time upper-class women devoted to theaters, concerts, dances, parties, and social calls could be more profitably spent in charitable enterprise, an avenue to the kind of self-esteem denied them by the society of the period. The association that she founded in 1832 was an institutional novelty. More important, it provided a model and initiated a network of orthodox Protestant women throughout Germany that engaged them in an exchange of skills and strategies for social leadership, mutual support, and the creation of a female consciousness. This aspect of Sieveking's accomplishment and its roots in the personal experience of overcoming social prescriptions, even more than the institutional impact of her career, was truly innovative. Sieveking addressed her appeal to women like herself who were financially secure and offered them the fruits of her personal struggle. The idea with which she first started was similar to Theodor Fliedner's: the introduction into German Protestantism of a charitable order for women. The Female Association developed in a way that in the end bore very little resemblance to her girlhood dream, but female leadership and female autonomy provided an element of continuity. Her unequivocal commitment to the goal of feminization as an end in itself, not as a means for achieving an ulterior confessional purpose, distinguished her work from Fliedner's. By virtue of the Sieveking association, orthodox Christian women in Germany joined their British and American sisters in the practice of philanthropy.

THE PATRICIAN CONTEXT AND THE
AWAKENING

Sieveking's accomplishment, both personal and public, is unimaginable outside the context of the Hamburg patriciate. During Amalie's own lifetime and still today, the Sievekings were among the first families of Hamburg. Amalie was the daughter and granddaughter of senators, niece of a syndic, and cousin of one of Hamburg's principal early-nineteenth-century diplomats.

The Female Association benefited from these contacts. The sense of responsible elitism which the Sieveking family cultivated reinforced the capacity for personal non-conformity, a major ingredient in Amalie's success.

One important legacy from her youth was an early exposure to educational discrimination. Raised in the company of brothers, a single daughter whose mother had died in her very early childhood, Amalie shared the house tutor as well as the recreation of her brothers until her father's death. At that time, in 1809, the children were dispersed among relatives. Amalie's school lessons, though not those of her brothers, were discontinued and she went to live as the companion to an invalid aunt. Her later advocacy of philanthropy as a vocation for women presupposed an improvement in the standards of women's education. She discovered her own talent as a teacher in her aunt's household where she instituted a series of six-year tutorial classes for girls which she continued through her entire life. They became a major source of her influence; her former pupils were dedicated disciples and ardent correspondents. She placed a number of them as tutors with prominent families throughout Germany. In this way she shaped the style of her subsequent activism, the marshalling of familial influence to advance her own conception of women's interests.[3]

A protracted period of personal turmoil and self-examination absorbed Sieveking's attention during her early twenties, a crisis evoked in part by the evident contradictions between contemporary expectations and the option of the single life for which she yearned. Much later she recalled:

It must have been about the year 1818 when I started to reflect on the specific fate of women, and when my inner calling began to be clear to me. The fatherly advice of Campe [the late-eighteenth-century moralist Joachim Heinrich Campe] to his daughter made a profound impression on me at that time and was, as I only later grasped, truly useful. Marriage was presented there [in Campe's book] as the only course for a girl, which contradicted an inner voice in me.... More and more it seemed clear to me that it was impossible that the bountiful Lord would bestow his blessing on one estate alone. Rather he would look with favor on all estates, even that of the ill-reputed old maid.[4]

In her spiritual diary she confided: "If not a happy wife and mother, then founder of an order of Sisters of Charity!"[5] This goal, in varying degrees of urgency, occupied her thoughts for the next decade.

Sieveking's fantasy, the creation of an order for Protestant women in Germany, was shaped by the religious awakening Hamburg experienced during and after the French occupation. Patriotism stimulated an enormously emotional revival, one that obscured confessional distinctions and sustained subjective forms of religious expression. The Sieveking family and many of their closest associates among Hamburg's religious and political elite were at the center of this movement. The pastor of the French Reformed Church in Hamburg, the mystic Henri Merle d'Aubigné, exercised a powerful influence in this circle, preaching that the one true Catholic church embraced all Christians, Catholics as well as Protestants, who had experienced conversion.[6] The Catholic legacy became particularly accessible to the Sieveking circle through the count Leopold Stolberg and the pastor Johannes Gossner, the one a recent convert to Catholicism, the other newly won to Protestantism. Both were residents of Hamburg during the post-war years. Stolberg's biography of St. Vincent de Paul introduced Amalie Sieveking to the historic milieu of the Catholic Sisters of Charity. The privileged relationship she enjoyed with Gossner in its emphasis on spiritual examination, growth, and social commitment is reminiscent of that between Vincent de Paul and the Daughters of Charity, on which it may indeed have been modeled.[7] Years later Sieveking urged her associates to

keep in mind that we are called to work in an area in the Evangelical Church that . . . has only been relatively little developed, namely the area of poor relief exercised by women. At the time of the Reformation, many a pious foundation went down . . . and nothing took its place. It seems to me particularly regrettable with respect to the Sisters of Charity who set as their life task to serve the Lord through his poor brothers. They became an ornament of the Catholic church which the Protestants might well envy. . . . Why do we let the Catholics shame us? . . . Ought not free Evangelical love give witness to a similar fruit?[8]

At the time of Gossner's departure from Hamburg, Sieveking accepted his blessing which formally solemnized her vow to make a reality of a Protestant Sisters of Charity.[9] In the end she moved in a very different direction, one determined by individual as well as social choices. Careful scrutiny of the statutes of the Bavarian order of Sisters of Charity which Gossner sent her roused a sense of skepticism. "The yoke is too slavish, the chains too restrictive," she wrote to Stein, the retired Prussian reformer.[10] To her brother she had once confessed: "From the bottom of my soul I hate all human organizations of authority in matters of faith, and I acknowledge evangelical freedom as one of the most exalted attributes of our church."[11] The Hamburg Awakening was fed from English Evangelicalism as well as from the Catholic renascence of the South, and it was this source that ultimately lent a more permanent mark to the institutional development of the city. The Hamburg-Altona Bible Society (1814), the Evangelical Missionary Society (1822), and the Lower Saxon Tractarian Society (1820) suggest the accuracy of one commentator who observed that English ideas, like English wares, flooded the city after the war.[12] Pastor Rautenberg of Trinity Church introduced the English Sunday school and his annual report of 1831 called the men of his congregation to adopt another English practice, that of benevolent visiting. Amalie Sieveking acknowledged no specific indebtedness to this report but it is more than likely it inspired the society she ultimately founded.[13] Benevolent visiting did not acquire much of a following among German men but as a consequence of Sieveking's commitment it was an area of Protestant philanthropy, like nursing, that women entered and then numerically dominated—or feminized.

The Awakening in Hamburg reinforced the historic interpenetration of sacred and secular. Membership in the several governing bodies of the city-republic depended upon wealth, religion, and kinship. Of the eighty-nine burgermasters since the Reformation, thirty-nine had been sons of senators. Legal citizenship itself was restricted to guild masters and to the three or four thousand owners of inherited property of stipulated value. The city was governed by a council and several colleges consisting of dignitaries whose position derived in part from their functions in the five major parishes of the city. There was also a citizens' assembly. Participation at any level of government was confined to Lutherans. Members of the Reformed and Roman Catholic communions could qualify for citizenship; Jews were excluded from government and citizenship alike although they constituted one-twentieth of the population.[14]

THE POOR RELIEF CRISIS

Two events in the life of contemporary Hamburg propelled Amalie Sieveking from the speculative course of her early life into social action. The first was a campaign launched by the press in 1830 to identify and publicize the failures of municipal poor relief in the city. The second was the cholera epidemic of 1831. During the first half of the nineteenth century Hamburg epitomized the contradictions and conflicts of modernizing Germany. At a time when only seventy cities in the German empire had counted more than 10,000 residents, Hamburg's population numbered 110,000; during the decades after the peace settlement, population increased at a rate of approximately 6 percent annually.[15] Seafaring tied Hamburg to the overseas world, particularly to England; during the war the city suffered as much from the interruption of English commerce as from the occupation by the French.[16] The restoration of commerce after the war acted as a magnet to the rural population; inordinate growth of the city kept wages low and drew the poor into increasingly miserable housing as the extension of wharfs and warehouses impinged upon their traditional quarters.[17] The poor relief administration was unable to accommodate these changes. At the end of the eighteenth century Hamburg supported a system of relief that was the envy of the European continent. Designed by Kaspar von Voght (1752–1839), it combined public and private resources with the goal of eliminating the conditions that produced poverty. The system depended upon close involvement with the poor, on training as well as penal provisions, and on the personal commitment of ranking government officials. Disrupted by the war when occupying officers banished poor people from the city, the poor relief administration never recovered its earlier character. In 1832 only 2846 families were regularly registered with the administration, an increase of just 540 since the turn of the century, a time span in which the total population was increasing at the rate of approximately 2000 persons a year. During the cholera epidemic, the inadequacy of the public relief system was scandalously apparent. A clear indication that a permanently alienated class was in the making was the record of illegitimacy, which in the years 1826–1835 numbered one in every five births. Residency requirements to meet the qualifications for legal marriage were, in other words, increasingly beyond reach. Many people were beyond the reach of the church as well; seldom were more than thirty or forty persons in attendance at any one of the city's five major churches.[18]

At the beginning of the century, citizens of Hamburg believed that theirs was a city of mutuality and interconnectedness. The guilds were one source of bonding, but by the early mid-nineteenth century their hold on the economy was no longer absolute. The post-war decades witnessed a rapid expansion of non-guild-controlled manufactures, among them tobacco wares, sugar products, umbrellas, and walking sticks. By 1856, 85 percent of all goods manufactured for export in Hamburg came out of factories rather than guild-controlled shops. The appearance of a class of small entrepreneurs accompanied this development, manufacturers who often shared few common interests with the guild masters, merchants, and shippers and whose participation in the government was negligible. A more visible evidence of change was the uncontrolled increase of unaffiliated workers, many of whom lived habitually on the borders of poverty and swelled the ranks of what was becoming a permanent, unassimilated underclass.[19]

Baron von Voght returned to the city in 1830 after a twenty-year absence and proceeded to attack the poor administration for its failure to deal with contemporary issues. He targeted the erosion of individual involvement on the part of the ruling circle, and the substitution of alms-giving for work and supervision. Conceding that the situation was beyond restitution, the poor administration called for a clear delineation between public and private responsibility and limited the commitment of the city to subsistence support only.[20]

Amalie Sieveking took this announcement as an invitation and a challenge. During the autumn of 1831 she had gained notoriety when she entered the infirmary of St. Ericus as a volunteer to care for female cholera patients. The medical service at first resented her intrusion; her social circle suspected her of courting deliberate martyrdom. She persevered, and when she completed her tour of duty she had established her credentials with the officialdom on which her future work would depend and won the reverential support of her peers.[21]

THE FEMALE ASSOCIATION ORGANIZES

On May 23, 1832 Sieveking was joined by twelve other women to found the Female Association for the Care of the Poor and Sick, a society for benevolent visiting. The aim of the association was to visit the households of impoverished invalids and their families on the basis of referrals from the public administration for poor relief, and to provide practical and material help as well as spiritual guidance. The statutes of the association recognized that the number of clients the association could expect to serve and the nature of its commitment would necessarily depend both on the number of members recruited and the financial resources at its disposal. No woman was to consider membership unless she could expect to devote herself to at least one and preferably two house calls each week, and to at least one meeting each week with other members of the association to review the results of their visits. Sieveking's preoccupation with the conventions of religious orders informed the new statutes: members were specifically instructed to remain in their customary life situation, to change neither their dress nor their appearance nor in any way draw attention to their calling. Their new corporate identity was to be reflected rather in their conduct: the obligations of sisterhood bound them to one another in prayer and love and in their work among the poor.[22] In her inaugural talk to the association, it is noteworthy that Sieveking invoked the general obligations of Christian charity; nowhere in her speech did she allude to womanly qualities or female spheres, nor did she cite the legacy of biblical women.[23] The imagery familiar to British and American benevolence was foreign to her and to conservative pre-revolutionary Germany. Socially, as well as spiritually and morally, Sieveking conceived of the charitable function as one of amelioration and integration, not one of change. Poverty, as she represented it, was one dimension of an educative plan ordained by God to improve the souls of the poor and instruct the rich in the virtues of mercy. Benevolent visiting took both dimensions of this plan into account. The visitor was expected to make a full assessment of the material and spiritual inventory of the household visited. She might donate goods and services but most important she must instruct the visited in the virtues of cleanliness, parsimony, sobriety, and the fear of God. Every visit included prayer and Bible reading. At the center of Sieveking's personal faith was a strong commitment to the doctrine of individual immortality and in her own visits she tried to awaken her clients to the promise of eternal life which, she believed, offered them an incentive to conduct better lives. As she wrote in the instructions to her colleagues: "Christian love ... points the way to future salvation but also recalls the condition to which the attainment of it is tied."[24] Sieveking, in other words, enlisted the supernatural in the service of social compliance.

Beyond the personal interaction of the visit itself, visits were the means the Female Association used to identify more extended commitments to its clientele: the distribution of clothing, of food donated by local provisioners, of coupons for the city's soup kitchen, and, most important, the assignment of work. The association itself functioned as an employer: it organized work among its own clientele such as repairs and maintenance, and it consigned put-out work, particularly work for home-bound women such as sewing, knitting, rag picking, and menial chores. Sieveking justified the distribution of piece work to impoverished mothers on the grounds that their continued presence at home would forestall the institutionalization of their children.[25] Sieveking operated within what was for Hamburg an increasingly obsolete household economy and she wanted to save rather than to change it. Her program provided no training component, no day care or infant schools to permit mothers to give up household handwork for manufacturing in the city. A voluntary effort in this direction awaited the organization of non-confessional women.

The poor Sieveking applauded in her annual reports were people who were willing to acknowledge that their own sinfulness played a role in their misery, those who displayed "the fear of God" and "child-like innocence," those who accepted aid "within the bounds of modesty."[26] In the economic crisis of the 1840s Sieveking recognized that, however virtuous, the male worker could scarcely support a family and she believed that the cause lay in the relentless drive of manufacturers to lower prices in order to seize the market. The surplus of laborers facilitated this practice. Sieveking barely contained her anger at the new bourgeoisie. The workers her organization supported were displaced artisans: carpenters displaced by the new construction industry and spinners put out of work by textile machinery. Given the constraints of her own education and position, Sieveking's observations were often acute, but strategies of change completely alluded her. "I see no way in the realm of human power and wisdom," she wrote, "to mitigate this poverty. . . . But I should at least like to draw it to the attention of the upper classes as an evil."[27]

In one of the messages she wrote to her "friends among the poor"—this time after violence had erupted in Paris and Berlin early in 1848—she equated the destruction of factories with the destruction of jobs. She reassured her ostensible audience that "our first statesmen" were seeking a solution to the crisis and urged the oppressed to forego the temptation to take the law into their own hands.[28]

Notwithstanding a commitment to the counsels of compliance, the association met with resistance at many levels when it was first founded. Baron von Voght himself doubted whether a society of "wives, mothers, housekeepers, sisters, and daughters" could undertake the requisite services: "the work of sisters of charity is suitable only to persons who are completely alone in the world and can devote themselves exclusively to their calling."[29] Relations between the association and the public administration remained fragile for years and demanded Sieveking's constant attention.

You have to know our local situation [she wrote in 1837]; the multitude of civic bureaucrats, the frequent changes among them, a prevalent republican spirit, and each one of them wishing to conduct his own area of competency with a kind of independent hegemony over which he is very jealous; then in the majority of our doctors a powerful partiality against the revived evangelical spirit which they equate with mysticism.[30]

Long after the existence of her association was assured, Sieveking remained poised for the counter-offensive. It is important to recognize the several sources of Sieveking's embattled righteousness. Perhaps it was a stance fueled in part by her earlier struggle to legitimate her personal and intellectual non-conformity. But it also suggests a particular perception of class and gender. Sieveking clearly exploited the advantage of her own station in the patriciate to anchor the work of her association in the routine of the city bureaucracy. The original design of the association, however, had embraced an inclusive membership with respect to class if not confession. Sieveking ultimately relinquished that goal in favor of a more limited constituency. Membership lists of the Female Association were not published, but Sieveking's manuscript notes taken in conjunction with the annual reports make it apparent that the women who joined her came from her own constellation, women whose families were politically and religiously powerful, who were frustrated by their own leisure and dismayed by the rise of poverty and the erosion of harmony in Hamburg society. Of the seventy members Sieveking recorded in her personal notebook in 1847, at least thirteen besides herself were wives or daughters of senators, ancients, or clergy. Their existence was interwoven with the oligarchy of the city.[31] The elitism of the association was a deliberate operational principle. Sieveking devoutly believed that "moral authority extends from the higher to the lower circles."[32]

Membership in the Sieveking association required non-conforming conduct: it was not customary for ladies to venture forth from their homes to visit the poor. But neither in her exercise of leadership nor in that of the women she recruited did Sieveking seek to alter the prevailing power relations between women and men. The premise of activity in the association was paternal or marital permission. Sieveking occasionally expressed her regret that men denied the women of their households the sanction to engage in charitable activities, even women who had dutifully absolved all of their household obligations, but she never challenged their right to do so.[33] The principle of women's autonomy within a sphere of her own was totally foreign to her. Just as Sieveking's concept of the Christian soul precluded a concept of woman's nature, her understanding of patriarchy precluded the division of public and private spheres. The enormous vindictiveness with which she later attacked the work of women aligned with non-orthodox associations suggests how vulnerable she apparently felt herself to be and how necessary she believed it was to reassure a society that was always potentially hostile that hers was truly a benign effort. She was clearly afraid that the appearance of organizations of women inimical to the social order might implicate her work and threaten her own access to public activity.

Positive support for the Sieveking association was nevertheless evident at many levels. From the original twelve members the society expanded to include fifty-three during its first decade, seventy on the eve of the revolution, and eighty-five at the time of Sieveking's death in 1859.[34] As the membership grew the case load expanded from an original eighty-five families to 256. Funded by voluntary contributions, the expendable income of the association increased from 1,332 marks the first year to 47,000 in 1859.[35] In 1837 a large anonymous endowment made possible a significant addition to the society's enterprises, the *Amalienstift*, a foundation that allowed for the construction of a building to provide both low-cost housing to the poor and a children's hospital. After the great Hamburg fire of 1842 destroyed a quarter of the city, advantageous funding permitted an extension of housing to families that had been burned out.[36]

"A PROPENSITY FOR DESPOTISM"

The governance of the Female Association reflected the predilections of its founder. Self-government and the democratic process were procedures Sieveking held in low esteem, and she intentionally retained absolute control of the association. She once wrote in her diary when she was still a young woman: "I believe I have the propensity to become truly despotic,"[37] and she was right. Later, referring to the association and her failure to delegate responsibility, she observed that although it did not "lie in my plan to do everything myself, and leave the abilities of my members unused, ... I have so far not yet found it feasible" to share responsibility. She was convinced that to relinquish "the conduct of affairs related to the direction of the whole enterprise would not be possible without threatening the unity and order of the entirety."[38] The work program of the association in the community—the purchase of raw materials and their distribution among the clients of the organization for manufacture—was implemented by the work committee. The finances of the association were managed by professionals, male acquaintances of Sieveking's in the Hamburg business community.

But in the administration of the association itself Sieveking acted alone. Her reelection at the annual meetings was pro forma; the executive committee and the general meeting exercised purely consultative authority. In case of admissions to membership, Sieveking in practice exercised the determining vote, although this violated the statutes. Major internal decisions as well as external relations Sieveking administered personally. She told an audience of women in Bremen who were planning to organize a club on the model of the association that punctuality, strict order, and subordination were the essentials to conducting an effective organization.[39] A decade later when the inter-confessional women of Hamburg had demonstrated that it was possible to conduct an effective organization within a collective leadership model, Sieveking justified her authority in different terms: "the Lord ... for the first time called into being through me the idea of a women's visiting society. It lies in the nature of the things," she argued, "that in Hamburg the administrative regime took on a patriarchal character."[40] The institutional model for the Female Association was obviously the city-republic of Hamburg itself.

In its membership the association, at least originally, was supposed to represent the various estates of contemporary society, which then in their functional connection with the poor and with each other would mirror the order of the wider community.[41] Just as all offices in the government of Hamburg were restricted to Lutherans, so Sieveking refused admission to her association to anyone whose religious orthodoxy was in doubt. It was on these grounds that Charlotte Paulsen (1799–1862) was refused membership in 1844. Paulsen was a member of a once-prominent merchant family; she was bitterly disillusioned by the rejection.[42] But the rejection was consequential both for progressive women in Hamburg and for the future of middle-class feminism in general because it turned her into the champion of a new form of women's philanthropy altogether. Paulsen's work reveals elements of continuity with the Sieveking association but the enterprise of Paulsen's inter-confessional associates was undertaken in a wholly different spirit, one that questioned the legitimacy both of the spiritual and of the structural premises of the Female Association.

Initially when she started the visiting society, Sieveking herself had viewed it as an expedient until such a time as she could mount the initiative to implement her earlier goal of a Protestant order. Apart from her success and "the affection I have come to feel for the association in its present form,"[43] a number of developments induced her to abandon her original plan. Decisive was the interchange with Fliedner. This legitimated her association in her own eyes and brought her to a full awareness of her place in the general context of female philanthropy. Fliedner offered Sieveking the position of Superintendent of the Motherhouse at Kaiserswerth in 1837. His letter described the hopes and realities of the incipient institution. Sieveking confessed to her brother that the offer was enormously tempting; in the end she refused in recognition of the ties she felt to her birthplace and her projects in Hamburg. Principal among these was obviously the benevolent society, but she also mentioned the deep commitment she felt to the girls in her classes and to women's education generally.[44] What is historically the most significant in Sieveking's rejection of Fliedner's overture, however, was the reinforcemnt it lent to the principle of female leadership independent of both male and ecclesiastical direction. At the same time Sieveking's refusal marked a self-conscious recognition on her part of her role as a philanthropic pioneer, the founder of an innovative institutional form that departed decisively from Catholic antecedents, vestiges of which were still evident in Fliedner's diaconate.

SIEVEKING'S SOCIETY: A NATIONAL MODEL

Already in 1837 in the interchange with Fliedner, Sieveking indicated that the Female Association was generating interest elsewhere in Germany. At least four similar societies had been established in other cities and more were anticipated. Sieveking's imitators found in her work not only the precedent for benevolent visiting as such but also the legitimation for a systematic recruitment of lay volunteer women, married as well as single, into the charitable enterprise. By 1842 there were more than fifteen associations that identified themselves as affiliates: they wrote to commiserate with Sieveking at the time of the Hamburg fire. The number of self-proclaimed affiliates was fifty-five by the outbreak of the revolution, forty-five of them in Germany. The proliferation of associations was confirmed in the pages of *Fly Leaves* (*Fliegende Blaetter aus dem Rauhen Haus*), the newspaper published by Johann Hinrich Wichern, which became the journal of the Inner Mission. The Sieveking affiliates adopted the practice of publishing annual reports only gradually and distribution was limited. The absence of a more formal structure among the several societies bothered Wichern, whose notions of order were global, but it was precisely this informality that proved the strength of the Sieveking coalition.[45] Personal networking created the impetus to organize and permitted women with little or no public exposure to come together without embarrassment and develop their talents through experience. Theirs was a loose bond forged primarily by correspondence with Sieveking and subscription to her annual report.

The initial overture to Sieveking was usually a request for copies of the statutes of the Hamburg association, for the instructions to benevolent visitors, or for annual reports. Women like the first chairman in Magdeburg hoped that close adherence to Hamburg procedures would compensate for their own inexperience and insure the successful recruitment of volunteers. What is striking among these correspondents is their relative diversity. Charlotte Ahlefeld-Lindau identified herself as a cloistered woman in Preetz who hoped to extend the nature of her work by creating a society like Sieveking's. Friederica Plau, a resident of Danzig whose familiarity with British experience prompted her interest, was grateful to Sieveking for demonstrating that an English practice could indeed be transferred to Germany. For her and the women she recruited, work with the poor had been a lesson in "fear of God, thankfulness, industry and modesty."[46] Sieveking's visit to Bremen stimulated a surge of correspondence; on that occasion she had for the first time formally appealed to an audience outside the confines of Hamburg. Her speech encouraged Henriette von Gruber to implement the desire for benevolent activity she had harbored ever since the War of Liberation.[47]

The deference with which Sieveking's correspondents addressed her suggest both her status and her originality. Sophie Behrens, who engaged in an extended interchange from Kiel, was positively reverential, exclaiming: "To think of actually possessing a few lines from Amalie Sieveking, directed to me!" Luise Gosche in Toenning compared her work to the work of martyrs. From Berlin, Sophie Erichmann thanked Sieveking for her encouragement and concluded that her most heart-felt prayers had been answered.[48]

Many of the letter writers asked for very practical forms of assistance. Frau Pastor Noltensius, for instance, asked Sieveking for the names of prayer books that were suitable for use with the sick; she also wanted to know how much the Hamburg association paid its home-bound workers for rag-picking. From Magdeburg came an inquiry about the number of poor calls each association member should be prepared to make and whether or not they should donate money to the households they visited.[49] All of the correspondents were awed by the accomplishment of the association in Hamburg. One woman spoke of the association in Cologne as "a little daughter" of the one in Hamburg; a correspondent in Kiel spoke of her society as a "weak little child" by comparison.[50]

As time passed, many of these associations gained in confidence and what had been an obsequious relationship became one of reciprocity. Gottfried Bagelmann, writing in 1841 not long after Sieveking's visit to Bremen, mentioned that the Bremen society assumed responsibility for providing food, wine, clothing, and care to fifteen families of impoverished invalids. Doris Esselbach in Schleswig spoke of twenty-five recipients of care from her society in 1845. Early in 1843 Ida Ahrenhold wrote that the Hanover association had purchased a house and garden where they provided more than twenty families with inexpensive rentals. Annual reports were increasingly exchanged rather than requested. Pastor Hugues sent the first printed report from Celle by the personal kindness of Frau von Voigt in 1842, and Elise Hunicke invited Sieveking's comments on the Bremen statutes in 1844.[51] In 1847, a poignant letter accompanied the report from Stettin.

It gives me particular pleasure to be able to send you, my dear lady, the enclosed report, for indeed your activity to relieve the need of the poor preceded ours and . . . your sleepless nights permitted our success. You in contrast to us, suffered much more anxiety than we for you founded your association at a time when much greater resistance prevailed. My sister workers ask you to accept their heartfelt thanks.[52]

In the course of their correspondence many of the women writing Sieveking were candid about their sense of personal inadequacy to deal with the problems they confronted, usually as chairpersons of their associations. Marianne von Voigt wrote from Celle in 1835: "A greater expansion under my aegis will be difficult, for my energies are insufficient for it."[53] Henriette von Gruber in Stralsund wrote that she would have liked to start a visiting association much sooner but until the Lord sent her a coworker in the person of the wife of Consul Bartels from Rostock who had previous experience, there was no one of sufficient stature to assume the chair. "I know," she added "that I do not possess your talents." Sophie Behrens called herself "still so inexperienced." Apparently leadership was the perennial problem. Ida Lempfert resigned from the female association in Altona for a while because she feared that her own weaknesses would bring discredit to the society. Emmy Pauli apparently became chairperson in Lubeck against her better judgment and wrote of her "many difficult hours." Helene Schulze, writing from

Ludwigslust, worried about whether she was following instructions accurately. From St. Georg outside of Hamburg, Maria Ide confided that the members of her association lacked the necessary independence and found it hard to get around by themselves in bad weather.[54] Some clubs experienced difficulty in reaching a consensus about what specific sector among the poor to target for assistance, the elderly or the young, the sick or the out-of-work.[55]

THE WORK OF WOMEN

There was a certain uniformity in the kind of issues that Sieveking's correspondence addressed and it was to these recurrent themes that the anonymous little volume *Work of Women in Associations for the Care of the Poor and Sick: An Exchange of Letters between Two Friends (Arbeit der Frauen in Vereinen fuer Armen- und Krankenpflege. Ein Briefwechsel zweier Freundinnen)*, was addressed.[56] The authors were, in reality, two close friends of Sieveking and Sieveking herself wrote the introduction. The purported exchange of letters echoes authentic letters in Sieveking's own files and were clearly designed as a guide to women in club work, perhaps to alleviate the personal burden Sieveking assumed when she personally answered the many requests for guidance. The sequence opens with "Clara's" election to the chair of her club and successively examines such issues as the best time and place for meetings, meeting strategies, procedures for visitations, personal qualities desirable for the successful interchange with clients, characteristic client problems, work suitable for home manufacture, and finally the management of club affairs as such: finances, records, and annual reports. Frequent mention is made of the value of the Hamburg reports as a precedent. It is apparent that the authors anticipated a reservoir of inexperience in their readership. Their purpose was to provide both a resource and a source of reassurance. Clara, for instance, confides: "I have just been introduced into the chairmanship and the meetings which in the beginning I used to anticipate with throbbing heart are now more or less easy and acceptable to me."[57] At another point, Clara deplores the fact that, while her coworkers acknowledge the importance of reading one another's reports of visits in the official bluebook each society kept, "how often is nothing read and virtually nothing written. . . . [Yet] how necessary it is that I don't lose my patience and bring upon myself the charge of pedantry in the service of orderliness."[58] *The Work of Women* delivered more substantive counsel as well:

Intervention on our part into the domestic and marital relations of our clients is something special and often something much more sensitive than our clients themselves behave as though it were. We cannot always entirely avoid involvement; the naiveté with which our poor commonly disclose their intimate relations and the motives of their conduct requires as great candor as it does caution in our ways of approaching such issues.[59]

The lady visitors learned the existence of another world, a world in which women workers would not, for example, attend church on Sundays if the piece work they had contracted to do at home were unfinished. The penalty was the sacrifice of wages for the entire week.[60] Yet, as Clara exclaimed:

We know that even for material need no relief is possible unless the poor learn to pray, and we consequently want everyone to reach this goal, but which paths lead there? Ah, dear Marie, here is where the diversity begins.[61]

A compendium of often sound observation, *The Work of Women* provided a hidden agenda. It reminded the reader that other Christian women were coping with similar problems and seeking bonds of mutual support, and that they could look for help from one another. This was the real achievement of the Sieveking coalition.[62]

Sieveking believed that the introduction of female benevolent visiting together with the implementation of female leadership were singular accomplishments, but as early as her speech to the women of Bremen she cautioned against "slavish imitation."[63] A review of her correspondence as well as of the notices in the *Fliegende Blaetter* make it apparent that the Sieveking coalition embraced a variety of charitable commitments and leadership patterns. Some of the affiliates were not even visiting societies: some adopted the model of the *Amalienstift*, Sieveking's foundation in Hamburg, and sponsored either children's hospitals or low-rent housing. Others, notably the society at Bremen, served a more limited clientele than Sieveking but preserved the principle of visitation. *The Work of Women* and Sieveking herself acknowledged that female leadership might not be possible in every case, and it is clear that it wasn't. The presence of clergy and clergy wives suggests that independence from the church was not always as fully achieved as it was in Hamburg.[64] Confusion about what distinguished the Sieveking coalition extended even to the *Frauen-Zeitung*, the feminist paper Louise Otto published in Saxony under the impetus of the revolution. Not long after the appearance of the first issue—but more than fifteen years after the founding of the Female Association for the Care of the Poor and Sick in Hamburg—the editor asked for more information about the society that seemed to be conducted in a spirit "out of keeping with our own," but which reputedly did good works.[65]

What did in fact distinguish the Sieveking coalition? What constituted the common ground among the various affiliates? Within the coalition there certainly was a growing consensus about the areas of charity that could be feminized, where women could be introduced without offense and ultimately prevail. For the most part they were new areas where male activity had not previously extended. There was also a consensus that this activity should develop within the tenets of Protestant orthodoxy. Beyond this Sieveking thought she represented a form of female emancipation.[66] Indeed she did, but it was a form of emancipation that addressed neither the basic class structure of society nor the social relationship between men and women. It envisaged the emancipation of privileged women compatible with traditional Christianity and subject to the acquiescence of the patriarchal family. In this regard, Sieveking is reminiscent of the British Quaker reformer Elizabeth Fry; contrary to conservative domestic feminism in America such as Catharine Beecher represented, Sieveking never imagined a sphere in which women would exercise autonomy. On a number of occasions she paid specific tribute to the husbands and fathers who gave permission to their wives and daughters to accept charitable responsibilities outside the home. She did not question their authority to do so.[67] The concept of woman's nature and a sphere in which women might be autonomous was alien to her thinking. Private and public were one. To legitimate women's charity Sieveking invoked not woman's nature but the analogue of the court whose moral example penetrated the entire *Residenz*.[68] Her opponents by contrast were able to develop a non-confessional basis for their effort and also to cultivate a family model that, by acknowledging the unique nature of woman and woman's distinctive sphere, permitted women autonomy within that sphere and allowed them increasingly to extend its boundaries by defining aspects of the public sphere in domestic terms. The sense of shared participation in woman's nature permitted them to develop both patterns of collective leadership among themselves and commitments to women of the popular classes inaccessible to Sieveking who was bound by the precepts of the Hamburg patriciate.

NOTES

1. Amalie Sieveking, "Vortrag in Bremen, gehalten am 25. Oktober 1841," *WVAK, 10. Bericht*, p. 73.

2. Ibid., p. 80.

3. [Emma Poel], *Denkwuerdigkeiten aus dem Leben von Amalie Sieveking in deren Auftrage von einer Freundin derselben verfasst* (Hamburg: Agentur des Rauhen Hauses, 1860), pp. 2–25, quotation from p. 84, a collection assembled shortly after Sieveking's death of excerpts from her letters and diary before they were deposited in the family archives in Hamburg; Verzeichnis III B, Die Schulerinnen, Nls AWS, StAr Hmbg; also Sieveking to Eduard and Louise Sieveking, 25 April 1832, citing family friends she approached, Nls AWS, StAr Hmbg.

4. [Poel], *Denkwuerdigkeiten*, pp. 116–17; see Joachim Heinrich Campe, *Vaeterlicher Rath fuer meine Tochter. Ein Gegenstueck zum Theophron. Der erwachsenen weiblichen Jugend gewidmet* (Brunswick: Schulbuchhandlung, 1791), especially pp. 85, 172.

5. Sonntagsunterhaltungen, entry for 18 April 1819, Nls AWS, StAr Hmbg.

6. Rudolf Kayser, "Henri Merle d'Aubigné und die Anfaenge der Erweckung in Hamburg," *ZVHG* 30 (1929): 125; Sieveking to Caroline Bertheau, 13 May 1836, confessed that she was in love in Merle, though none of her biographies to my knowledge refer to this disclosure, Nls AWS, StAr Hmbg.

7. Kayser, "Friedrich Perthes und seine katholischen Freunde," *ZVHG* 34 (1934): 9–10; [Poel], *Denkwuerdigkeiten*, pp. 85, 117, 131–34; Sieveking to Senator Dr. Volkmann, 25 July 1828, Nls AWS, StAr Hmbg; Friedrich Leopold Graf von Stolberg *Leben des heiligen Vincentius von Paulus* (Vienna: C. Gerold 1819), especially pp. 102–7.

8. *WVAK, 20. Bericht*, pp. 60–61.

9. Hermann Dalton, *Johannes Gossner. Ein Lebensbild aus der Kirche des neunzehnten Jahrhunderts* (Berlin: Gossner, 1874), pp. 297–98.

10. Sieveking to Freiherr v. Stein, 14 Sept. 1830, Nls AWS, StAr Hmbg.

11. [Poel], *Denkwuerdigkeiten*, p. 167.

12. Kayser, "Henri Merle d'Aubigné," p. 129; Hans Georg Bergemann, *Staat und Kirche in Hamburg waehrend des 19. Jahrhunderts* (Hamburg: Friedrich Wittig Verlag, 1958), pp. 41–42.

13. Martin Gerhardt, *Johann Hinrich Wichern: Ein Lebensbild*, 3 vols. (Hamburg: Buchhandlung des Rauhen Hauses, 1927–31), 1: 118, 257.

14. Ingrid Lahrsen, "Beitraege zum kirchlichen und religioesen Leben Hamburgs zur Zeit der Erweckungsbewegung" (Dissertation, Hamburg, 1957), pp. 1–5; Kayser, "Henri Merle d'Aubigné," pp. 118–27; Percy Ernst Schramm, *Hamburg, Deutschland und die Welt. Leistung und Grenzen hanseatischen Buergertums in der Zeit zwischen Napoleon und Bismarck* (Munich: Georg D. W. Calwey, 1943), pp. 27, 17, 417; Dirk Baverdamm, *Von der Revolution zur Reform. Die Verfassungspolitik des hamburgischen Senats 1849–50* (Berlin: Duncker und Humblot, 1969), pp. 18–19 explains the intricate interconnections between church and state; Antje Kraus, *Die Unterschichten Hamburgs in der ersten Haelfte des 19. Jahrhunderts: Entstehung, Struktur und Lebensverhaeltnisse* (Stuttgart: G. Fischer, 1965) pp. 24–27 indicates that the convocations of legal citizenry were poorly attended early in the century.

15. Karl Obermann, "Die deutsche Bevoelkerungsstatistik und die Bevoelkerungsstruktur des Deutschen Bundes in den Jahren um 1815," *Bevoelkerungsgeschichte*, ed. Wolfgang Koellmann and Peter Marschalck (Cologne: Keipenheuer und Witsch, 1972), p. 196; Schramm, *Hamburg*, p. 27; with forty-one millionaires, Hamburg was a match for the capital of the Empire, Vienna, ibid., p. 26; Kraus, *Unterschichten*, p. 34.

16. Schramm, *Hamburg*, pp. 243, 269.

17. Kraus, *Unterschichten*, pp. 36, 31.

18. Caspar Freiherr von Voght, *Account of the Management of the Poor in Hamburg since the Year 1788* (London: reprinted by G. Davidson, 1817); Hermann Joachim, *Historische Arbeit aus seinem Nachlass* (Hamburg: Hans Christians Verlag, 1936), p. 127; Kraus, *Unterschichten*, pp. 47–49; Elisabeth Haupt, *Amalie Sieveking als Gruenderin des weiblichen*

Vereins fuer Armen- und Krankenpflege in Hamburg (Berlin-Spandau: Wichern Verlag, 1933), pp. 20, 22, 77; Lahrsen, "Beitraege," pp. 98–100.

19. Schramm, *Hamburg,* p. 29; Ernst Baasch, *Geschichte Hamburgs 1814–1918,* 2 vols. (Gotha-Stuttgart: F. A. Perthes, 1924–25), 1: 20; Kraus, *Unterschichten,* pp. 1, 51.

20. Haupt, *Amalie Sieveking,* pp. 20–24.

21. Ibid., pp. 19–20; Hudtwalcker, *Ein halbes Jahrhundert* 3: 387–88.

22. Haupt, *Amalie Sieveking,* p. 20; *WVAK, 2. Bericht,* pp. 1–5.

23. A. Sieveking, "Erste Anrede an die Mitglieder des weiblichen Vereins fuer Armen-und Krankenpflege, den 23. Mai 1832," *WVAK, 10. Bericht,* pp. 56–68.

24. *WVAK, 2. Bericht,* pp. 27–29; *9. Bericht,* pp. 50–66, quotation from pp. 62–63.

25. *WVAK, 12. Bericht,* pp. 40–41, 80; *14. Bericht,* pp. 74–75; *17. Bericht,* pp. 19; *22. Bericht,* p. 24; when the association sold goods made by the poor, they were priced at prevailing prices to preclude undercutting market pricing, see *WVAK, 6 Bericht,* pp. 43–44; Haupt, *Amalie Sieveking,* pp. 53–54 summarizes Sieveking's stance on placing children in orphanages; also *WVAK, 18. Bericht,* 49–50, on dilemmas of the working mother.

26. *WVAK, 11. Bericht,* pp. 33–35.

27. *WVAK, 16. Bericht,* pp. 47–48; *17. Bericht,* p. 19; *6. Bericht,* pp. 42–45, quotation from p. 43.

28. *WVAK, 16. Bericht,* pp. 48, 58.

29. Voght is quoted in Heinrich Sieveking, "Zur Geschichte der Geistigen Bewegung in Hamburg nach den Freiheitskriegen," *ZVHG* 38 (1927): 141.

30. Sieveking to Theodor Fliedner, 28 Aug. 1837, FlAr.

31. [Poel], *Denkwuerdigkeiten,* p. 209; Archiv des weiblichen [Sievekingschen] Vereins fuer Armen-und Krankenpflege, small notebook in Sieveking's hand which unfortunately includes only last names, StAr Hmbg; Bavendamm, *Revolution zur Reform,* p. 284, a chart indicating familial relationships among Senate members.

32. *WVAK, 5. Bericht,* p. 14.

33. *WVAK, 17. Bericht,* p. 66; [Poel], *Denkwuerdigkeiten,* p. 350.

34. *WVAK, 10. Bericht,* p. 11; *15. Bericht,* p. 39; Richard Remé, *Amalie Sieveking. Eine Vorkaempferin der christlichen Frauenbewegung* (Hamburg: Agentur des Rauhen Hauses, 1911), p. 28.

35. *WVAK, 1. Bericht,* pp. 6–7; Remé, *Amalie Sieveking,* p. 28. The municipal poor administration in 1832 estimated minimum subsistence for a family of five at 420 to 440 marks yearly. Contemporaries agreed that a yearly income of 1000 marks was *knapp* or tight. These estimates

may be useful to interpret the relative value of later figures as well. Helga Krohn, *Die Juden in Hamburg 1800–1850. Ihre soziale, kulturelle und politische Entwicklung waehrend der Emanzipationszeit* (Frankfurt a.M.: Europaeische Verlagsanstalt, 1967), p. 51.

36. Haupt, *Amalie Sieveking*, pp. 48–50.

37. [Poel], *Denkwuerdigkeiten*, p. 78.

38. Ibid., p. 228; see also Haupt, *Amalie Sieveking*, p. 29, where she makes a similar point to her brother.

39. *WVAK, 10. Bericht*, p. 92; Haupt, *Amalie Sieveking*, p. 48 discusses how opposition to the acceptance of the *Amalienstift* was overridden by Sieveking; Elise Geerdtz to Sieveking, two letters of 4 March 1841 and Louise Monckeberg geb. Schroder to Sieveking, also 4 March 1841, protest her arbitrary handling of the admission of Therese v. Bacheracht, the writer, opposed by these and other members, Nls AWS, StAr Hmbg.

40. *WVAK, 19. Bericht*, p. 30.

41. [Poel], *Denkwuerdigkeiten*, pp. 208–9.

42. Charlotte Paulsen to Sieveking, 8 June 1844, Nls AWS, StAr Hmbg.

43. Sieveking to Prof. Karl von Raumer, 18 Jan. 1832, in Haupt, *Amalie Sieveking*, p. 59; quotation from *WVAK, 10. Bericht*, p. 77.

44. Fliedner's original invitation and Sieveking's first response of 27 March 1837, in Anna Sticker, *Friedericke Fliedner und die Anfaenge der Frauendiakonie. Ein Quellenbuch*, 2d ed. (Neukirchen-Vluyn: Buchhandlung des Erziehungsvereins, 1963), pp. 331–34, 109–10; [Poel], *Denkwuerdigkeiten*, pp. 237–42, letters describing her decision; the final letter, Sieveking to Theodor Fliedner, 28 Aug. 1837, FlAr; Sieveking to Eduard Sieveking, Jr., 8 April 1855, looking back on role of Hamburg in decision, Nls AWS, StAr Hmbg.

45. *WVAK, 10. Bericht*, pp. 28–29; "Nach dem Muster des Hamburger Vereins an anderen Orten gegruendete Frauenvereine," Verzeichnis, Nls AWS, StAr Hmbg, pp. 60–63; *Fliegende Blaetter* 4 (1847): 228.

46. Bertha Sack to Sieveking, 16 Feb. 1848, Charlotte Ahlefeld-Lindau to Sieveking, 7 Nov. 1841, Frederica Plau to Sieveking, 19 April 1849, Nls AWS, StAr Hmbg; "Weiblicher Verein fuer Armen und Krankenpflege in Danzig," *AuKF* 3 (March-April 1851): 20.

47. Henriette von Gruber to Sieveking, 1 June 1847, Nls AWS, StAr Hmbg.

48. Sophie Behrens to Sieveking, 11 Nov. 1845, Luise Gosche to Sieveking, 22 March 1858, Sophie Erichmann to Sieveking, 20 Aug.

1844, Nls AWS, StAr Hmbg. See also Julie Hartmann, a woman in Hildesheim, to Sieveking, 17 July 1845, who is profusely thankful for the Hamburg statutes, and Sidonie, Pastorin Zernial, to Sieveking, 16 March 1845, who apologizes for writing when she does not know her, Nls AWS, StAr Hmbg.

49. Frau Pastor Therese Noltensius to Sieveking, 23 Dec. 1842, Bertha Sack to Sieveking, 20 Jan. 1848, Nls AWS, StAr Hmbg.

50. Emilie Lehmann to Sieveking, 22 Nov. 1849, Sophie Behrens to Sieveking, 17 Sept. 1845, Nls AWS, StAr Hmbg.

51. Gottfried Bagelmann to Sieveking, 18 Nov. 1841, Doris Esselbach to Sieveking, Montag Abend [1845], Ida Ahrenhold to Sieveking, 25 Jan. 1843, Pastor Hugues to Sieveking, 2 Feb. 1842, Elise Hunicke to Sieveking, 14 Dec. 1844, Nls AWS, StAr Hmbg.

52. Emilie Brehmer to Sieveking, 23 Feb. 1847, Nls AWS, StAr Hmbg.

53. Marianne von Voigt (in correspondence from Emilie Schlepegrell) to Sieveking, Aug. 1835, Nls AWS, StAr Hmbg.

54. Henriette von Gruber to Sieveking, 1 June 1847, Sophie Behrens to Sieveking, 17 Sept. 1845, Ida Lempfert to Sieveking, im Fruehjahr 1843, Emmy Pauli to Sieveking, 10 Feb. 1848, Helene Schulze to Sieveking, 9 Nov. 1843, Maria Ide to Sieveking, 17 Nov. 1856, Nls AWS, StAr Hmbg.

55. Henriette von Gruber to Sieveking, 1 June 1847, Helene Schulze to Sieveking, 3 March 1843, Nls AWS, StAr Hmbg.

56. [Emma Poel and Sophie Wattenbach] *Arbeit der Frauen in Vereinen fuer Armen-und Krankenpflege. Ein Briefwechsel zweier Freundinnen* (Berlin: Hertz, 1854).

57. Ibid., pp. 18, 27, quotation from p. 72.

58. Ibid., p. 33.

59. Ibid., p. 145.

60. Ibid., p. 61.

61. Ibid., p. 59.

62. Ibid., p. 31; *WVAK, 19. Bericht*, p. 21, Sieveking herself applauded the value of collective action over "the isolated efforts of individuals."

63. "Vortrag gehalten am 25. Oktober 1841 in Bremen," *WVAK, 10. Bericht*, p. 69; also Amalie Sieveking to "Geehrte Vorsteherinnen des cellischen Frauenvereins," 27 March 1836, Nls AWS, StAr Hmbg.

64. Helene Schulze to Sieveking, 3 March 1843, Frau Pastor Elise Ahrendts to Sieveking, 26 March 1852, Nls AWS, StAr Hmbg; "Neuestes aus Frauenvereinen," *Fliegende Blaetter* 13 (1856): 239–51; *Arbeit der Frauen*, pp. 76–79; *WVAK, 12. Bericht*, p. 25.

65. "Briefkasten," *FZ* 1, no. 11 (30 June 1849): 8.
66. *WVAK, 17. Bericht*, p. 55.
67. Ibid., p. 66; *18. Bericht*, p. 27; [Poel], *Denkwuerdigkeiten*, p. 350.
68. *WVAK, 5. Bericht*, p. 14.

CHAPTER 3

Inter-Confessional Expectations of Women in Hamburg

Hamburg was the cradle of the mid-nineteenth-century women's inter-confessional initiative. A number of circumstances were particularly hospitable to this development. The most obvious was the precedent of leadership by Sieveking's association, headquarters of the network for orthodox women in northern Germany and beyond. The philanthropic agenda of the inter-confessional women developed at first as an alternative to the work of Sieveking's association, and then became a national model on its own. The success of the German-Catholic—or free-Christian—congregation in Hamburg was also a major factor in promoting the distinctive interests of inter-confessional women. Elsewhere there were German-Catholic congregations of greater size, but none had so large and gifted a constituency of women. The importance of the Jewish population in Hamburg and the strength of its commitment to assimilation also figures prominently in the consolidation of an inter-confessional consciousness. Last and perhaps most important, the revolution in Hamburg followed a distinctive course both in political tone and chronological rhythm. It did not synchronize with the pattern of revolutions elsewhere in the German confederation and this difference became central to the women's movement as a whole, propelling the Hamburg circle into a brief but critical leadership role. This chapter and the next consider the way these circumstances interacted to produce an inter-confessional consciousness and the impetus for institutional reform.

THE SOCIAL CONTEXT

The same complexities of economic and social class structure that fostered the establishment of the orthodox women's movement in Hamburg also contributed to the organization of inter-confessional women. Salient here was the existence of an urban society that could support numbers of women detached from the productive economy on the one hand, and on the other, the consolidation of a permanent underclass alienated not only by poverty but by culture as well from the legal citizenry. There were certainly women among the middle class of Hamburg who shared the kind of oppressive leisure that Amalie Sieveking so aptly described in the lives of her own peers. They were also moved by the plight of the poor. But these women, or at least many of them, did not have the access, however vicarious, to the municipal and clerical establishment of Hamburg, which Sieveking and her friends enjoyed. They were not married to senators or masters of major guilds; they were not daughters of the established property owners. Their sense of alienation was enhanced by Sieveking herself and the elitism of her organization. When Sieveking first founded the Female Association for the Care of the Poor and Sick, she talked about creating a microcosm within her association that would reflect all the orders of external society. She had assumed that the majority of the association would be drawn from the middle class because, as she put it, they were closer to the poor. But in time she dropped this idea, claiming that the cultivation of the upper class was a better assurance of good judgment.[1] Clearly women such as Emilie Bieber of the photographic studio or Frau Hadersold who managed a small hotel[2] lacked the cultivation Sieveking thought was desirable; in the end when the inter-confessional women's movement was finally in place, many of its principal members were not leisured women at all. If they were oppressed it was not by dissociation from the productive economy, but rather from the values that Sieveking herself represented.[3] The crucial criterion was religion, however, not class, as the case of Charlotte Thornton Paulsen illustrates.

Paulsen came from a family of British ancestry, whose commercial house during the eighteenth century was the major English business in Hamburg. The Thornton family itself fled to England during the French occupation; company business suffered because the French accused its members of harboring spies. When the Thorntons returned with their eighteen children after the war, the husband chosen for sixteen-year-old Charlotte, twenty years her senior, satisfied one creditor and helped secure the family fortunes. The Thorntons were in many respects peers of the Sievekings.[4] In 1844, as a woman of forty-five, Charlotte Paulsen applied for admission to the Sieveking organization. To her surprise and humiliation she was rejected. "I have today wept hot tears of disappointment," she wrote to Sieveking.[5] Paulsen did not believe in personal immortality; she had an interest in what was called critical religion. She read David Friedrich Strauss who replaced the function of the miraculous in the life of Jesus with the function of myth; she studied Ludwig Feuerbach who considered religion a form of anthropology. To Sieveking these were reprehensible interests. Denial of personal immortality was blasphemous; besides, she believed, it deprived the poor of a reason for living. Sieveking's rejection of Paulsen was a consequential moment in the history of women's organizations in Hamburg because it induced Paulsen to develop new forms of philanthropy altogether when circumstances were more propitious.

THE ADVENT OF GERMAN-CATHOLICISM

The immediate catalyst for the non-confessional women's initiative in Hamburg was the appearance of Johannes Ronge, the charismatic leader of the national German-Catholic movement, in the autumn of 1846. His first public appearance was a speech delivered in the Tonhalle, packed for the occasion. On November 29, 1846 he celebrated mass according to his new rite: forty-seven people converted to the German-Catholic confession and joined in founding a new congregation.[6]

The German-Catholic protest was a repudiation on nationalist and religious grounds of both contemporary ultramontanism and the policy of the new Prussian monarch, which lent support to the mystic-conservative sector of Protestantism as well as to Catholic ultramontanist politics. One of a number of critical responses, the German-Catholic movement offered the greatest prospect of permanence and one most cordial to the involvement of women. In creed, the new sect adopted an essentially rationalist-theist position, acknowledging the Scriptures interpreted by the powers of reason as the only legitimate source of belief. All but two of the Catholic sacraments were eliminated, and German rather than Latin became the language of worship. A loose national ecclesiastical structure left each congregation independent with respect to the specifics of belief, liturgy, and criteria for membership. Pastors and lay officers were elected within the congregation, thereby creating one of the most truly populist organizations in contemporary Germany. The movement rapidly abandoned its Catholic origins. It entertained close ties with independent Protestant congregations; membership within the German-Catholic church itself was soon nearly half Protestant in origin.[7]

The congregation at Hamburg reflected the wider German experience. Of the original forty-seven converts, twelve were Protestants; within a year, membership had doubled and former Protestants were in the majority. When Karl Scholl, a radical Young Hegelian from Mannheim presented himself as a candidate for the office of pastor, Franz Schuselka (1812–1889), the literary exile from Vienna and a convert, persuaded the congregation to elect Georg Weigelt, a Protestant theological candidate from Schleswig-Holstein, instead, to insure continued support from moderates in the community.[8] Weigelt himself ultimately moved to a much more critical, post-Hegelian position, following Strauss and Feuerbach. He led his congregation to examine traditional dogma "in the spirit of scientific criticism" and to inform "all levels of human existence in the state, the society and in the family" with the new ideology, a member of the congregation reported.[9] This shift from a supernatural religion to a belief in the immanence of God replicated the general experience of German-Catholic congregations elsewhere.

The membership of the Hamburg congregation also resembled the over-all German-Catholic social profile. The original German-Catholics in Hamburg, by all accounts, were not affluent. There was one notable exception: Heinrich Christian Meyer, the city-republic's enormously successful and successfully advertised self-made man. Meyer had come to Hamburg in 1803 from Hanover as the six-year-old son of a carpenter. He soon began to peddle his father's walking sticks near the Town Hall. The factory that Meyer himself subsequently founded to manufacture walking sticks was the first in Hamburg to use steam power; by 1839, he employed 200 workers. Meyer's canes were works of art featuring inlays of ivory, tortoise shell, mother of pearl and other exotic materials that he imported and also sold. "*Stock*-Meyer," as he was called, though a proponent of free enterprise, created a system of social insurance for his employees that invited comparison with that of the British socialist Robert Owen (1771–1858). Involved in countless schemes for the improvement of the city from harbor projects to the introduction of railroad lines, Meyer refused to be considered for high government office even after he was eligible, arguing that he could serve the city best in his factory. When Ronge came to Hamburg, *Stock*-Meyer was his patron.[10]

The presence of entrepreneurs like Meyer in the German-Catholic movement was not unusual. In a society which precluded political opposition, German-Catholicism offered an opportunity for protest that attracted a hybrid collection of supporters. In cities like Hamburg where they found themselves in opposition to the guilds, it was not uncommon for factory owners and unaffiliated workers to take common cause. Laissez-faire in their economic orientation and often oriented specifically toward England, they found in German-Catholicism an affirmation of freedom of conscience and dissent congenial with that tradition. Concurrently, small tradespeople everywhere who supported the dissenters did so out of a resentment against the wealth and hierarchy of both established churches, as well as from more purely spiritual motives.[11] At the same time in Prussia, and in Wuerttemberg as well, representatives of traditional interests and local corporations supported the German-Catholic movement as an expression of generalized opposition to centralism. In regions such as Saxony or the city-republic of Hamburg where Roman Catholics were in an extreme minority, German-Catholicism drew its Catholic constituency from people who wanted to assimilate with the majority while preserving something of their distinctive legacy.[12] For the poor, the new sect offered economic advantages: there were no fees for many of the church's services, which elsewhere were taxed. Nor did the German-Catholics exact pew fees; seating was without charge. The sense of egalitarian community that characterized many congregations was itself a point of attraction to some members.[13]

There were a number of features of the Hamburg dissenting congregation that gave it a special prominence. One was Schuselka's presence. A native Austrian, Schuselka not only converted to German-Catholicism but distinguished himself as a major proselytizer. National unification, he believed, required the religious involvement of the masses; German-Catholicism offered a potentially popular alternative to the confessional division of the German states. Another distinction of the Hamburg congregation was Johannes Ronge's particular interest, based perhaps on his liaison with one of Meyer's daughters, Bertha Traun. Finally, German-Catholics were not persecuted in Hamburg, as was often the case elsewhere. To gain state recognition, the Senate merely required the congregation to furnish proof of its financial ability to support a house of worship and a pastor.[14]

FEMALE BONDING AND THE CAPACITY FOR INTER-CONFESSIONAL COMMITMENT

The Women's Association for the Support of the German-Catholics (*Frauen-Verein zur Unterstuetzung der Deutsch- Katholiken*) raised the funds to realize the Senate conditions. As its report for 1848 declared: "If the men of Germany greeted this first appearance of a free [religious] direction with enthusiasm and promised it final victory, so it seemed the right of women through persistence and exertion to protect the weak and often threatened beginnings of the new church." Known among its members as the Women's Club of 1847, the auxiliary organized shortly after the congregation was founded and held its first meeting December 12, 1846. It was the pilot project of the mid-century inter-confessional women's initiative. Within a year it collected 7000 marks through benefits and solicitations. The auxiliary provided the salary for a resident clergyman and transferred its remaining funds to the congregation to finance a place of worship and a regular schedule of services and liturgical music. For its own members, the auxiliary supported a lecture series.[15]

The membership of the auxiliary was in itself an interesting phenomenon. At the outset, eighty women enlisted in the organization, nearly twice the initial enrollment of the congregation. Many auxiliary members, in other words, did not join the congregation or convert to German-Catholicism. Jewish names were conspicuous in the membership list; so were liberal Protestants. Some of the women who supported the German-Catholics were even members of government families.[16] German-Catholicism clearly tapped a latent reservoir of sentiment and expectation far more comprehensive than the immediate program of its converts. Evidence about the women in the rank and file of the auxiliary is fragmentary, but it is at least possible to reconstruct a profile of the leadership.

The women instrumental in founding and directing the association of 1847 shared a number of qualities in common. They were all married women in their middle years. Their husbands were men of the manufacturing and commercial class of Hamburg: prosperous but not among the first rank merchants. They were men who had made their own way. They were not members of the patriciate but relative newcomers to the city. Their businesses as well as their residences adjoined one another and in this way they first became friends. The husband of Emilie Wuestenfeld was an exporter of goods to Australia and South America who had moved from rural Hanover shortly after the couple married. Andreas Christian Paulsen, Charlotte's husband, was a broker. Bertha Traun and Amalie Westendarp, as well as Marguerite Meyer, a younger sister, were all daughters of Heinrich Christian Meyer. The spouses of both Traun and Westendarp worked for their father-in-law. Johanna Goldschmidt came from propertied Jewish parents, the Schwabes, who had emigrated to Hamburg from rural Hanover when she was seven, in 1813; her husband Moritz Goldschmidt was a businessman.[17]

Even before the German-Catholic congregation gave them a common enterprise and a single religious focus, these women shared a sufficiently similar spiritual orientation to forge a bond of mutual attraction. In their personal lives and in their social concerns, religion was central. But while the constructs of their thinking were religious, they shunned conventional orthodox institutions and forms of behavior. In the small anonymous volume, *Amalie and Rebecca: Correspondence of a Christian Noblewoman and a Jewess, On Issues of Our Life and Times* (*Amalie und Rebekka: Briefwechsel einer christlichen Adligen und einer Israelitin ueber Zeit- und Lebensfragen*), published in 1847, Johanna Goldschmidt provided the most articulate evidence of a quality shared by the entire group: the subordination of orthodoxy to more general ethical concerns. The tract sought to demonstrate that among Jewish and Christian women there was a common moral ground. Goldschmidt was personally unknown to Amalie Westendarp when Westendarp first read the Goldschmidt book. It was her first exposure to the phenomenon of Jewish oppression and she wrote Goldschmidt to convey the appreciation she felt for her new insight. This was the start of an intimacy that ultimately inspired the coalition for women against religious prejudice (*Frauenverein zur Bekaempfung und Ausgleichung religioeser Vorurteile*).[18] Charlotte Paulsen developed a similar religious orientation. Suspect in Amalie Sieveking's eyes and often viewing herself as an atheist, her struggle with ambivalence expressed itself not only in her interchange with Sieveking but also in moments of emotional turmoil when she had recourse to the language and imagery of tradition. On the occasion of her father's death, for example, she confided to her daughter: "With a full soul I am indebted to him for everything. I praise him joyfully that he may occupy a place in heaven."[19] Yet it was her association that ultimately created the reality of Jewish-Christian collaboration for women. The tension between opportunity and conscience in the life of Emilie Wuestenfeld was equally apparent before the advent of German-Catholicism. She joined the Bible society when she first came to Hamburg but found its orthodoxy intolerable; she yearned to be active in the manner of the Sieveking association but was repelled by what she considered the hypocrisy of the lady visitors who exacted piety in exchange for material help.[20] Many years later the pastor of the German-Catholic congregation wrote of her:

> However decisive her renunciation of the images of the divinity might be, no less firm was her belief in the purpose and power of the godly in the world. . . . Devotion ceased but there remained a pious spirit . . . a deep spirit, a strong feeling seeking substitution for the lost objects of devotion and finding them in the cult of human love.[21]

This was a comment that could have as well been made of any one of the leaders of the Woman's Club of 1847.

Their particular kind of piety moved these women to engage themselves in a variety of inter-confessional organizations even before their involvement with German-Catholicism. Charlotte Paulsen, for instance, became active in the Pestalozzi foundation, a society for abandoned children, and the first non-confessional society founded in Hamburg. Emilie Wuestenfeld was a leading member of the Society for Social and Political Interests of the Jews (*Gesellschaft fuer soziale- und politische Interessen der Juden*), an organization commited to social assimilation as distinct from, but supportive of, legal emancipation. Dr. Anton Rée, director of the independent Hebrew school, was a moving spirit in this society, where his leadership insured not only an integrated membership of Jews and Christians, but also of men and women. The collaboration of Rée with Emilie Wuestenfeld in this enterprise was the beginning of a long and fruitful partnership. It anticipated both Wuestenfeld's role in the women's alliance against religious prejudice and Rée's later commitment to the founding of a college for women in Hamburg.[22]

The Hamburg circle enjoyed a particular kind of claim on the sympathy of contemporary German feminists, one derived from the life experience of two of its members. Emilie Wuestenfeld and Bertha Traun were women whose religious convictions increasingly acted to erode their marriages. Wuestenfeld, for her part, was charged in court by her husband with evading her domestic responsibilities; he called attention to her failure to entertain his business clients. Her preoccupation with public concerns exercised in the name of religion usurped her time and energy, he believed, and he came to view her as a fanatic. She in turn refused to reside in his household any longer, and in Hamburg, failure to cohabit was grounds for divorce. Bertha Traun articulated her own position with unambivalence and poignancy. In a private letter to her spouse, which ultimately made its way as legal evidence against her, she announced her refusal to be a martyr to convention. "Love," she wrote, "cannot be construed as a duty but is itself the life of the soul;" "love is the only ethical ground for marriage." As a German-Catholic convert she had come to believe that "God is the process of the striving after truth;" "God within the world and within the human spirit is the highest revelation." Traun, like Paulsen and most of the contemporary married women of her class, was partner to an arranged marriage, one that, like Paulsen's, had served her father's business interests. Only sixteen when she married, she recalled having neither a mother nor woman friend to advise her. She conceded she had once believed that respect for her husband's character and love for her children would compensate for the absence of affection between her and her spouse. She found she could no longer defend the flawed grounds of an arranged marriage in these terms. She divorced Traun to become the wife of Johannes Ronge, and ultimately went into exile with him.[23]

The cases of Traun and Wuestenfeld shared a number of similarities with the widely publicized life-story of Luise Aston (1814–1871). Aston, in much the same fashion as Traun and Paulsen, had been given in marriage to a rich industrialist in Saxony by her father, an important figure in the Protestant church hierarchy. In her volume *My Emancipation: Proscription and Justification* (*Meine Emancipation: Verweisung und Rechtfertigung*) of 1846, she described with great bitterness her struggle for divorce and custody of her child and her sense of betrayal at the hand of the church. Her subsequent novels and poetry defended her practice of free love as an alternative to marriage, which Aston came to believe was intrinsically coercive for women. In her spiritual life she traversed a course from the orthodoxy of her father to "critical religion"—specifically the position of Feuerbach which accounted for the evolution of all religions in terms of human need.[24]

Mathilde Franziska Anneke's life (1817–1884) embraced striking parallels. Aston became Anneke's correspondent and an increasing figure of identification. At the age of nineteen Mathilde had been her father's last remaining asset. He had over-speculated in railroad stocks and so he married his daughter off to a rich Rhenish nobleman in order to reestablish his position. After a single year of marriage and the birth of a daughter Mathilde Franziska left her husband and set out to support herself by her own writing. She experienced a period of devout Catholicism, a kind of reconversion, which resulted in her volume of prayers for Roman Catholic women, a collection endorsed by the Archbishop of Cologne. Her belief in the unique character of female piety and the special capacity of women for faith, suffering, and sacrifice permeated this phase of her life. Emancipation from orthodoxy came as a consequence of Anneke's introduction to the life story of Luise Aston. Her essay *Woman in Conflict with Social Convention* (*Das Weib im Conflict mit den socialen Verhaeltnissen*) was a tribute to Aston's work.[25]

In their public impact, the trials of Traun and Wuestenfeld were most immediately consequential for German-Catholics in Hamburg. The fundamental statutes of the congregation were modified to incorporate a conception of marriage totally at variance with conventional practice. No marriage of arrangement could be celebrated within the congregation and the principle of equality between marriage partners was acknowledged by congregational mandate. For German-Catholics, these resolutions did not, however, reflect an idiosyncratic position. Karl Scholl, the German-Catholic pastor once considered as a candidate by the Hamburg congregation, devoted a major speech to the oppression of women and the issue of marriage within the church during a proselytizing tour of Austria in the winter of 1848–49. He examined the practices of celibacy and confession as devices for controlling women and exposed the hypocrisy of a system of divorce that not only prohibited remarriage but effectively impoverished the female partner as well.[26]

The cases of Traun and Wuestenfeld were symptomatic of a current debate that increasingly polarized contemporary opinion. As a religious and political issue, it set the more orthodox members of the ecclesiastical hierarchy against existing civil law, which permitted remarriage in some cases as well as divorce.[27]

As a woman's issue, it stimulated a literature of protest against arranged marriages and incited women against the complicity of the church in this practice. The convention of arranged marriage offered feminists an unequivocal target, one on which moderates and radicals could agree however they might disagree on the relative merits of companionate marriage and free love. Partnership by choice united feminist discourse. A major segment of the feminist press was devoted to the issue. Correspondents in Louise Otto's *Frauen-Zeitung* frequently alluded to it; so did distinguished contemporary novelists, as we shall see.[28] In this respect the personal lives of Traun and Wuestenfeld located them within the mainstream of contemporary feminist issues.

Another theme that runs common to the lives of the Hamburg women was the importance they attached to motherhood. From their situation as mothers all of them derived an essential aspect of their personal identity. Motherhood for them was not simply a biological and psychological condition; it was also a moral and pedagogical status. In their private correspondence and journals as well as their public writings and activities this theme is a constant. Emilie Wuestenfeld's biographer claims that she was profoundly influenced by her own mother who raised the family as an early widow, an iron-willed and unconventional rural woman who boasted that the true demonstration of womanhood was the ability to combine the roles of mother and father.[29] Charlotte Paulsen's most profound attachment was to her daughter and only child, Elisabeth. As she once wrote: "The most precious thing for me and certainly for any mother is when she can rest on the heart of her child." Whenever she was separated from Elisabeth, she found that "sadness overwhelmed" her. Through her life she repeatedly multiplied the private as well as public opportunities for maternal expression. She breast-fed one of her mother's infants when Elisabeth was a baby; she adopted the daughter of an unmarried friend and raised her as Marie Paulsen. She herself assumed full responsibility for the education of Elisabeth at home. Philanthropy for Paulsen extended the ethical and educative components of motherhood. Symbolically, when her husband died in 1855, she took up residence in the children's home that she had founded.[30]

In the work of Johanna Goldschmidt the professional potentiality of a maternal identity is most apparent. As author of two books, she was intellectually the most productive of the Hamburg circle. Her *Amalie and Rebecca* addressed issues of concern shared by Jewish and Christian women. She argued for the elimination of obstacles to women's education, and proposed the creation of an organization in which the moral sensitivity of the female sex would be mobilized to persuade prosperous women of both confessions to take up the cause of working women. Goldschmidt's book appeared in print two years before the inter-confessional philanthropy that Paulsen founded; *Amalie and Rebecca* could almost have been a blueprint. Goldschmidt's second book, *The Delights and Cares of Motherhood* (*Mutter-Sorgen und Mutter-Freuden*), published in 1848, shared with Paulsen the conviction that an exploration of the common elements of woman's experience would promote both the achievement of inter-confessionalism and advance the cause of women.[31]

The *Delights and Cares* was an early entry into what was becoming a genre: a literature that developed the possibilities of motherhood as a source of expression and power for women, a vocation that was gradually absorbing most of the functions of the father of the traditional or patriarchal family. This literature both reflected and molded the emerging bourgeois family in which the mother governed the household as a function of "woman's nature," and created a sphere that men sustained financially but in which they otherwise played a minimal role.

The experiences of these mothers can be followed in the pages of the short-lived periodical *Pedagogical Announcements for Parents and Teachers* (*Paedagogische Mittheilungen fuer Eltern und Lehrer*), which gave way to the equally short-lived *Our Children* (*Unsere Kinder*). Some of these mothers, like Goldschmidt herself, moved from the personal experience of motherhood in the home to a professional advocacy of mothering. Others, such as Auguste Herz, who developed her career in the context of revolutionary Saxony, wrote about the qualities of motherhood on the basis of their experience in philanthropy. Goldschmidt's *Delights and Cares* shared a number of features common to all of these works. In terms of religion they were non-confessional, optimistic, and inspired by a profound belief in the distinctiveness of woman's nature as well as in the hope of national regeneration through women and children. They categorically rejected the Christian doctrine of original sin and the view that life on earth was valuable primarily as a preparation for salvation, the view which characterized contemporary Christian pedagogy. The appearance of motherhood manuals during the middle years of the century fostered a climate for the reception of the educational theorist Friedrich Froebel (1782–1852), who as an old man emerged after decades of relative obscurity to promote the end of male-controlled and confessionally-oriented early childhood education. Goldschmidt herself was apparently unfamiliar with the Froebel literature until the summer of 1848, after her own book was published. She became one of his principal advocates.[32]

Goldschmidt believed in the theory of maternal impression or the formative power of events in the environment of the pregnant mother to shape the unborn child. On this premise she developed a system of early childhood training involving the symbiosis of mother and child and a belief in the interaction of physical and psychological elements in the early development of the child. She stressed close observation on the part of the mother and the recognition of individual tendencies in the child's imagination that the mother should direct but not force: "Until the thirst develops, do not offer drink." She believed in a religious cultivation of the spirit without reference to confessional specificity; she excluded biblical stories and fairy tales from her recommended instructional materials. Education, Goldschmidt argued, should discourage superstition and foster an understanding of nature and of nature's laws. Respect and piety must arise from conscience rather than from indoctrination. The theme of national training reinforced that of non-sectarianism, and in this regard Goldschmidt, like her contemporary and sister-author Auguste Herz, reflected concerns of the times. She emphasized the dangers of introducing foreign language training into the world of the child who must first incorporate the rhythms of its own tongue into its expression. Her book was an appeal to bourgeois women to raise their children themselves and thereby avoid the dangers inherent in the employment of nursemaids, particularly foreign ones. By emphasizing the importance of infancy, Goldschmidt claimed motherhood as a distinction for women and an alternative to the subordination of wifehood. In the Women's Club of 1847 Goldschmidt secured for herself a forum through which she could develop some of the implications of her own ideas, ideas which in their implementation supplanted Christian orthodoxy with the new womanhood, rooted in the concept of woman's nature.[33]

The original aim of the Woman's Club of 1847 in which all of these women were active was realized when the Senate of the city-republic granted state recognition to the Hamburg German-Catholic congregation on March 3, 1848. The women themselves ascribed this legalization as much to the impact of contemporary politics as to their role in meeting the original financial stipulations of the Senate.[34]

THE REVOLUTION IN HAMBURG

For this discussion it is important to appreciate the wider political life of Hamburg in 1848 and particularly to document the idiosyncratic rhythm of events in the city-republic that made the experience of the revolution different in Hamburg from what it was elsewhere in Germany. This absence of synchronization provides an important clue to the way in which the religious interests of the Hamburg Women's Club of 1847 exerted an unanticipated impact upon the nascent bourgeois women's movement associated with the revolution in the rest of Germany.

News of the overthrow of the French king in February 1848 and the bloody demonstrations against the Prussian royal family in Berlin in March 1848 as well as the formulation of the so-called March demands throughout Germany accelerated the introduction of freedom of worship in Hamburg and with it the specific recognition of the German-Catholic congregation. Hamburg had in fact been caught up in a movement of political reform since the spring of 1842, a movement in which confessional issues played a vital part. In early May 1842 Hamburg experienced a catastrophic fire that destroyed a third of the city center, left 20,000 people homeless, and annihilated property estimated at some fifty million marks.[35] The fire exposed the inadequacy of public services, which in turn destroyed citizen confidence in the government. Within a matter of days the demand for reform extended beyond issues concerning the fire department and the water supply to embrace a comprehensive overhaul of the constitution. A number of constituencies—"patriots," lawyers, property owners—organized clubs, among them the Society for Social and Political Interests of the Jews. Separation of the judiciary from the administration, accountability in the Senate and body of elders to the citizenry, and modification of the legislative system in general to permit the inclusion of a younger contingent of delegates, were among the demands. So was the separation of civil rights from religious affiliation. The government had itself taken a step in this direction when, under the financial pressure of the crisis, it revoked the prohibition against Jewish property ownership in certain sections of the city to facilitate the unrestricted sale of holdings damaged by the fire. Jews, who numbered about one-twentieth of the city's inhabitants, enjoyed a particularly ambivalent status in Hamburg. They shared with minority Christians—all Christians except Lutherans, that is—ineligibility for government office. Additionally they enjoyed no civil rights. They were citizens of their own congregation or community (*Gemeinde*), hence ineligible for citizenship in the city or for any of the rights and privileges pertaining to citizenship. The denial of citizenship penalized Jews at many levels in the economic and social life as well as in the political life of the city. Jews, for instance, were assimilated into the English trade but excluded from overseas commerce. Jews provided much of the city's industrial capital and financed railroad construction, but Jews were denied membership in the brotherhood of "the honorable merchant." Jews plied all kinds of trades as peddlars but traditional crafts were closed to them because they were ineligible for guilds, a restriction that often affected women adversely. Jewish lawyers, of whom there were many, conducted their practices in the name of Christian partners. Particularly since 1830 Jews had vigorously sought emancipation in Hamburg; the reform movement that started in 1842 embraced the cause of Jewish emancipation in the larger cause of liberal reform.[36]

The Senate, accustomed to a passive citizenry, resisted change except on issues narrowly related to the management of the fire. In March 1848 the cause of constitutional reform in Hamburg itself was engulfed in the larger cause, that of German liberation.

The Hamburg Senate was compelled to lift censorship, to widen the press laws, and to appoint a constitutional commission. Proposals included not only responsible government and separation of religion from civic status but also the right of free assembly, the abolition of the special cooptive privileges by which the Senate controlled its own membership, and universal education. In the larger context they included the incorporation of Hamburg into the institution of a national German state governed by a national and liberal parliament and served by a national army and navy. In April 1848 Hamburg was represented in the national pre-parliament and at the end of the month held elections according to the national prescription that required general male suffrage for all taxpayers. In Hamburg Jews were thereby for the first time permitted to participate in a civil election and to select representatives for the national parliament. With respect to these events, then, Hamburg shared the experience of the rest of revolutionary Germany.

In contrast to many areas of Germany, however, there was no outbreak of violence in Hamburg in the spring of 1848. The men who sat in the Frankfurt Parliament for Hamburg represented moderate to conservative positions. The public in Hamburg patiently awaited the outcome of the deliberations at Frankfurt and the results of the local constitutional commission. Finally in August Hamburg was radicalized by impatience. A huge meeting of all the opposition clubs met on August 17, 1848 and demanded the immediate convocation of a constituent assembly recognized as competent by both the Senate and by the corporate citizenry. Elections for this assembly favored the radical democrats. On December 22, when this assembly had barely started its work, the Frankfurt National Parliament published its Fundamental Rights of the German People. Among them was the elimination of religion as a determinant of political and civil rights. The implications of this provision for Jews in Hamburg was specifically confirmed in the Hamburg law of February 21, 1849. The constitution proposed by the Hamburg constituent assembly, like that of the Frankfurt National Parliament, devoted much attention to fundamental rights. Essentially it anticipated a government modeled on the concept of the separation of powers and designed to replace the elaborate system of interlocking political and religious bodies that historically governed Hamburg. There was also a proposal to reduce the age of the governing authorities and limit the perpetuation of family power. The attainment of citizenship was eased and elections were to be based on a more general suffrage. The intention was to introduce the new constitution in July of 1849, and although the old Senate delayed the transfer of power, the Hamburg radicals remained optimistic that the new constitution would be implemented.[37]

In this respect the rhythm of the revolution in Hamburg differed markedly from its rhythm elsewhere. For in Prussia the so-called imposed constitution was already a reality in December of 1848 after the restoration of the monarchy and the forceful dissolution of the Berlin constituent parliament. The Frankfurt Parliament was disowned by the greater German powers, Prussia and Austria, in April 1849 when Frederick William IV refused to accept the imperial crown of the proposed new federation. And in April and May of 1849 popular democratic uprisings in South Germany and in Dresden were brutally put down by the military might of Prussia. Democrats indeed were fleeing from elsewhere to Hamburg. As late as August 1849 when Prussia insisted on garrisoning troops in Hamburg on their return from Schleswig-Holstein, the Hamburg Senate, however it may have obstructed internal change, refused to submit to Prussia's efforts at intimidation.[38] Hamburg was in fact a relative haven for political democrats for at least another two years.

For the inter-confessional women of Hamburg, the new era was punctuated by the two great changes in religious policy: the legalization of German-Catholicism early in 1848 and the emancipation of Hamburg Jewry a year later. These two acts of legislation shaped the distinctive style and focus of the Women's Club of 1847 and its wider circle during the critical years that ensued.

NOTES

1. [Emma Poel], *Denkwuerdigkeiten aus dem Leben von Amalie Sieveking in deren Auftrage von einer Freunde derselben verfasst* (Hamburg: Agentur des Rauhen Haus, 1860), p. 209.

2. See below, Chapter 4, note 9.

3. *WVAK, 19. Bericht*, p. 30.

4. Rudolf Kayser, "Charlotte Paulsen," *Hamburgische Geschichts-und Heimatsblaetter* 1, no. 2 (June 1926): 33–35; Anna Wohlwill, "Charlotte Paulsen," Jahresbericht der Schule des Paulsenstifts 1900, Schule des Paulsenstifts, StAr Hmbg, pp. 1–4, a condensation of handwritten notes by the author deposited in the archive file Paulsenstiftschule, Manuskripte Anna Wohlwill. According to Kayser, Paulsen's original diary deposited in the StAr Hmbg has disappeared.

5. Paulsen to Sieveking, 8 June [1844], Nls AWS, StAr Hmbg.

6. Kayser, "Die deutsch-katholische Bewegung in Hamburg," *ZVHG* 26 (1925): 147–50.

7. Catherine M. Prelinger, "Religious Dissent, Women's Rights and the Hamburger Hochschule fuer das weibliche Gechlecht in Mid-Nineteenth-Century Germany," *Church History* 45 (1976): 42–46.

8. Kayser, "Deutsch-katholische Bewegung," pp. 150–53.

9. Malwida von Meysenbug, *Memoiren einer Idealistin*, Volksausgabe, 3 vols. in 2 (Berlin and Leipzig: Schuster und Loeffler, 1907), 1: 305.

10. Heinrich Ad. Meyer, *Erinnerungen an Heinrich Christian Meyer— Stockmeyer* (Hamburg: Gesellschaft Hamburgischer Kunstfreunde, 1900), pp. xi–xiv, 54 and *passim*; Percy Ernst Schramm, *Hamburg, Deutschland und die Welt. Leistung und Grenzen hanseatischen Buergertum in der Zeit zwischen Napoleon und Bismarck* (Munich: G.D.W. Calwey, 1943), p. 171; Marie Kortmann, *Emilie Wuestenfeld. Eine Hamburger Buergerin* (Hamburg: Georg Westermann, 1927), p. 19, for Ronge's contact with Meyer as well as modest circumstances of the original Hamburg German-Catholics. Kortmann was Wuestenfeld's niece.

11. The diverse social composition of the German-Catholic movement is apparent from a variety of sources. In Offenbach, for example, where the largest German-Catholic congregation after Breslau's was established, the founder was a manufacturer of strings for musical instruments. He had been a Catholic; his wife, Protestant. The first service of worship was held in the warehouse of a hauling concern whose owner was sympathetic; artisans of every sort worked to produce an appropriate setting. Subsequently land was given the congregation by the owner of a factory manufacturing oil cloth, Max Gehrmann, *Geschichte der frei religioesen Gemeinde in Offenbach am Main* (Offenbach a.M.: Offenbacher Geschichtsverein, 1968), pp. 1–24. Abt 356/566 Die kirchlichen Verhaeltnisse der deutsch-katholischen Gemeinde in Heidelberg 1845–1865. Grossherzoglich Badisches Oberamt Heidelberg. Verwaltungs-Sachen. Ort: Heidelberg. Rubrik X: Kirchensachen, GlAr Krlsr, indicates that the leading officers of that congregation were a

prominent lawyer, a physician, an apothecary, a master-baker, and a minerologist. Winter, the burgermaster, and the theologian Heinrich Paulus always figure prominently in literature about the Heidelberg congregation. In "Demokratische Opposition in religioesem Gewande" (Dissertation, Karl Marx Universitaet Leipzig, 1964) pp. 50–57, Guenter Kolbe identifies the membership of the congregations in Saxony with the impact of mechanization; in some cases they were cottage workers disadvantaged by the new competition, in others, workers resentful of new demands on their methods of work.

12. Catherine M. Prelinger, "The German-Catholic Church: From National Hope to Regional Reality," *The Consortium on Revolutionary Europe Proceedings 1976* (Athens, Ga.: The Consortium on Revolutionary Europe, 1978), pp. 88–101; Veit Valentin, *Geschichte der deutschen Revolution*, 2 vols. (Berlin: Verlag Ullstein, 1930–1) 1: 219, specially mentions lower-middle-class Catholics approaching their liberal middle-class neighbors.

13. The monthly from Breslau, *Volkspiegel* 2 (1847), p. 92, reported that Roman Catholic clergy would not perform burials without a fee so that the poor occasionally joined the German-Catholics out of grim necessity. See Prelinger, "The German-Catholic Church," p. 91 for the concept of the congregation as a community of life; also Meysenbug, *Memoiren*, 1: 304–9.

14. Franz Schuselka, *Deutsche Worte eines Oesterreichers* (Hamburg; Hoffmann und Campe, 1843); idem, *Die neue Kirche und die alte Politik* (Leipzig: Weidmann'sche Buchhandlung, 1845), especially pp. 83–86 where he criticizes the left-wing Hegelians for their failure to recognize the popular sources of German-Catholicism; Prelinger, "The German-Catholic Church," p. 93, and Carl Wilhelm Wuppermann, *Kurhessen seit dem Freiheitskriege* (Cassel: Theodor Fischer, 1850), pp. 505–7, on persecution; Kayser, "Deutsch-katholische Bewegung," p. 150; "Hamburg," *FCL*: 154–55.

15. "Bericht des Frauen-Vereins zur Unterstuetzung der Deutsch-Katholiken [Hamburg]," Februar 1848, Nls EW, StAr Hmbg.

16. Ibid.; Kortmann, *Emilie Wuestenfeld*, pp. 20–21, for the membership list. There was at least one member of the Sieveking circle here, Louise Lappenberg; Amalie Siemers was the wife of an *Oberalter*. Two women were wives of Protestant clergy: Pauline Alt and a Frau Schwenzen. One woman, Fanny Schlueter, was the mother of an early candidate for the Kaiserswerth diaconate; there are at least six Jewish women. Another feature of interest on the list: there are at least ten sets of female relatives.

17. Kortmann, *Emilie Wuestenfeld*, pp. 16–17; Wohlwill, "Charlotte

Paulsen," StAr Hmbg, p. 4; Meyer, *Erinnerungen*, p. viii; "Johanna Gold-schmidt aus der *Frauen-Zeitung*, 27 December 1884," typescript copy, PFVAr. Other members of the executive committee included Auguste Burmester, who came from the merchant family of C. H. Burmester; Johanna Jahncke was the daughter of J. P. N. Jahncke, a gold changer by profession; Jenny Beinhauer came from the family of Bernhard R. Beinhauer who traded in jewelry, hardware, and cigars. Personal communication of Dr. Schneider, StAr Hmbg archivist.

18. "Johanna Goldschmidt," PFVAr; searches in both the BDR and the DDR have failed to uncover an extant copy of *Amalie und Rebekka: Briefwechsel einer christlichen Adligen und einer Israelitin ueber Zeit- und Lebenfragen*; Kortmann, *Emilie Wuestenfeld*, pp. 48, 26–28.

19. Wohlwill, "Charlotte Paulsen," StAr Hmbg, p. 5.

20. Kortmann, *Emilie Wuestenfeld*, pp. 17–18.

21. Georg Weigelt, *Christliche und humane Menschenliebe. Zur Erinnerung an Frau Emilie Wuestenfeld* (Hamburg: Otto Meissner, 1875), pp. 32–33.

22. Kayser, "Charlotte Paulsen," p. 37; Joseph Feiner, *Anton Rée. Ein Kaempfer fuer Fortschritt und Recht* (Hamburg: A. Janssen, 1916), pp. 20–29; Gesellschaft fuer soziale und politische Interessen der Juden, "Programm," Nls EW, StAr Hmbg. Rée and Wuestenfeld continued to collaborate on issues of conscience even into the period of reaction through the Verein zur Foerderung der Gewissensfreiheit, Nls EW, StAr Hmbg.

23. Niedergericht B 1301 Acta in Sachen Marie Wuestenfeld geb. Capelle, StAr Hmbg. A higher court reversed the decision, records of which did not survive World War II, personal communication, Dr. Schneider. Also in Sieveking to Princess von Hohenlohe-Schillings-fuerst, Sept. 1850, Nls AWS, Sieveking claimed Wuestenfeld's associational activities had made her "a stranger in her own house, and her husband complained that when he occasionally entertained, his wife appeared for an hour at most." Niedergericht B1226 Acta in Sachen Herrn Dr. juris Carl Petersen mandati nomine Bertha Traun geb. Meyer, Beklagten, StAr Hmbg. On refusal to cohabit as grounds for divorce, see H. Baumeister, *Das Privatrecht der freien und Hansestadt Hamburg*, 2 vols. (Hamburg: Hoffmann und Campe, 1856), 2: 34–37, 106–7.

24. Luise Aston, *Meine Emancipation: Verweisung und Rechtfertigung* (Brussels: C. G. Vogler, 1846), and Renate Moehrmann, *Frauenemancipation im deutschen Vormaerz. Texte und Dokumente* (Stuttgart: Philipp Reclam Jun, 1978), pp. 65–81, 225–29.

25. Henriette Heinzen and Hertha Anneke Sanne, Biographical notes in Commemoration of Fritz and Mathilde Franziska Anneke,

typescript in 2 vols., Fritz and Mathilde Anneke Papers, State Historical Society of Wisconsin Archives; her *Das Weib im Conflikt mit den socialen Verhaeltnissen*, evidently written in 1846 or 1847, is also here in typescript; excerpts in Moehrmann, *Frauenemancipation*, pp. 82–87; *Der Meister ist da und rufet Dich: Ein vollstaendiges Gebet- und Erbauungsbuch fuer die gebildete christliche Frauenwelt*, published in 1843, is not extant but sections of it are quoted in Hermann Boppe, "Mathilde Franziska Anneke . . . ," *Amerikanische Turnzeitung*, Jan. 4–25, 1885; I am grateful to Maria Wagner, editor of *Mathilde Franziska Anneke in Selbstzeugnissen und Dokumenten* (Frankfurt a.M.: Fischer-Taschenbuch Verlag, 1980), for this reference.

26. Johannes Ronge, *Aufruf an die deutschen Maenner und Frauen nebst Grundstimmungen der freien Kirche* (Hamburg: G. W. Niemeyer 1850), p. 15, Articles 30–33; Gerlinde Hummel-Haasis, ed., *Schwestern zerreisst eure Ketten. Zeugnisse zur Geschichte der Frauen in der Revolution von 1848–49* (Munich: Deutscher Taschenbuch Verlag, 1982), pp. 155–60.

27. The literature representing various shades of contemporary male opinion is reviewed in the *Allgemeine Literatur Zeitung* 135 (July 1843): 418–22, 425–64; Ute Gerhard, *Verhaeltnisse und Verhinderungen. Frauenarbeit, Familie und Rechte der Frauen im 19. Jahrhundert. Mit Dokumenten* (Frankfurt a.M.: Suhrkamp Verlag, 1978), pp. 167–75.

28. For example, see excerpts in *"Dem Reich der Freiheit werb' ich Buergerinnen." Die Frauen-Zeitung von Louise Otto*, ed. Ute Gerhard and others (Frankfurt a.M.: Syndikat, 1979), pp. 223, 244, 309, 146, 150–51; "Die Liebe und der Pietismus," *FZ* 3, no. 8 (21 March 1852): 58–60; and the discussion in Chapter 5 below.

29. Kortmann, *Emilie Wuestenfeld*, p. 11.

30. Wohlwill, "Charlotte Paulsen," StAr Hmbg, pp. 5, 10.

31. P. G., "Bemerkungen einer Mutter. Ueber die bei Hoffmann und Campe in Hamburg erschienene Schrift "Mutter-Sorgen und Mutter-Freuden. Worte der Liebe und des Ernstes ueber Kindheitspflege von einer Mutter," *FZ* 2, no. 34 (24 Aug. 1850): 3–5, a detailed account of the book which, I believe, is no longer extant; for the preface, by Friedrich Adolf Wilhelm Diesterweg, which also summarizes the spirit and content, Karl Mueller, *Kulturreaktion in Preussen im 19. Jahrhundert. Mit einem Anhang: Briefe Froebels und Diesterwegs* (Berlin: Verlag fuer Kulturpolitik, 1929), pp. 110–15; the only extant publication of Johanna Goldschmidt in Hamburg, according to Dr. Schneider, the archivist, is an 1866 report of the Paulsen foundation children's shelter.

32. *Unsere Kinder. Vereins-Schrift . . . fuer Eltern, Lehrer, Lehrerinnen . . .* 1 (1849): 234–35, on Thekla von Gompertz, who moved from educating children in her own household to producing children's literature; in

the same journal, for instance, "Die Mutter Handbibliothek," pp. 146–55, 377–81, a series continued from the predecessor of the journal, *Padagogische Mittheilungen fuer Eltern und Lehrer* 1 and 2 (1846–47); "Hauserziehung und Kindergarten. Vortraege fuer Frauen und Jung-frauen welche fuer die Familie oder den Kindergarten sich zu Erzieh-erinnen bilden wollen (Leipzig: Ernst Keil, 1851)," *FZ* 3, no. 32 (16 Aug. 1851): 221–22, a review; also "Urtheil einer deutschen Mutter ueber die Froebelische Erziehlehre," *Der Freischuetz* 25, no. 75 (18 Sept. 1849): 298. Diesterweg's letters to Goldschmidt of 20 June 1849 and 1 July 1849 in Mueller, *Kulturreaktion*, pp. 115–17, indicate the sequence of their respective acquaintances with Froebel. Goldschmidt knew his work first, Diesterweg met him first in person.

33. P. G. "Bemerkungen einer Mutter," *FZ* 2, no. 34 (24 Aug. 1850): 3–5.

34. Kortmann, *Emilie Wuestenfeld*, p. 23.

35. Schramm, *Hamburg*, p. 195.

36. Ernst Rudolf Huber, *Deutsche Verfassungsgeschichte seit 1789*, 2 vols., 2d ed. (Stuttgart, Berlin, Cologne, Mainz: W. Kohlhammer, 1960), 2: 545; Schramm, *Hamburg*, p. 417; Helga Krohn, *Juden in Hamburg 1800–1850. Ihre soziale, kulturelle und politische Entwicklung waehrend der Emanzipationszeit* (Frankfurt a.M.: Europaeische Verlagsanstalt, 1967), pp. 52–57, 64, 77.

37. Dirk Bavendamm, *Von der Revolution zur Reform. Die Verfassungs-politik des hamburgischen Senats 1849–50* (Berlin: Duncker und Humblot, 1969), pp. 20–26, 34–35; Krohn, *Die Juden in Hamburg. Die politische, soziale und kulturelle Entwicklung einer juedischen Grossstadtgemeinde nach der Emanzipation 1848–1918* (Hamburg: Hans Christians Verlag, 1974), pp. 19–26; idem, *Juden in Hamburg 1800–1850*, p. 73.

38. Bavendamm, *Von der Revolution*, pp. 31–33, 95–101.

CHAPTER 4

Philanthropy and Education: An Agenda for Women Allied Against Prejudice

The revolution brought in its wake a general proliferation of clubs in Hamburg reflecting various specific concerns and addressing a variety of distinctive issues. Associations within the community of progressive women represented one aspect of this development. The new women's societies shared a number of qualities. In each case they were deeply committed to the principle of collective leadership, reflecting strong ties of friendship as well as intense conviction. Each of the associations was headed by a consortium of leaders rather than by a single individual woman. At general meetings of the membership the exercise of democratic procedures recognized that debate and the exercise of majority rule were inherently educational opportunities as well as occasions for the development of intellectual independence and confidence. Meetings, in other words, were designed to be more than forums for the dispatch of business.[1]

The substantive programs of the new associations intersected and overlapped at several points. Each was engaged in some form of charity, early childhood education, or women's education—occasionally all three. But what differentiated these women from their patrician contemporaries was not only their procedural style but the intention of their programs as well. Philanthropy was in each case the starting point, but women from the inter-confessional community increasingly recognized the practice of philanthropy as a means to their own self-realization and personal emancipation. They were determined to reinterpret and extend the boundaries of charity to embrace social change as well as social service.

The concession of legal status to the German-Catholic congregation was a signal to the Women's Club of 1847 to enlarge the sphere of its mandate. The club remained primarily a fundraising society, but extended its practice of distributing funds locally to embrace German-Catholic and independent Protestant congregations throughout Germany. It also donated money to a number of public causes arising from revolutionary emergencies. Ultimately the Women's Club of 1847 adopted an openly feminist posture and directed its funds to programs designed to advance the position and status of women. Because all of these programs were non-confessional they concurrently promoted the assimilation of Jewish women. Increasingly the association came to believe in the intimate connectedness of spiritual freedom and the development of a female consciousness, for, as its executive committee reported:

For three years we vigorously sought to further the cause of religious reform. We cannot, however, struggle for freedom of conscience without becoming free ourselves. For it is the blessing of all true human striving that a human being wins his own spiritual power when he works for the general good. The more clearly and self-consciously we came to an appreciation of the significance of our own spiritual lives, the more we felt called upon with joy and commitment to work for the intellectual and material well-being of our own sex.[2]

The emancipation of the Jews created the environment for both non-confessional philanthropy and for a kind of feminism: the consciousness of a common oppression and shared interest which Johanna Goldschmidt articulated and progressive women could support. Just as Jewish emancipation signalled a new definition of citizenship, one unrestricted by confessional distinctions, it also permitted women to think of themselves collectively as members of a gender rather than simply as adherents to a confession. Earlier in the century Gabriel Riesser, the Jewish leader from Hamburg, had pointed out the futility of philanthropy among impoverished Jews. Indoctrination in the impor-

tance of self-help and self-support among the community of Jews
was meaningless so long as occupational choice itself was predicated on a definition of citizenship from which Jews were excluded.[3] The development of a self-consciousness among women
had been stunted in a similar manner by confessional division.

THE WOMEN'S ASSOCIATION FOR THE
SUPPORT OF POOR RELIEF

Charlotte Paulsen was first among the members of the Wom-
en's Club of 1847 to formulate an institutional response to Jewish
emancipation in Hamburg. In March 1849 she laid the ground-
work for a society of her own to relieve the poor. Hers was also,
then, in some sense a response to the policies and practices of
the Sieveking association. More than the other societies of progressive women, it revealed the dialectic link between the activity
of orthodox women and those who saw themselves as ecumenical. There were no confessional restrictions on either the membership of the Paulsen association or on its clientele. Paulsen
recruited her members both from the Women's Club of 1847
and from the Society for Social and Political Interests of the
Jews. Emilie Wuestenfeld was vice-president, her sister Pauline
Kortmann was treasurer, and Johanna Goldschmidt, with
Amalie Westendarp, supervised the education program.[4] The
aim of the new association was to "further to the best of its ability
the material and moral well-being of the poor entrusted to its
care."[5] By stimulating confidence and initiative among its adult
clients and by providing day-time shelter, care, and instruction
to the children of working parents, Paulsen and her associates
hoped to accomplish their goal. The organization was called the
Women's Association for the Support of Poor Relief (*Frauenverein zur Unterstuetzung der Armenpflege*). Visitation, as in the
Sieveking association, was a major point of contact with the poor,
but so were the day-care center and the school. Like the Sieveking association, the Paulsen society operated on the basis of
referrals from the municipal poor administration. Contrary to
the Sieveking association, however, negotiations with city authorities were a corporate rather than an individual responsibility. The Paulsen association assigned superintendents to each

of eleven municipal districts; these women together comprised the executive committee and represented the association to the city. This was one of several ways in which the association endeavored to cultivate the qualities of leadership among its members.

Paulsen's humiliation in 1844 at Sieveking's behest did not end all contact between the two women. An occasional letter, an occasional donation to the *Amalienstift* were indications that Paulsen continued to acknowledge some measure of continuity in the activity of the two associations.[6] Her own work was, however, undertaken in a very different spirit. Committed to the principle of confessional inclusiveness, Paulsen's society invoked a different rationale: woman's nature took the place of the Christian spirit. The first annual report includes a categorical statement of the conviction that inspired Paulsen and her associates: "The more tender, gentler and more reconciling faculty of women and their experience as housekeepers, spouses and mothers eminently equips them ... to practice benevolence."[7] The original membership of the Paulsen society numbered fifty-two women, who met with "ridicule, blame [and] rejection" when they first solicited the public for support.[8]

Paulsen's women came from a very different social stratum than the members of the Sieveking society. Besides the members of the executive committee—Wuestenfeld, Kortmann, Paulsen herself, and Goldschmidt and Westendarp who were linked to the business community—it was small business women and artisan women who were prominent among the charter members and supervisors. Emilie Bieber ran a photography studio, Jenny Berghauer was a piano teacher, Amalie Niemeyer worked with her husband in a music shop, Frau Gotzel had a husband who built organs, the widow Frau Havemann ran a shop for Dutch wares, and Frau Hadersold managed a small hotel.[9] The trades that these women practiced had one feature in common: none was conducted within the system of guilds, a powerful bond in the political reality of Hamburg society and one shared with the Jewish trades as well as with such manufacturing entrepreneurs as the Meyer family. Paulsen's daughter Elisabeth Schulz was also active in the association as were the wives of two doctors, the wife of a liberal Protestant pastor, and the wife of a church school supervisor. The differing demands of business, in which some of these women were engaged, and domesticity, which fully occupied others, apparently did not interfere with the development of a collective ethos. A statement in the eighth annual report was the closest the association came to a self-conscious representation of the issue of class. Addressing the cause of prejudice against women's clubs, the report concluded:

Perhaps the fear has now diminished that women and girls will be alienated from their domestic obligations by club work because it is now apparent that rich ladies who have substantial help and little to do often lack the time for fulfilling uncustomary obligations. By contrast our simple women with their many household burdens and completely inadequate or non-existent household personnel find that visiting with the poor is their favorite mode of recuperation.[10]

The annual budget of the Paulsen association was less than one-fifth that of the Sieveking society—3607 marks in 1850 as compared with more than 15,656 for the Sieveking society in 1847. Some funds went for direct assistance to clients and the society accepted food donations for immediate distribution: mothers recovering from childbirth were the particular target of this program.

The care of women recently delivered we find especially important for the health of the family. The mother is indispensible to the prosperity of the entire family and certainly under oppressive conditions is the more threatened in childbed.[11]

Special concern for the welfare of mothers distinguished the Paulsen from the Sieveking society.

Beyond this, the Paulsen enterprise focused on projects that permitted the poor to work. The association established a fund to purchase materials for its clients to manufacture into inexpensive, serviceable clothing; second-hand objects were also collected for repair. An on-going sale made these articles available to the public and proved an effective source of re-funding for the entire scheme. No provision was made, however, to produce or distribute garments for church attendance, a practice that nicely highlights the difference between Paulsen's emphasis and that of Sieveking: the Sieveking clubs often distributed clothing to enable their clients to attend church services.[12] A recurrent outlay from the Paulsen treasury went to subsidize application fees for legal residency. Since legal residence was the pre-condition to any claim on the city from the legalization of marriage to free schooling and occupational licensing, the Paulsen association supported these applications whenever possible, out of motives that combined moral as often as pragmatic considerations.[13]

Because the budget of the Paulsen association was so limited, the organization relied heavily on personal contact, counselling, and instruction. As an employment agency, Paulsen's association built a more substantial reputation than the Sieveking society, a record consonant with its general purpose.[14] For while Sieveking invoked resignation among her clientele, cautioned them against protest and held out the promise of eternal salvation, the Paulsen association was firmly anchored in the concerns of the contemporary secular world.

Like other members of her milieu, whether artisan or entrepreneurial, Paulsen believed that social stability depended upon a continual expansion of the middle class to forestall the formation of a proletariat. The term proletariat had both material and moral connotations. It signified rootlessness as well as dependency. Reform efforts in general during the revolutionary decade characteristically included moral as well as economic dimensions; they were channelled through clubs—clubs for education, for savings, for recreation—because these clubs were thought of as a replacement for the old corporative institutions that were gradually being undercut by new forms of socio-economic organization.[15] In this context, the children of the poor represented a particular challenge to Paulsen.

Notwithstanding the many free schools established by the state, large segments among the children of our poor find themselves sadly ignorant [her second annual report announced]. We must actively entertain the possibility of extending the educational institution we started last year. . . . Through improved instruction we believe we can most effectively forestall the corruption of the poor as well as the formation of a proletariat, for both in our experience are the fruit of ignorance.[16]

When the police shut down the Paulsen school a few years later, the association sought legal redress in similar terms: "The poor and needy should be strengthened and sustained in the struggle against the adversities of life, through ethical guidance and instruction, and through the introduction and mediation of work," not frustrated in their efforts at self-improvement.[17]

The heart of the Women's Association for the Support of Poor Relief and the first stage of its training program was the children's shelter. This was Paulsen's own pet project.[18]

We particularly direct our attention to helpless children, to removing these poor innocent creatures from their damp, unhealthy living quarters where inadequate supervision and poor nourishment condemn them to certain destruction.[19]

Contrary to the Sieveking practice of trying to keep infants at home even at the cost of distributing meaningless work to their mothers, Paulsen's shelter recruited and cared for the young children of working parents. From early morning until late evening, while their mothers were at work, children between the ages of two and six were supervised, bathed, and fed. Confident in the belief that the child "is of nature pure and without sin," Paulsen and her colleagues in the ecumenical nursery adopted a pedagogical stance distinctly at odds with the tenets of contemporary orthodox Christianity. They assumed the moral obligation to train bodies as well as minds and celebrated the accomplishments of children who "developed their limbs through outdoor play, their ears through song, and their sense of nature's law through the mastery of simple arithmetic rules."[20]

Children could graduate from the shelter of the Paulsen association directly into its school, where, for a small fee, they continued their education until confirmation. Tuition support was one of the regular goals of fund-raising.[21] There was no compulsory schooling in Hamburg; private schools were out of reach for the poor. Free schools were overcrowded and available only to legal residents. The Woman's Association started its school with twenty girls and rapidly expanded to a coeducated student body of 100. The trained teaching staff, all volunteer, numbered seven; this staff was augmented by fourteen girls and women who were members of the association. Johanna Gold-schmidt and Amalie Westendarp shared the responsibility of supervising the school as representatives of the association. Classes were conducted in basic academic subjects, gymnastics, and singing. No formal instruction was offered in religion; when the full impact of the reaction reached Hamburg, it was on this ground that the school was forced to shut down.[22] An ancestor of the girls' trade school in Hamburg, Paulsen's school reflected her overriding concern for girls and women. She deplored the prevalence of illiteracy among girls of fifteen and sixteen who had been allowed to slip through confirmation instruction without being taught to read. The same girls were often ignorant of the most elementary domestic tasks, yet they were abandoned to a labor market where they were expected to earn their living in domestic service.

FEMINIST INITIATIVES: THE DOMESTIC INSTITUTE AND THE SOCIAL CLUB

To address the circumstances of women fated to become domestic servants, the Paulsen association entered into a cooperative arrangement with the "domestic institute"—the Association for the Training of Capable Servants (*Verein zur Bildung der tuechtigen Dienstmaedchen*) was its full name. This was the first project of the Women's Club of 1847 singularly aimed at helping women. Paulsen herself was an enthusiast.[23] The domestic institute was modeled after a similar program that the Society for Social and Political Interests of the Jews had sponsored in the years before emancipation. The Jewish program recognized that immigrant girls needed what their brothers had long enjoyed: an institutional apparatus to ease the transition from country to city and a recognized means of training and placement for employment.[24]

With the organization of the domestic institute we are located squarely in the world of the bourgeois family, a world populated and controlled by women. Self-serving as these programs may appear to the modern reader, they also succeed in conveying the enormous confidence these women vested in the moral and educative potential of their own domesticity. They were appar-

ently unconcerned that relations within the family—father/
mother, mother/servant—duplicated and reinforced the power
relations of the public economy, and that the autonomy of the
mother in the household was illusory, deriving as it did from
the economic power of the absent father. These were corollaries
to the generally held belief in unlimited economic expansion
and social mobility. The bourgeois family depended on servants
but the serving girls whose stories found their way into the reports of the Women's Club of 1847 were girls whose training in
the domestic institute enabled them to move out from domestic
service into the vocation of child care and early childhood education. The lines between home and workplace, private and
public were not rigidly drawn. The mothers understood their
households not as barriers but as means of access to further
education and vocational opportunity. Their conviction shaped
the agenda of the Women's Association to Combat and Reduce
Religious Prejudice (*Frauenverein zur Bekaempfung und Ausgleichung religioeser Vorurteile*)—what its membership called the Social
Club—one more of the societies like the Paulsen association and
the Women's Club of 1847 that availed themselves of the revolutionary ferment in 1848–49 to promote women's issues.[25]

The Social Club, like Paulsen's association, represented a wom-
en's response to the emancipation of Hamburg Jewry and, like
so much of their activity, originated in the recognition that the
experience of men and that of women of the same class was very
different. Emilie Wuestenfeld spoke for the Social Club when
she argued that Protestant businessmen could associate with Jewish men in the context of daily commercial life while Protestant
women enjoyed no comparable access to their Jewish sisters. The
Social Club was designed to amend this deficiency. At the same
time it aimed to profit from the differences perpetrated among
women by differing religious traditions to identify the common
concerns of gender and to address these concerns with an agenda
for action. Through such a program the Social Club hoped to
promote the self-realization of women and to enhance their contemporary stature in society. An inaugural meeting at Wuestenfeld's house targeted two principal concerns: early childhood
education and the higher education of women.[26] What I will call
the Froebel initiative addressed the first of these concerns; the

Hochschule initiative addressed the second. The Paulsen association actively engaged in the Froebel initiative with the Social
Club; the Women's Club of 1847 and the Social Club piloted the
Hochschule initiative until a specific sponsoring association with
national ties could be established. The Froebel initiative proposed to bring Friedrich Froebel (1782–1852), the founder of
the modern kindergarten, to Hamburg to conduct a six-month
training program. The *Hochschule* initiative proposed to implement the prospectus composed by another branch of the Froebel
family, Karl Froebel (1807–1894) and his wife Johanna, for a
women's college. In this campaign, with the combined resources
of several associations and its double objective, the inter-confessional women's movement in Hamburg came to maturity and
ultimately provided both purpose and structure to a network of
progressive women throughout Germany.

EARLY CHILDHOOD EDUCATION: THE
FROEBEL INITIATIVE

Johanna Goldschmidt, writer, philanthropist, and interpreter
of Jewish women to those who were nominally Christian, was
pivotal to the Froebel initiative. The publication of her book,
The Delights and Cares of Motherhood, had propelled Goldschmidt
into prominence as an early childhood educator.[27] Instrumental
in her success was the recognition accorded to her by Adolf
Diesterweg (1790–1866), Germany's leading progressive educational theorist. When *Delights and Cares* was still in manuscript,
Goldschmidt sent it to Diesterweg; he not only read it with enthusiasm but offered to write a preface to the book, one that
was extremely laudatory. Goldschmidt's volume also initiated a
chain of events that ultimately brought Diesterweg into personal
contact with Friedrich Froebel, a fruitful encounter for both men
and one that also induced Diesterweg to give the weight of his
support to the Hamburg enterprise. At the time Goldschmidt
wrote to Froebel in March 1849 she was acquainted with him
through his work but not in person. What she proposed was that
he offer a series of lectures and demonstrations to women interested in the kindergarten movement; she invited him to sub-

mit a proposal for consideration by the Social Club, the coalition of women against prejudice.[28]

Froebel was by now an old man. He had been involved with pedagogy since the early decades of the century. Under the influence of Pestalozzi, he published a treatise called *Human Education* (*Die Menschenerziehung*), but nothing he wrote then or later offers a full or coherent theory. His preoccupation with small children was more recent. The institute for early childhood education he conducted at Keilhau in Saxony consisted of an extended family comprising his own immediate family and those of his brother and brother-in-law, augmented by a number of nieces and other young people interested in absorbing his theory and practice. Part of his entourage joined him in Dresden for a six-month session of instruction during the winter of 1848–49. The succeeding summer he won the patronage of the duchess of Leiningen and brought his institute to Bad Liebenstein near Marienthal at her behest. Materials and equipment for the distinctive Froebel method were manufactured by artisans in neighboring Blankenburg; local children were his subjects. Froebel did not represent a theory so much as a practice. A review of his principles, however, makes it apparent why he was so enthusiastically courted by Johanna Goldschmidt and her associates in the Social Club—indeed by women in general who were committed to developing a concept of motherhood based on woman's nature rather than one rooted in Christianity.[29]

The basic concept of the Froebel system was the conviction that human growth, both physical and intellectual, came essentially from within, and represented a process of unfolding and developing rather than one of receiving and accommodating.

Not through what one early receives and assimilates from without does the human being develop himself and become cultivated for the attainment of his destination and his vocation, but overwhelmingly more through that which he unravels and conceives out of himself.[30]

In this sense the Froebel theory was profoundly secular. Froebel categorically rejected the concept of original sin; he was equally disinclined to the doctrine of personal immortality which, he believed, falsely distinguished between the physical and the spiritual in human nature. In his own system the two were inextricably bound one to the other. The child, according to Froebel, was born with the mental as well as physical drive for activity; it wanted to make use of its limbs and to exercise its spirit. The aim of the kindergarten was to develop the child's own strivings, to stimulate harmonious development of body, mind, and spirit. Froebel intentionally discarded the term "school" in conjunction with programs using his methods and his name. "Little children, particularly children before they are ready for school should be neither trained nor schooled but developed."[31]

The term "kindergarten" not only suggested the location Froebel liked best for his program—a facility with access to an actual garden where children could observe and cultivate growing things—but it also evoked his imagery, in which the acorn and the oak were standard metaphors for the child and the adult. The function of the kindergarten was to convert the child's indigenous drive for activity into purposeful activity; the means: play. Froebel spoke of play as a representation of the child's inner life and the foreplay of human existence itself. Since the favorite plaything of a child was another child, Froebel believed child-play was a means of creating community. The preferred mode of play was the game that engaged the greatest number of the child's faculties.[32] The Froebel system embraced the practical as well as the ideal in pedagogy. To support and implement his theory of childhood, Froebel developed an elaborate, graduated repertoire of exercises and play objects designed to cultivate mind and body in a single organic process. His *Mother and Play Songs* (*Mutter- und Kose-Lieder:Dichtung und Bilder zur edlen Pflege des Kindheitslebens*) and his "gifts": the ball, the cube, and the cylinder, were conceived as both devices to structure children's play and as strategies to cultivate the mental processes of abstraction and reconciliation. He spoke, for example, of the cylinder as a model to "mediate" the ball and the cube. As the repertoire of play equipment was elaborated, Froebel believed the child received the means to derive for itself the laws of nature. Here, as elsewhere, Froebel conveyed the essential pantheism of his own belief.

Conceptually, the Froebel system was rooted in a division of human nature by gender. Women were central to the theory and function of the kindergarten. The kindergarten teacher performed a dual role in the human drama: she was at once a surrogate for the mothers of her pupils and a student of mothering skills and attitudes for her own future motherhood. To insure continuity in the primary growth of the child with respect to its mother, kindergarten participation was restricted to a few hours each day; mothers were encourged to attend. The rhythmic exercises and the distinctive play objects that became hallmarks of the Froebel system were intentionally designed for introduction by women, mothers, and teachers alike.[33]

Reverence for women permeated all of Froebel's relationships. Henriette Breymann, a young grand-niece and Froebel trainee who later in the century led the kindergarten movement in Berlin, reported in her diary that

they [meaning her uncle and his male associates] always thought of us women differently from most men; that they consider us worthy even outside of marriage to assume a respectable place as guardians of childhood, that we even as unmarried women can collaborate with understanding and consciousness in the ennobling of human society, that we could be and become something for ourselves.[34]

The dignity and social importance ascribed, particularly, to single women by the Froebel system was virtually unique among male contemporaries, as Breymann recognized. Similarly the role assigned to the mother as family tutor and spiritual interpreter usurped the moral and pedagogical authority of the father, prescribed in *Hausvater* literature since the time of Luther.[35]

Reliance on women created serious resistance to the reception of the Froebel method on a national level. The Frankfurt National Parliament addressed the issue of a national system of education during the summer of 1848. In the hope that his own system might be incorporated into the national constitution, Froebel issued a public invitation to statesmen and teachers to a two-day demonstration at Rudolstadt in Saxony.[36] Elaborate preparations preceded the affair. In an auditorium garlanded with flowers and the Froebel motto: "Come, let us live for our children" (*"Kommt, lasst uns unsern Kindern leben"*), women trained by Froebel illustrated his techniques by exercises with local children and Froebel himself delivered lectures and interpretations.[37] Henriette Breymann, who was very loyal to her uncle, postponed writing her parents for a full two weeks, so conflicted did she feel about a meeting that could only be described as a disaster. Froebel, never an effective public speaker, had become confused on the platform, and "this interminable play," Breymann observed, had simply not been the appropriate way to convey his ideas. "I must say that some of it even seems ridiculous to me."[38] A delegate sent by the ministry in Saxony, at that point a liberal government put into power by the revolution, declared: "I look into Froebel's creative spirit as into a holy chaos."[39]

But what in the end most antagonized the assemblage was the role of women in the Froebel scheme. A delegate from Dresden remarked:

Froebel expects that his *Kindergaerten*, from which he promises such great consequences for the elevation of human society, will be led by women, that therefore his philosophic ideas should be carried through by women. I must, however, say that I shudder at philosophic women.[40]

The remark galvanized the women present. Johanna Kuestner jumped to her feet and demanded "that women be treated as human beings. They are laying claim to a totally new form of education...and they are quite capable of pursuing scientific and philosophic studies."[41] Kuestner seized the opportunity to implement her convictions the following year. She and her husband, Karl Froebel, drafted the founding proposal for the women's college in Hamburg (*Hamburger Hochschule fuer das weibliche Geschlecht*), the institution created by the second initiative of the Social Club or coalition of women against prejudice, and Kuestner herself acted as an administrator.

For the moment, however, the Rudolstadt conference represented a severe setback to Friedrich Froebel's credibility. Froebel continued to conduct seminars in Saxony but the hope that the national political movement would embrace his system evaporated. The inquiry from Johanna Goldschmidt, by extending the support of an organized women's association in one of Germany's major urban centers, promised to reverse his fortunes. It was also a particularly important instance of the way in which the distinctive pace of revolutionary events in Hamburg shaped the movement of progressive women. Goldschmidt's letter was a product of Jewish emancipation, a radical victory in Hamburg achieved at a moment when elsewhere radicalism was on the defensive and the revolution was in retreat. Adolf Diesterweg was delighted by Goldschmidt's action. As he confided to her: "I am very anxious about [Froebel]. Most men will not understand him nor commit themselves to his thinking. The women must save him."[42]

Diesterweg credited Goldschmidt with his own conversion to Froebel's principles. On her suggestion he had sought out the old man in the hills of Saxony at Bad Liebenstein in July 1849; Goldschmidt herself visited Bad Liebenstein in August. Of this sojourn, Diesterweg wrote:

If you had done no other service but make me aware of this excellent, noble, profound man, I would never forget it. I have become a student again and am delighted to be one.... [Froebel] is a jewel, a pearl.[43]

From a position of skepticism toward the Froebel system, the *Rhenish Reports for Education and Instruction* (*Rheinische Blaetter fuer Erziehung und Unterricht*), Diesterweg's journal, became a significant source of support. As Diesterweg again wrote to Goldschmidt: "It would be an eternal pity if the treasures which lie in F. F. were to go forgotten."[44] This was precisely the legitimation Froebel needed. Goldschmidt was able to supply something else: contact with a wide circle of women, which could afford Froebel the exposure and recognition that years of effort on his own part had failed to accomplish.

Froebel himself welcomed the overture from Goldschmidt and endorsed the goal of the coalition against prejudice with an extravagance bordering on unintelligibility.

[Y]our ... attention and that of your highly esteemed club to this prospect ... [t]he unification of the world of women, is a truly world-concept, one of humanity which in order to achieve realization must emerge freely out of the world and soul of women themselves.[45]

The pedagogy of the kindergarten and the ecumenism of the Social Club in Hamburg held out the possibility of mutual reinforcement.

The love of children, children's love, the nurturing of childhood and with it the nurturing of humanity is actually the basic sentiment and unifying feeling of the female being. Through the cultivation of this feeling in girls, young women and mature women you wish to unite the worlds of young women and women divided by custom, tradition and prejudice and wish to annihilate and eradicate the thousand year gulf among and between them.[46]

This concept of woman's nature resonated well with the convictions of Goldschmidt and the members of the Social Club because it seemed to anchor their moral and educational goals in a primary source of legitimation antecedent to Christianity and Judaism. It offered an alternative, an apparent guarantee against the divisiveness of confessionalism. In the interests of ecumenism, the evident limitations of a theory that both purported to offer a rationale for emancipation in terms of gender difference and all but equated woman's nature with child-nurture were not addressed.

Negotiations between Goldschmidt and Froebel coincided with the efforts of Allwine Middendorff, Froebel's grand-niece, to introduce a kindergarten within the curriculum of the girls' school in Hamburg directed by Doris Luetkens. The Social Club agreed to make contact with this project, but no collaboration developed. Allwine's correspondence unintentionally clarifies why. The Christian dogma of Incarnation was central to Luetkens' personal faith and her household opposed Jewish emancipation. Luetkens acknowledged that Froebel's religious orientation differed from her own but claimed that his pedagogy was nevertheless compatible with Christianity. Although she was an accomplished polemicist on Froebel's behalf, Froebel himself had reservations about her adaptation of his system, and when he wrote to her, he discussed the need for mediation and reconciliation.[47] Another more immediate controversy impinged on his interchange with Goldschmidt. Froebel attached conditions to his appearance in Hamburg: detachment from the proposed women's college and detachment from his nephew Karl. Although the proposed curriculum of the college was essentially humanistic, it also embraced an early childhood component. Karl Froebel as author of the curriculum was commited to the professionalization of women. This was just one of the ways in which he construed the concept of woman's nature that his uncle found unacceptable.[48]

HIGHER EDUCATION FOR WOMEN

The *Hochschule* initiative expressed a need long recognized among progressive women in Hamburg. In this regard they were not unique. Amalie Sieveking herself had frequently articulated her concern about the absence of advanced education for women. Doris Luetkens' periodicals also promoted the cause of higher education for girls, but to these women, a confessional context was desirable. Progressive women, Christian and Jewish alike, on the contrary, concurred in their conviction that it was the monopoly of women's education by confessional institutions that held the training of women to the contemporary level of mediocrity. Interest escalated when the Social Club received a brochure entitled *Universities for Girls, and Kindergartens as Segments of a Comprehensive Educational Institution which Unites Education for Family and School Instruction (Hochschulen fuer Maedchen und Kindergaerten als Glieder einer vollstaendigen Bildungsanstalt welche Erziehung fuer Familie und Unterricht der Schule verbindet)*, which the authors, Karl Froebel and his wife Johanna Kuestner Froebel sent to the association in search of a sponsor.[49] Johanna Kuestner was the woman who had spoken so forcibly in favor of women's education at the earlier Rudolstadt convention; she had since married Karl Froebel. Emilie Wuestenfeld and Bertha Traun assumed responsibility for exploring the feasibility of the Froebel prospectus. Neither had the kind of credentials that made Goldschmidt so ideal a negotiator with Friedrich Froebel. Wuestenfeld, however, in a statement she circulated in Hamburg, amply conveyed the depth of her commitment to the project and the command of pertinent issues that made her so valuable an advocate.

Wuestenfeld deplored the absence of involvement by women

in contemporary issues and the indifference to the significance of their role as "guardians of the next generation." She blamed "the false apostle of femininity," which restricted women to the narrow confines of their households.

More than ever [she continued] the last few years have once again made apparent the uncertainty of material property and external relationships, and have confirmed the premise that thorough, basic education is the only certain dowry for life, in that it permits independence from within as well as from without. In the male sex this premise has long since been put into actual practice; in the female sex—in half of humankind—it is only very occasionally implemented. Indeed from many voices worthy of respect the demand for basic instruction [in the various disciplines] is expressed, as an essential basis for the independent development of character.[50]

Neither the pursuit of domesticity nor the external polish of music and the languages—only higher education—could equip women for what Wuestenfeld viewed as their future life work.

Both Wuestenfeld and Traun were charter members of the executive committee of the Women's Club of 1847. Beyond the original commitment to religious radicalism this group had long entertained the possibility of a project in higher education for women. One of the annual reports of the Women's Club of 1847 had so forcefully made the point that in working for the liberation of others, women had become aware of the need to be free and self-sufficient themselves.[51] But the Women's Club of 1847 hesitated to overextend its resources. However, under the aegis of the more recent Social Club, the coalition aligned against religious prejudice, a campaign to improve women's education seemed eminently appropriate. The inadequacies of women's education in mid-nineteenth-century Germany were so closely linked to the tenacity of confessionalism that change in one area invited challenge in the other. Hence the impetus that finally produced the *Hamburger Hochschule fuer das weibliche Geschlecht*, the single German institution approaching the actuality of a women's university during the entire century, developed within the agenda of an association designed to combat religious prejudice on the one hand and as a sequel to a series of initiatives in the realm of religious dissent and philanthropy on the other. The Froebel proposal under review by the Social Club embraced an entire critique of society, one that would have introduced a network of interconnected age- and sex-specific communities to replace the existing family. The prospectus had been rejected by municipal authorities in Zurich and the Froebels were soliciting sponsorship in Hamburg for a more limited segment of their proposal, devoted to women and children, where the redress of social neglect was most urgent.

The Froebels derived their pedagogy from a concept of innate sexual difference. At one level their theory differed very little from that of Friedrich Froebel. In their application of what they understood to be inborn attributes of women, their theory represented a radical departure. According to Karl Froebel, the differences between woman and man corresponded to those between nature and culture, one involving unconscious creativity, the other conscious manufacture. The highest goal of women, Froebel believed, was making the ideal or the intellectual concrete, whereas man's goal was the reverse: the intellectualization of the concrete. Woman was by nature concerned with the individual, the specific; man with the general, the abstract.[52] Froebel drew a number of rather arbitrary conclusions from his dichotomy that were to govern activities and forms of training appropriate to the two sexes.

Both sexes, Froebel argued, were committed to the improvement of society, but women were interested in preserving the beautiful and the good that already existed, whereas men were committed to transforming society into what it ought to become. Froebel denied any intrinsic difference in the rational capacities of the sexes: "If women in general lag behind men in knowledge, artistic achievement and accomplishment," he wrote, "the reason lies partly in the fact that they are offered fewer opportunities to demonstrate their achievements, but much more in their disadvantageous training."[53]

If equivalent time and means were provided for women's education, their contribution to society, however different, would be as substantial as men's. Froebel believed that society in fact could not be transformed without the full participation of women since their ability to mediate the abstract and to concretize the ideal was necessary in the process of realizing the goals envisaged by men.

However problematic the theoretical underpinning, the actual curriculum of the Froebel prospectus was designed with the explicit aim of liberating women from the economic necessity of precipitous marriage. Short-term careers, Froebel argued, should be available to women so that they could prolong the conventional period of singlehood; if marriage was not in their future they should be equipped to develop occupations that would offer dignity and security for their entire lives. The Froebel curriculum emphasized practical sciences such as arithmetic, chemistry, and physiology—disciplines that would be useful to the management of a household and also to cultivating the rudiments of hygiene and health care. Froebel believed that philosophy for women was the most important formal discipline since an understanding of the states of human evolution and the development of self-consciousness preceded the intelligent rearing and education of children. Philosophy also assumed the place of formal religion in the curriculum. The concepts of God, Nature, Spirit, and Immortality were counted among the modes of philosophic expression.[54]

The prospectus included an essay on the social significance of the kindergarten by Johanna Froebel. The theme she developed most fully was the fallacy of the assumption that woman's instinct constituted an adequate basis for the rearing and management of children. Three elements, she believed, were essential to the development of the young personality: reason, free will, and love. Women who relied exclusively on their personal capacity to love, though, failed to support the developemnt of the other two capacities in children. Like Friedrich Froebel, she emphasized the essential relationship between physical and emotional development, and the use of geometric objects and of prescribed body movements to cultivate the growing capacity of the young child. Johanna Froebel acknowledged the value of the kindergarten as a training program for motherhood but she also believed in training women for certain professions, and she was convinced that employment in the kindergarten offered some women an avenue of social and political expression. The Zurich Froebels envisaged the kindergarten as an integral part of any women's college and they thought of both as components of a comprehensive educational enterprise that would contribute to the fundamental reform of society.[55]

In its emphasis on an education beyond confessions, the Froebel proposal resonated with the interests and goals of the Social Club. Wuestenfeld and Traun were commissioned to transact the necessary arrangements in Zurich and engage the Froebels to implement their plan. During their sojourn, however, the entire project very nearly foundered, first, on Friedrich Froebel's own intransigence with respect to his nephew, and second, on the apprehensions of a faction within the Social Club itself. This group feared the over-commitment of resources and argued, in the absence of the two principal advocates of the college, that the Froebel seminar deserved priority. The college project was saved by an affirmation of solidarity and the creation of a new society designed for the express purpose of supporting inter-confessional education, the Hamburg Education Association (*Hamburger Bildungsverein*).[56]

The Education Association deliberately enlarged the sponsorship of the women's college in two directions: it solicited the membership of foreigners—residents of other parts of Germany—and it opened its ranks to men. A stipulation that two-thirds of the directorate must consist of women at all times safeguarded the principle of female leadership. The new society was predicated on the assumption of a national constituency with an extended institutional structure, headquartered in Hamburg. Johannes Ronge was probably responsible for this scheme. He was fully conversant with the possibilities of national organization and he was a staunch advocate of women's education. The machinery of the Education Association permitted the Hamburg women to extend their influence into the national arena. Under its auspices they expanded their more conventional commitments to charity and early childhood education to embrace the larger challenge of advanced education for women.

The potentiality of the Hamburg Association was immediately recognized by Johanna Froebel. In November 1849, shortly after her relocation in Hamburg, she wrote to Louise Dittmar, the feminist disciple of Feuerbach who had promoted education as an alternative to marriage, that the most persuasive element in her decision to support the women's college project in Hamburg was "the wide-branching Education Association" with its promise of "penetrating the widest and most distinctive circles of German women."[57] Those circles coincided with the readership of Louise Otto's *Frauen-Zeitung*.

NOTES

1. Der Vorstand des Frauen-Vereins von 1847 zur Unterstuetzung deutschkatholischer Gemeinden und zur Foerderung humaner Zwecke, "Bericht," [1850], Nls EW, StAr Hmbg.
2. Der Vorstand des Frauen-Vereins von 1847 zur Unterstuetzung der freien Gemeinden und zur Foerderung humaner Zwecke, "Bericht," [1851], Nls EW, StAr Hmbg.
3. Helga Krohn, *Juden in Hamburg 1800–1850. Ihre soziale, kulturelle und politische Entwicklung waehrend der Emanzipationszeit* (Frankfurt a.M.: Europaeische Verlagsanstalt, 1967), p. 62.
4. Marie Kortmann, *Emilie Wuestenfeld. Eine Hamburger Buergerin* (Hamburg: Georg Westermann, 1927), pp. 43, 48.
5. "Revidirte Statuten des Frauen-Vereins zur Unterstuetzung der Armenpflege," *FVUA, 3. Jahres-Bericht*, p. 6.
6. Charlotte Paulsen to Amalie Sieveking, 8 Jan. 1845, 15 May 1849, 15 Nov. 1849, Nls AWS, StAr Hmbg.
7. *FVUA, 1. Jahres-Bericht*, p. 3.
8. Wohlwill, "Charlotte Paulsen," Schule des Paulsenstiftes, StAr Hmbg, p. 8.
9. Kortmann, *Emilie Wuestenfeld*, p. 44.
10. *FVUA, 8. Jahres-Bericht*, p. 11.
11. *FVUA, 3. Jahres-Bericht*, p. 9.
12. *FVUA, 2. Jahres-Bericht*, p. 5; on Sieveking, see [Emma Poel and Sophie Wattenbach], *Arbeit der Frauen in Vereinen fuer Armen- und Krankenpflege. Ein Briefwechsel zweier Freundinnen* (Berlin: Hertz, 1854), pp. 61, 69.
13. *FVUA, 2. Jahres-Bericht*, p. 5; Kortmann, *Emilie Wuestenfeld*, p. 45n.
14. *FVUA, 3. Jahres-Bericht*, p. 6; *WVAK, 15. Bericht*, p. 9; Kayser, "Die Deutsch-katholische Bewegung in Hamburg," *ZVHG* 26 (1925): 157.
15. James J. Sheehan, *German Liberalism in the Nineteenth Century* (Chicago and London: University of Chicago Press, 1978), pp. 26–33; Her-

bert Freudenthal, *Vereine in Hamburg. Ein Beitrag zur Geschichte und Volkskunde der Geselligkeit* (Hamburg: Museum fuer Hamburgische Geschichte, 1968), pp. 129–30.

16. "Bericht ueber die Schule des Paulsenstifts zu Hamburg erstattet bei Gelegenheit des 25. jaehrigen Bestehens der Anstalt 1891," p. 3, and Johanna Goldschmidt, "Bericht ueber die Bewahranstalt und Schule des Frauenvereins zur Unterstuetzung der Armenpflege," Hamburg: Druck von Carl Reefe, 1866, Schule des Paulsenstifts, StAr Hmbg.

17. "Die Schliessung des Unterrichts-Cursus des Frauen-Vereins. Aktenstuecke," Hamburg, June 1854, p. 5, Polizeiliche Untersuchungsakten Serie VI, Unterrichtsanstalten des sog. Frauen-Vereins, StAr Hmbg.

18. Wohlwill, "Charlotte Paulsen," StAr Hmbg, p. 8.

19. Quoted in Fritzi Liecks, "Charlotte Paulsen, geb. Thornton 1797–1862," 100-Jahr-Feier in der Charlotte Paulsen Schule Hamburg-Wandsbeck im November 1949, Schule des Paulsenstifts, StAr Hmbg, p. 10.

20. Wohlwill, "Charlotte Paulsen," StAr Hmbg, pp. 8–9; Der Vorstand der Frauen-Vereins von 1847, "Zur Unterstuetzung deutschkatholischer Gemeinden und zur Foerderung humaner Zwecke," [1850] Nls EW, StAr Hmbg; Martin Gerhardt, *Theodor Fliedner. Ein Lebensbild*, 2 vols. (Duesseldorf-Kaiserswerth: Verlag der Buchhandlung der Diakonissen-Anstalt, 1937), 1: 349.

21. *FVUA, 2. Jahres-Bericht*, p. 6.

22. "Bericht ueber die Schule des Paulsenstifts zu Hamburg . . . 1891," StAr Hmbg, pp. 3–5.

23. *FVUA, 2. Jahres-Bericht*, pp. 6–7.

24. Gesellschaft fuer soziale und politische Interessen der Juden, "Auszug aus den Statuten der Commission fuer weibliche Dienstboten," Nls EW, StAr Hmbg.

25. Der Vorstand des Frauen-Vereins 1847 zur Unterstuetzung der freien christlichen Gemeinden und zur Foederung humaner Zwecke, "Bericht," [1851], Nls EW, StAr Hmbg, mentioned a girl originally enrolled in the domestic program who became a student in the Friedrich Froebel seminar; another who showed proficiency in the language classes at the domestic institute was placed in a French-speaking family to train as a French teacher, Gesellschaft fuer soziale und politische Interessen der Juden, "Programm," Nls EW, StAr Hmbg.

26. Kortmann, *Emilie Wuestenfeld*, p. 26; Anna Warburg, "Vortrag: Friedrich Froebel und Hamburg (aus alten Berichten, Briefen und Buechern zusammengestellt), gehalten am 18. April 1932, anlaesslich des 150. Geburtstages Friedrich Froebel," typescript, PFVAr.

27. *See* Chapter 3 note 33 above.

28. Karl Mueller, *Kulturreaktion in Preussen im 19. Jahrhundert. Mit einem Anhang: Briefe Froebels und Diesterwegs* (Berlin: Verlag fuer Kulturpolitik, 1929), pp. 110–15; Friedrich Froebel to Johanna Goldschmidt, 17 March 1849, typescript copy, PFVAr. Goldschmidt's letter has to be extrapolated from Froebel's answer; in this case, as in her correspondence with Diesterweg, the letters of the men were preserved while hers were not. This letter is not included in the Mueller appendix, where the remaining correspondence may be found.

29. "Friedrich Froebel," *Allgemeine Deutsche Biographie*; Anna Wiener-Pappenheim, "Froebels Idee der Muetterbildung in ihrer geschichtlichen Entwicklung," *Kindergarten* 68 (1927): 241–46; Mary J. Lyschinska, *Henriette Schrader-Breymann. Ihr Leben aus Briefen und Tagebuechern*, 2 vols. (Berlin and Leipzig: Walter de Gruyter u. Co., 1922), 1: 47–147.

30. "Froebel Worte," typescript copy, PFVAr.

31. Froebel to Ida Seele, 14 March 1847, Hermann Poesche, ed. *Friedrich Froebels Kindergarten Briefe* (Vienna and Leipzig: Pichlers Wwe. und Sohn, 1887), pp. 223–24. Seele was one of Froebel's followers, herself a gifted kindergarten teacher.

32. "Froebel Worte," PFVAr.

33. Doris Luetkens, "Die Froebel'sche Klein-Kinder Spiele, als Bildungs- und Erziehungsmittel," *Paedagogische Mittheilungen . . . 2*, no. 10 (16 May 1847): 150 StAr Hmbg; Friedrich Adolf Wilhelm Diesterweg, "Friedrich Froebel und die Goethe Stiftung," "Friedrich Froebel," *Saemtliche Werke*, ed. Heinrich Deiters and others, 15 vols. to date (Berlin: Volk und Wissen Volkseigener Verlag, 1956–), 8: 157–64, 9: 58–74, an extensively but not reliably footnoted edition.

34. Lyschinska, *Henriette Schrader-Breymann*, 1: 80. Froebel was also autocratic. Ida Seele had an opportunity to learn French but he insisted she decline; foreign languages interfered with his conception of the mother tongue. See Ida Seele, "Meine Erinnerungen an Friedrich Froebel," *Kindergarten* 27 (1886): 132.

35. Marilyn Chapin Massey, *Feminine Soul: The Fate of an Ideal* (Boston: Beacon Press, 1985), pp. 47–48.

36. *Allgemeine Schulzeitung* no. 120 (30 July 1848): 969. That summer Froebel wrote to Seele that there were sixteen *Kindergaerten* in existence; this makes the movement sound far more effective than it was up to that point. These were essentially little groups ephemerally gathered around specific individuals. Until it was championed by the progressive women and the free religious movement, Froebel's movement had met no significant public response. The letter to Seele in Poesche, ed., *Friedrich Froebels Kindergarten Briefe*, p. 144.

37. *Allgemeine Schulzeitung* no. 166 (19 Oktober 1848): 1337–40.

38. Lyschinska, *Henriette Schrader-Breymann*, 1: 71–83.

39. Quoted in ibid., p. 78.

40. Quoted in ibid., p. 79.

41. Quoted in ibid., p. 80.

42. Mueller, *Kulturreaktion*, p. 122.

43. Ibid.

44. Ibid. Among the pieces in the Diesterweg journal, "Friedrich Froebel," *Rheinische Blaetter fuer Erziehung und Unterricht*, N. F. 40, no. 3 (Nov.-Dec. 1849): 291–344, "Der Kinderfreund in Bad Liebenstein," ibid., 43, no. 1 (Jan.-Feb. 1851): 116–22; "Die Kindergaerten in Hamburg und das Wirken Friedrich Froebels," ibid., no. 2 (March-April 1851): 153–57; Henriette Breymann recognized the importance of Diesterweg's presence and endorsement to the Froebel enterprise, Lyschinska, *Henriette Schrader-Breymann*, 1: 134–35; also of Goldschmidt, ibid., pp. 140–41, whom she referred to as famous because she had initiated the first steps to bring Jews and Christians together.

45. Friedrich Froebel to Goldschmidt, 17 March 1849, PFVAr.

46. Ibid.

47. Anna Warburg, "Vortrag," Allwine Middendorff to Friedrich Froebel, 13 Feb. 1849, typescript copy, PFVAr; "Antwort der Herausgeberin," *Paedagogische Mittheilungen* 2, no. 7 (1 April 1847): 106–11; "Wie kann ein auf biblischem Standpunkte fussender Lehrer sich mit dem Froebelschen System vereinigten?" *Unsere Kinder* 1 (1849): 74–82, one of many examples of the position fostered here; Doris Luetkens, *Froebel'sche Kindergaerten. Eine Beantwortung der kleinen Schrift von J. Foelsing "Froebel'sche Kindergaerten,"* (Hamburg: Perthes, Besser und Mauke, 1849); Poesche, ed., *Friedrich Froebels Kindergarten Briefe*, p. 225–36.

48. Friedrich Froebel to the "honorable executive of the highly esteemed club of German Women in Hamburg," quoted in Mueller, *Kulturreaktion*, pp. 105–7; Kortmann, *Emilie Wuestenfeld*, pp. 33–34; Lyschinska, *Henriette Schrader-Breymann*, 1: 111, describes the fundamental differences between the two Froebels (and Julius as well) in a letter to her mother of 27 Feb. 1849.

49. Karl Froebel and Johanna Froebel geb. Kuestner, *Hochschulen fuer Maedchen und Kindergaerten als Glieder einer vollstaendigen Bildungsanstalt, . . . nebst Briefen ueber diesen Gegenstand als Programm zu den Plaenen der Hochschule fuer das weibliche Geschlecht in Hamburg* (Hamburg: G. W. Niemeyer, 1849).

50. Quoted in Marie Kortmann, "Aus den Anfaengen sozialer Frauenarbeit," *Frau. Monatsschrift fuer das gesammte Frauenleben unserer Zeit* 20 (1913): 427–28.

51. Vorstand des Frauen-Vereins von 1847 zur Unterstuetzung der freien christlichen Gemeinden und zur Foerderung humaner Zwecke, "Bericht," [1850], Nls EW, StAr Hmbg.

52. Froebel and Froebel, *Hochschulen fuer Maedchen*, pp. 14–15.

53. Ibid., p. 16.

54. Ibid., pp. 17–20, 40.

55. Ibid., pp. 25–31.

56. Kortmann, *Emilie Wuestenfeld*, pp. 30–39; Der Vorstand des Frauen-Vereins von 1847 zur Unterstuetzung deutschkatholischer Gemeinden und zur Foerderung humaner Zwecke, "Bericht [1850], 'Statuten des allgemeinen Bildungsvereins deutscher Frauen,' " Nls EW, StAr Hmbg.

57. Froebel and Froebel, *Hochschulen fuer Maedchen*, p. 50; the case for the education of women for singlehood Johanna Froebel presented with particular force, p. 53.

CHAPTER 5

From Hamburg to Germany: Appeal to the Feminist Press

Coverage in the *Frauen-Zeitung*, or *Women's News*, was the one certain access to a national audience of progressive women in the Germany of 1849. The Hamburg Education Association adopted this route to transform a local commitment into a national one, and to convert the vision of a women's initiative into a reality. The collaboration proved decisive. For the Hamburg Education Association it provided exposure and support for a campaign to create a women's college with a national constituency. For the readership of the *Frauen-Zeitung* it held out the promise of collective action particularly at a time when confidence in the efficacy of political activity was on the wane. The Education Association called for a coalition of auxiliaries dedicated to the women's college; it proposed to extend educational and professional opportunities in the field of early childhood education and to coordinate the charitable networks of progressive women on the local and the national level. It anticipated the transformation of philanthropy from a focus on evangelization and preparation for personal immortality to genuine social work. The manifesto issued by the Hamburg Education Association in the *Frauen-Zeitung* announced this three-pronged effort. The collaboration of journalism and self-conscious social action stimulated the discussion of issues hardly anticipated when Otto first launched her newspaper.

The *Frauen-Zeitung* commenced publication in April 1849. Unlike the magazines for women that preceded it, magazines published by men and catering to the entertainment of women, the *Frauen-Zeitung* had as its major purpose to disseminate information of a political and social character specifically relating to women and to function as a forum for opinions and discussions of the rights and duties of women in society.[1] Its goal was expressed in Otto's slogan on the mast-head: "For the empire of freedom I recruit female citizens" (*Dem Reich der Freiheit werb' ich Buergerinnen*). Otto proclaimed in her first trial issue that the people whom history forgets are those who forget to think about themselves. She summoned her sisters to join her in the forward struggle of all humanity, "of which we are one half."[2] She declared for the indivisibility of freedom, indicating the contradictions that inevitably accompanied a demand for freedom of conscience separate from a concomitant commitment to political freedom, the demand for republican institutions without an equivalent concern for social justice, or the liberation of males without the correlative liberation of females.[3]

At the same time, Otto elaborately dissociated herself from the so-called emancipated women like Luise Aston and George Sand, whom she accused of behaving like caricatures of men. Luise Aston, in fact, came in for virulent criticism in the pages of the *Frauen-Zeitung* for what purported to be her libertinism. Nor was Otto reliably generous in her appraisal of other contemporary German feminists. At one time or another, she or her paper attacked Louise Dittmar, Ida Frick (1824–c.1900), and Fanny Lewald (1811–1889). She was apparently unfamiliar with Mathilde Franziska Anneke whose own *Frauen-Zeitung* succeeded in producing only a single issue before it was suppressed.[4] Although Otto's journal elicited a wide range of women's participation and comment—in this regard it was tolerant and supportive of difference—there was an ideological uniformity within its editorial position and the work of its regular contributors. Otto was impatient of women's demands if they required different priorities from the program of the radical democrats involved in the immediate politics of the revolution and to this extent her feminism was certainly flawed. She argued forcefully for the participation of women in the public sphere but at the same time insisted that this participation assume "a *different* character and [occupy] a *different* realm" from that of men.[5] What she meant by this was never clear.

For herself, she presumably meant the investigative and expository role of the journalist, a career she performed with great effectiveness and one in which she apparently felt no compunction about entering alongside of men. Her own girlhood had been abruptly interrupted with the early deaths of her parents in 1835, followed closely by the death of the man she planned to marry. A small legacy gave her some financial independence, but essentially Otto supported herself by her writing. Ernst Keil, for whose periodicals *Our Planet (Unser Planet)*, *Comet (Wandelstern)*, and *Lighthouse (Leuchtturm)* she wrote, considered her a gifted journalist. In 1843 Otto published the essay for which she is particularly remembered where she argued that, contrary to popular opinion, women indeed had a responsibility to the public sphere. This article put her in the limelight of Saxon radicalism. One of her subsequent novels, *Castle and Factory (Schloss und Fabrik)*, was withdrawn from public distribution by the censor. In the wake of the revolution, Otto made two incursions into direct political action. One was an appeal to the new Saxon commission on labor to include the female as well as the male labor force in its investigative mandate. The other was a petition to the Berlin convention of male workers developing a platform of collective action, demanding that they help less experienced women workers adopt similar strategies. Otto's long essay on the female work force was reprinted in the *Frauen-Zeitung* late in 1849.[6]

IN REVOLUTIONARY SAXONY

The inauguration of the *Frauen-Zeitung* was symptomatic of the relatively advanced political and economic situation of Saxony with respect to the rest of Germany. It must be seen within this context as well as within that of the political revolution that had reached a point of crisis when the *Frauen-Zeitung* appeared. More than half of the population of Saxony was engaged in handicraft or industrial enterprise, a condition found in the rest of Germany only in the 1870s. Iron mining and production and textile manufacture were the historic Saxon occupations: mechanization changed the nature but not the importance of these two industries. By the 1840s there was already one factory employing 3000 people in Chemnitz; cotton and wool manufacture were introduced. The putting-out system employed large numbers of women in cottage textile manufacture; cotton replaced linen as the product of the domestic weaving industry, which employed men and women alike. The contrast between the lives of the factory owners and those of the women of the town of Oederan who hurried to their spinning mills before dawn captured Louise Otto's attention when she visited her sister in the Erzgebirge and inspired the commitment to women workers that marked her early journalistic career. She immortalized another group of women workers in her poem "The Lacemakers" (*Die Kloepplerinnen*). In the years just before the revolution the plight of the working class was exacerbated by a number of developments. The appearance of a surplus labor supply created by the accelerated application of technology and by the increased entrance of peasants and miners into cottage industry drove wages down. At the same time, crop failures in 1846–47 drove up the price of food.

Industrialization stimulated urban life in Saxony. A new bourgeoisie was grafted onto the historic middle class of such cities as Leipzig, traditional center of markets, fairs, and the international publishing and printing trades. During the years before the revolution Leipzig served as a magnet for liberal and radical journalism and a rallying point for opponents of the government resident in Dresden.

In 1830 the state of Saxony succeeded in acquiring a constitution that provided for a bicameral system of government. During the 1840s, however, feudal elements controlled the ministry and the heir to the throne was an ultra-conservative in close touch with the Prussian crown. In 1842 the introduction of censorship and the suppression of associations restricted the legitimate organization of political opposition. In Saxony as in the other German states, the revolution of 1848 was triggered by the news of revolution in Paris. Representatives from Leipzig and other cities threatened to march on Dresden. They were discouraged by the mobilization of the military but sufficiently persuasive in their solidarity to force the formation of a new ministry, one of moderate liberal complexion, and the promise of a new electoral law. Radicals made further demands for the creation of a popular militia, total abolition of remaining feudal dues and services, and reform of the tax structure. Like Hamburg, Saxony also witnessed an accelerated growth of clubs, the forerunner of political parties. Leipzig became the center of a labor movement that the government could not fail to address and when a labor commission was created, it was to this body that Louise Otto directed her appeal on behalf of the female work force. By November 1848 the sessions of the legislative chambers of the government were regularized the liberal legislation governing the militia, judicial proceedings, the right of assembly, and freedom of the press were enacted. Saxony contributed substantially to the radical and extreme radical contingent at the Frankfurt National Parliament.[7]

Notwithstanding their exclusion from the national electoral process, women were a conspicuous if small presence as observers at the national assembly. In his letters home, Robert Blum, the Saxon radical, expressed his surprise at the fanaticism of the women "here in the south and their ways of participating reach incredible lengths!" Some of this was pure theater but political curiosity and conviction was there as well. Political women who sat through the sessions at Frankfurt tended to be self-selecting and for obvious reasons, radical. They formed a noisy support group for the Frankfurt left, and also apparently had the temerity to confront the delegates periodically about the tedious pace of their deliberations.[8] The Declaration of Fundamental Rights, issues at the very core of the March demands on which virtually everyone agreed, were not enacted until December 1848.

By the time the *Frauen-Zeitung* appeared late in April 1849 to take advantage of the new press law in Saxony, the revolution was in retreat. In the fall of 1848, Prussia capitulated to the disadvantageous armistice of Malmoe, thereby disclaiming accountability to the national parliament at Frankfurt and its goal of annexing Schleswig-Holstein. Radicals, in response, increasingly engaged in initiatives to seize direction of the revolution outside the new legislative process, and shifted their emphasis from political to social grievances. These initiatives included the various violent uprisings in Frankfurt and in Baden as well as the two democratic congresses and the counter-parliament. The formation of women's democratic clubs paralleled this devel- opment and usually had as their object the collection of funds or the circulation of petitions to support the growing number of prisoners and their families, as well as the widows and orphans of radicals. In October the reaction gained ascendency in Aus- tria-Hungary. Robert Blum left his seat in the Frankfurt Parlia- ment to join forces on the barricades of Vienna; he was captured and summarily tried and executed. For Saxon democrats, Blum's death was a moment of special despair; Louise Otto was one of Blum's close friends and his death affected her acutely. The triumph of reaction in Austria destroyed the remnant of hope that a new Germany would embrace the greater German solu- tion. It also annihilated the brief but impressive existence of one of the few contemporary feminist initiatives to embrace both middle- and working-class women. Bourgeois women organized a vigorous democratic women's club in Vienna in August 1848 to affirm their "solidarity with women workers," whose strike against the reduction of their wages had been brutally dispersed by the military a few days earlier.[9]

With the revolution defeated in Austria, the future of the new German federation depended on the Prussian response. Fred- erick William IV dealt the decisive blow to the forces of national liberation when he declined the imperial crown offered him from Frankfurt. He had already dismissed the Prussian parlia- ment and imposed a constitution on his own territories. That was on April 3, 1848. The Saxon uprising in Dresden of early May and the one in Baden which ended at the siege of Rastatt in July were final desperate efforts on the part of radicals to compel governments in power to honor earlier promises. Women were highly visible in these confrontations. The nature of their participation, particularly in the Baden revolution, cap- tured the attention of the press and for a long time historians all but equated the female role in Baden with the female di- mension of the entire revolution. Emma Hegwegh (1817–1904), for example, reconnoitered for the German Democratic Legion in its march from Paris, dressed variously in men's clothing and a Spanish costume; Matilde Franziska Anneke and Elise Blenker

(1824–1908) appeared on horseback among the volunteers. Ka-thinka Zitz (1801–1877), the writer from Mainz, twice visited scenes of battle in order to take account of the captured and their needs. The radical insurrections were overwhelmed by su-perior forces, in each case with Prussian collaboration. Those captured were either executed, forced into exile, or sentenced to long prison terms. Within this political context the *Frauen-Zeitung* first entered the public arena, an arena, in other words, in which revolutionary radicalism and its feminist component were fighting a rear-guard action.[10]

THE FRAUEN-ZEITUNG

During the first six months of its existence Otto's paper pub-lished a multitude of reports and letters on the involvement of women in the revolution, answering what the reader "Adelaide" identified as a "deeply felt need." The democratic press offered coverage to women's activities, but the papers themselves were circulated in clubs restricted to men.[11] A number of women's clubs organized expressly to aid refugees and prisoners of the Baden and Saxon uprisings; their subscriptions supported the wives of those condemned for political reasons such as Adolph von Truetschler and Gottfried Kinkel. The clubs Humania, Con-cordia, and Germania were notable in this enterprise. The dev-astation of Dresden produced a massive relief effort; women were recognized for heroic acts in their care of the wounded. One of the most courageous commitments was to tend the graves of the radical dead, because it identified those involved so un-ambiguously in the eyes of the government. For radical emi-grants going into exile, women raised money and wrote verses.[12] Although the activities chronicled by the *Frauen-Zeitung* entailed a high risk for the women involved, they were not necessarily innovative. Relief work for the soldiers and families of revolu-tionaries fell into the same category as the activities German women had performed during the War of Liberation at the be-ginning of the century. Emergency measures of short duration, they required no new understanding of women's roles.

If a chronicle of women's participation in the relief work of the revolution had been all the *Frauen-Zeitung* produced, the newspaper would not have enjoyed the passionate loyalty that characterized its readership and an apparently ever-expanding circulation. *Frauen-Zeitung* lifted women out of their isolation and put them in touch not only with the world of democratic activities but with one another. Across Silesia and in Berlin, women formed literary groups of their own to read the *Frauen-Zeitung* together aloud. "A worker" wrote that she counted her intellectual salvation from the day she first read *Frauen-Zeitung*.[13] In the letters and in the column "Round Robin" *(Blicke in die Runde)* readers exchanged ideas. A consensus developed along the lines of a poem, submitted by "Anna," which heralded women's struggle for freedom as one that could succeed only through the struggle of individual women themselves.[14]

The *Frauen-Zeitung* served this process of self-realization; it both molded and reflected the opinion and activity of an important sector of German womanhood. At the close of the year 1850, when Louise Otto thought that changes in the Saxon press law would force the suspension of her journal altogether, she was "overwhelmed with requests and proposals" to continue. An ingenious transfer of legal responsibility to the publisher permitted the journal to survive for another two years but political expression was severely curtailed.[15]

A CALL FOR ACTION

Long before external pressure dictated political caution, however, and following the first feverish months of rescue work, the explicit wish surfaced in the readership of the *Frauen-Zeitung* for opportunities to associate collectively with a sisterly rather than a political agenda. "Wouldn't it be wonderful," one woman wrote, "if, without the usual accompaniment of clinking tankards, we could all join hands in a firm and loyal sisterhood. Then we would cease to be a weak sex and through ourselves we would become great, strong and free."[16] The manifesto of the Hamburg Education Association tapped this sentiment when it appeared four months later, in November. It coincided with the publication of a piece by one of the regular correspondents of the *Frauen-Zeitung*, "Georgine," called "Reform of the Family" *(Reform der Familie)*. Georgine advocated education for women in terms reminiscent of the earlier American ideal of Republican Motherhood, to teach recognition of the "duties towards the fatherland as the most sacred" rather than "imitating the trivia of the genteel."[17] Georgine, like the Hamburg manifesto, anticipated the reality of a mother-centered sphere. The Hamburg statement invited women to look beyond domesticity but it did so in a way that conformed to domestic, even religious, ideology which many women found more congenial than politics.

The Hamburg Education Association published its appeal in the form of a circular letter, "To all German Women and Women's Associations," over the signature of the German-Catholic pastor, Johannes Ronge. It announced the goal of "creating that place in society for the female sex which it ought to assume," a goal accomplished by the three-tiered program of charity, early childhood education, and higher education for women. While Ronge dissociated himself from any theory of emancipation, his appeal defended the right of women to "self-determination" in order to achieve full self-consciousness and personality. Women, he wrote, "in our times are called upon to direct their gaze out over the narrow confines of the family and, according to the extent of their powers, take part in the solution of the great tasks of the times." The powers of the female spirit previously held captive by "childish etiquette and a destructive restriction on its sphere of activity, should be free to develop and evolve." Women had already taken a first step toward realizing the solution of contemporary problems in the associations they had organized to aid and educate children of the poor, to visit the sick, and to train young women in the domestic arts. Through these efforts they gained insight into the nature of the school system and social institutions generally, and, he continued, "while you would render help to others your own inner life is itself enriched." But, the appeal went on, "in order to exercise the full claim of the personality and . . . correspond to the demand of the spirit of the age or world-history—that is to the spirit of God—you must above all give consideration to fundamental and timely education for female youth."[18] Appended to the pronouncement was the exchange of letters between the representatives of the Social Club in Hamburg and the two Froebels in Zurich proposing the creation of the women's college.

Subsequent circular letters announced the creation of a regional administration of women's associations with national headquarters in Hamburg, and provincial centers in the women's clubs of Hanau, Nuernberg, and Breslau. Formal organization, Ronge suggested, was designed to supplement, not supercede, the informal communications maintained through correspondence and through the pages of the *Frauen-Zeitung*. Its purpose was to enable the Education Association in Hamburg to draw more effective support from its affiliates and to provide better service. Branch associations were expected to raise money and to recruit candidates for the women's college. At the same time the Education Association in Hamburg stood prepared to assist other associations financially and personally in the sponsorship of kindergartens and primary schools, a campaign they were urged to initiate on a local level. Ronge added some rhetoric of his own: he described his dream of a living chain of women's clubs encircling the Fatherland, "more beautiful, more genuine than a string of diamonds."[19]

The glitter of Ronge's rhetoric belied an earnest commitment to women's education, one that surfaced in response to the complaints he claimed he had heard from women everywhere he lectured in Germany about the quality of female education and the monopoly of girls' schools by Jesuits and Pietists. Ronge was known throughout Germany both for his religious activities and for his political involvement at Frankfurt and in Berlin; more recently, an enormously successful speaking tour had taken him through the southwest in the summer of 1849. By publishing their manifesto in Ronge's name, the association in Hamburg clearly hoped to harness Ronge's national reputation as well as the attention of German women, whose support Ronge enjoyed.[20] It also recognized Louise Otto's early endorsement of Ronge and her affinity for his cause.

THE PERSISTENCE OF OTTO'S PIETY

Contemporary scholarship has served to obscure the traditionalistic aspects of Otto's viewpoint during the revolutionary years. The enormously important function religion played in her first decade as a writer and journalist has neither been adequately documented nor analyzed, perhaps because of her decidedly secular character in later years. Four years after her article in Robert Blum's newspaper in Saxony where Otto proclaimed women's responsibility in the public sphere, she tried to assess the progress women had made during the interim. She concluded, "It is above all the religious movement to which we are indebted for the rapid advance of female participation in the issues of the times." She attributed the effectiveness of religious separatism, particularly of the German-Catholic movement—for this is what she meant by the religious movement—to what she considered the characteristically religious temperament of women. Otto shared with her contemporaries the virtually universal conviction that piety was an intrinsic part of a woman's character, and that a woman failing in piety "has lost her entire hold on life, sacrificed a part of her heart and her femininity." Certainly the major cause for the ideological rift between Otto and Aston, two major voices of mid-century feminism, was religious. For the still pious Otto, Aston's self-proclaimed atheism was insufferable.[21]

In the prospectus Otto submitted to the very first issue of the *Frauen-Zeitung* she expressed the hope that she would be compared to the Mary of the Mary and Martha story, the woman whom Jesus praised for taking the better part because she tried to absorb the meaning of the new teaching while Martha bustled about the household. When Otto delivered her address to the democratic women of Oederan, she mentioned Mary again and then held up Katharina Luther as a model for imitation. These occasions were public and required caution but they also suggest that Otto may well have believed that for women the appropriate form of participation in the public sphere, the activity of "a *different* character and [occupying] a *different* realm" was, in the broadest sense, religious or ethical.[22]

The Jesuits were a major target of Otto's early journalism. The flowering of her own reputation was linked with the poem "Roman and German" *(Roemisch und Deutsch)*, which appeared first on the front page of the *Comet* in February 1845. She herself seemed to acknowledge the connection between this theme and her own fame when she used the title over a different poem in the second issue of the *Frauen-Zeitung*. The original "Roman and

German" welcomed "German-Catholic" as a word of reconciliation and the new church as a model for German unification. As Otto's career had advanced, her Leipzig coterie of progressive writers convinced her that prose fiction might be a more effective vehicle for her social criticism than poetry. In one of her early efforts in the newly adopted medium, a four-volume work of contemporary historical fiction about Johannes Ronge's impact on Germany published in 1847, she used the title *Roman and German* for the second time.[23] The incentive for this work came from a sense of urgency which the new religious movement inspired in Otto, an awakening that she described in an essay, "Another Word about the 30th of November in Dresden," where she was "enthralled, inspired, overpowered" by Ronge's words.[24] The novel *Roman and German* was more than a statement of support for Ronge. It was a work of propaganda designed to win converts, particularly women converts, to the German-Catholic church.

With the novel *Roman and German* Otto lent her own talents to the growing sub-genre of anti-clerical fiction composed by women who were beginning to identify and focus on the issues of an emergent feminism. Besides Otto's work, *A Question of Life (Eine Lebensfrage)* by Fanny Lewald and the *Mirage (Fata Morgana)* by Claire von Gluemer (1825–1906) as well as much of the work of the contemporary novelists Kathinka Zitz, Ida Frick, and Luise Aston belonged in this category. These narratives characteristically uncovered a clerical conspiracy at the root of an arranged marriage, a flawed divorce, or a life of unwilling celibacy. Sometimes a sexual motive was predominant; often the motive was political advantage or the control of wealth. The hypocrisy of the Catholic clergy commonly contrasted with the moral stature of various skeptics. In von Gluemer's novel, for instance, the young girl destined by her Catholic mentors for a nunnery discovered to her surprise the moral superiority of a heretic whom she ultimately marries.[25] In Lewald's *A Question of Life* the author gave voice to her anger in the words of the story's hero:

Those ties that are contracted out of acquisitiveness and a thousand other considerations, and sanctify with the honorable name of a legitimate marriage the unharnessed freedom of depravity, repel me. . . . I hold marriage in its present form in great disrespect. A price is set on reciprocal love, feeling is bridled until such an hour as a strange man, a priest, permits one person to belong to the other.[26]

The function of marriage in conventional religion as well as the complicity of the clergy convinced Luise Aston that free love afforded women the only viable means of companionate partnership. In her poetry and in her life, Aston defended her choice, drawing on the anthropological theology and rhetoric of Feuerbach. Marriage as an institution was not, however, necessarily disparaged in contemporary feminist literature; Louise Otto, in fact, was severely critical of Aston, believing as she did that conjugal love sanctified the institution of marriage and that free love, as sin, was the reverse of freedom. When the Frankfurt Parliament enacted legislation that recognized civil marriage as the only marriage contract valid in the eye of the law, Otto's response was to commission one of the German-Catholic pastors who served as a delegate to the parliament to explicate the new legislation for the readership of the *Frauen-Zeitung*.[27]

Arranged marriage, with the implicit absence of choice legitimated by the collaboration of the church, was the issue on which all feminists, moderate or radical, could agree with conviction. It was a frequent, indeed major, literary theme. A related theme was the issue of marriage as a recourse from economic necessity. Von Gluemer scrutinized this custom and the consequent need for women's higher education in a discussion between Werner, the hero of *Mirage* who attended the Frankfurt Parliament, and his daughter. This fragment ultimately found its way into the pages of the *Frauen-Zeitung*. The interchange closed with the assertion that women must seek training of all kinds, humanistic and technical, in order to acquire the expertise for raising future generations.[28] Ida Frick's *Slavery and Freedom of Women (Der Frauen Sclaventhum und Freiheit)* involved the fantasy of a woman who is turned to stone because of her fleeting wish that instead of marriage she were free to be educated in the idealized academy of her dreams, whose principal distinction was that it excluded all instruction in social polish.[29]

In her novel *Roman and German*, the patriotic theme of Otto's earlier writing under this title is linked to the feminist theme of seduction and exploitation by the Catholic clergy. The German-Catholic ideology of marriage based on mutuality and love is juxtaposed against both the hypocrisy of celibacy and the immorality of marriage arrangement. Admittedly a work of persuasion, the novel suggests at least some of the reasons why German-Catholicism might appeal to women and offers Otto's solution to the kind of conflicts posed in the work of Lewald and von Gluemer. There is also an interesting sub-plot that dramatizes the struggle of a Protestant woman of good works in a hostile Roman Catholic environment, a woman whose fictional frustrations illustrate perhaps better than the realities of history the political importance attached to women's philanthropy, both by the women themselves and by their opponents. The opening scene of the novel finds its heroine Gabriele subjected to a diatribe against contemporary women in the course of a mass celebrating the ascension of the Virgin Mary. The celebrant, we learn, has himself fathered two sons by two different women whose lives he has ruined. The two sons conspire to avenge their mothers. Gabriele experiences a feminist as well as a German-Catholic conversion. She recognizes in her father's friendship with the priest the threat both of incarceration in a convent school and the arrangement of a distasteful marriage. The novel captures the social composition of the typical German-Catholic population, which includes a cross-section of the contemporary urban scene: artisans of various trades and statuses, factory workers as well as a liberal factory owner, intellectuals, and women, married and single, from across the class spectrum. In Otto's novel German-Catholicism succeeds in mediating the religious and social obstacles that stand in the way of inter-marriage among the six principals of the story, women and men whose relationships are characterized by a heady component of idealism and mutual love. The novel ends with a multiple marriage ceremony, which would be a caricature save for the evident seriousness of the author and the centrality of the issue to contemporary women.[30]

FEMINIST EXPECTATIONS FROM RELIGIOUS NON-CONFORMITY

But Otto's endorsement of German-Catholicism had expressed a wider expectation. Otto had assumed that the democratic structure of the German-Catholic congregations would offer women a forum for public participation and an agency for exacting their own demands from society. This hope was realized in part. In Breslau a liturgical book, *Lieder meiner Kirche*, was composed by a woman, Ida von Dueringsfeld (1815–1876), the writer.[31] Women exercised suffrage in most German-Catholic congregations; in all but one of the ecclesiastical provinces in Prussia, they also enjoyed the right to hold office. Their absence from the ranks of leadership reflected custom rather than statute. One of the congregations in the province of Silesia where German-Catholicism was particularly strong, in fact, listed two women as elders.[32] The process of revolution itself, taken in conjunction with the manifest success of the separate structure of women's associations supporting German-Catholic congregations acted to accelerate the entrance of women into public, if not necessarily political, life.

What can be said about the women involved in the German-Catholic movement and what kind of assessment can be made about the nature of their commitment? Comments from regions as different as Baden and Berlin suggest a preponderance of women who both worshipped and enrolled in German-Catholic congregations. Karl Kerbler, the pastor, created a spectacle when he rode with twenty-five women in the head carriage of a wagon train from Kreuznach where he had founded a German-Catholic congregation.[33] Far more impressive, however, is the fact that women were apparently willing both to depart from convention and to put themselves at risk in the interest of German-Catholicism. In Leipzig and in Dresden, the two most important German-Catholic congregations in Saxony, a significant number of the married women members—thirty-one out of ninety in the case of Leipzig, sixteen out of seventy-eight in the case of Dresden—enrolled without their spouses. At Gernsheim on the Rhine, two women testified in court as witnesses for the defense of two German-Catholic pastors, charged with inciting a riot on the landing dock; they ascribed the outbreak of violence instead to the machinations of a Roman Catholic priest. Kathinka Zitz, the writer, herself a former Roman Catholic and resident of Mainz, contributed support to three different German-Catholic congregations, those at Offenbach, Darmstadt, and Mannheim.[34]

The outpouring of sympathy, particularly at the start of the movement, came overwhelmingly from Protestant women, like those in Hamburg, who may or may not have finally enrolled in dissident congregations. In Worms, it took the form of the gift of a wristwatch for Ronge; in Berlin, a silver service to the wife of the first German-Catholic cleric to renounce celibacy. Protestant women in Dresden mounted a campaign to build a church for the German-Catholics; in Berlin, they contributed land for a cemetery. In Heidelberg, Babetta Landfried donated her personal chapel. Countless bazaars and benefits were organized.[35]

What lay behind this demonstrative outpouring? Certainly outright hostility to Roman Catholicism played a role: Ronge's own rhetoric included the concept of the second Reformation. Louise Otto, for her part, urged women to assume the moral obligation of rescuing their Catholic sisters from the grip of Rome.[36] Beyond this, however, was an undercurrent among less traditional Protestant women of resentment against the unremitting patriarchalism of the Protestant faith. The feeling surfaced with great urgency in a letter Henriette Breymann wrote to her father, a Lutheran pastor:

We had lost our good mother nature as well as her daughter Mary (the mother of Jesus). We have (in Protestantism) only the father and the son, and from hence it comes that women have been given a totally false place in life, . . . [37]

In a similar vein, Hedwig and Eleanore Wallot of Heidelberg, poets and sisters who converted to German-Catholicism, in an article entitled "What does 'Woman' Mean?" *(Was heisst Frau?)*, observed: "Maria and Christus, representatives of both sexes, used to be highly revered. Then came Luther and destroyed the Maria."[38] The sense of Protestant impoverishment, of the erosion of Christianity by the patriarchalism of the Reformation, is palpable.

Ronge capitalized on this sentiment in his tract, *Mary, or the Place of Women in Ancient and Modern Times (Maria, oder die Stellung der Frauen der alten und neuen Zeit)*, published at the same time as the appeal of the Hamburg Education Association. The tract combined a refutation of the recent papal encyclical on veneration of the Virgin with a celebration of the vocation of contemporary women which Ronge equated with modern Marianism. He called upon German women to imitate Mary in her confident commitment to an appointed mission. "German daughters, hold yourselves in high esteem," he wrote; "you must become conscious of your free human dignity and struggle for the right of self-determination for yourselves." He urged them to break their "unholy bondage under which you often count as mere objects," and act in a community of interest. Ronge identified the lot of women as that of aiding the oppressed peoples of the nation and urged his readers to

begin... by concerning yourselves with the children of those of your brothers and sisters who have been reduced by public conditions, and try to transform them into human beings. [You should also attend] the sick beds of those abandoned ones who have been thrown from earliest childhood into a hard, cold struggle for existence.[39]

To Marian imagery Ronge linked not only women's philanthropic obligation but also their right to higher and secular education.

This right the Education Association of Hamburg intended to realize in the women's college, the *Hamburger Hochschule fuer das weibliche Geschlecht*. By the close of the year 1849, the initiative coming from Hamburg turned from propaganda and promotion to implementation.

NOTES

1. Ruth-Ellen Boetcher Joeres, "Louise Otto and her Journals: A Chapter in Nineteenth-Century German Feminism," *Internationales Archiv fuer Sozialgeschichte der deutschen Literatur* 4 (1979): 100–129. Many of the articles cited from the *Frauen-Zeitung* may also be found in *"Dem Reich der Freiheit werb' ich Buergerinnen." Die Frauen-Zeitung von Louise Otto*, ed. Ute Gerhard and others (Frankfurt a.M.: Syndikat, 1979); original citations, however, follow.

2. Louise Otto, "Programm," *FZ* 1, no. 1 (21 April 1849): 1.

3. "Die Freiheit ist untheilbar," ibid., p. 2.

4. Anna, "Aufruf an deutsche Frauen und Jungfrauen zur Begruendung einer aecht weiblichen Emancipation," ibid., p. 5; Emilie Spreu, "An Louise Aston," ibid., no. 23 (23 Sept. 1849), pp. 6–7; un-

signed review of Aston's *Freischaerler*, ibid., no. 21 (8 Sept. 1849), pp. 5–6, possibly by Otto herself; "Buecherschau," ibid., no. 22 (15 Sept. 1849), pp. 4–5, with a negative footnote by Otto, p. 4; L. O., "Buecherschau: *Soziale Reform*," ibid., no. 5 (19 May 1849), pp. 7–8, a congratulatory comment, but Helene, "Seitenstueck," *FZ* 3, no. 49 (28 Dec. 1851): 358–59, is very hostile; "Buecherschau: *Keine Politik*," ibid., no. 13 (5 April 1851), p. 71; Otto, "Ueber Robert Blum...zur Berichtigung Fanny Lewalds," *FZ* 2, no. 21 (25 May 1850): 1–3.

5. "Vortrag," *FZ* 1, no. 11 (30 June 1849): 4.

6. Joeres, "Louise Otto and her Journals," pp. 104–6; Margrit Twellmann, *Die deutsche Frauenbewegung. Ihre Anfaenge und erste Entwicklung*, vol. 2, *Quellen 1843–1869* (Meisenheim am Glan: Anton Hain, 1972), pp. 1–3; Otto, "Sendschreiben an alle Verbruederten," *FZ* 1, no. 3 (5 May 1849): 6–7; "Association fuer Alle," ibid., no. 4 (12 May 1849), pp. 4–5; "Fuer die Arbeiterinnen," ibid., no. 20 (1 Sept. 1849), pp. 1–3, no. 21 (8 Sept. 1849), pp. 1–3, no. 34 (8 Dec. 1849), pp. 1–3, no. 35 (15 Dec. 1849), pp. 1–2.

7. Ernst Rudolf Huber, *Deutsche Verfassungsgeschichte seit 1789*, 2 vols. (Stuttgart, Berlin, Cologne, Mainz: W. Kohlhammer Verlag, 1960), 2: 77–83, 410–11, 526–29, 617–19, 687–709, 774–83, 866–77, for pre-revolutionary Saxony, the Saxon revolution, and the revolution generally; Gerhard, *"Dem Reich der Freiheit"*, pp. 7–12; Twellmann, *Die deutsche Frauenbewegung*, 2: 23–24, 28.

8. Gerlinde Hummel-Haasis, ed., *Schwestern, zerreisst eure Ketten. Zeugnisse zur Geschichte der Frauen in der Revolution von 1848–49* (Munich: Deutscher Taschenbuch Verlag, 1982), pp. 40, 39.

9. Ibid., pp. 240–58.

10. Ibid., pp. 185–240, 281–98; Anna Blos, *Die Frauen der Revolution von 1848. Zehn Lebensbilder und ein Vorwort* (Dresden: Kaden, 1928), is an example of women's history of this kind.

11. "Briefe," *FZ* 1, no. 4 (12 May 1849): 5–6; *Heidelberger Journal* 7, no. 32 (8 Feb., 1849), no. 121 (25 May 1849), no. 122 (26 May 1849), no. 124 (28 May 1849), no. 141 (17 June 1849); also, Hummel, ed. *Schwestern*, index.

12. *Der Demokrat* [Mainz], no. 34 (17 May 1849): 153–54; *Mainzer Tagblatt und Fremden-Anzeiger*, no. 125 (26 May 1849); *Mainzer Zeitung*, no. 97 (23 April 1850): 1; "Briefe," *FZ* 1, no. 22 (15 Sept. 1849): 4; ibid., no. 14 (21 July 1849), pp. 6–7; "Blicke in die Runde," ibid., no. 5 (19 May 1849), p. 8; Otto, "Zum Trost," ibid., no. 6 (26 May 1849), pp. 6–7; "Buecherschau," ibid., no. 3 (5 May 1849), pp. 7–8; also, Hummel, ed., *Schwestern*, pp. 302–27.

13. "Blicke in die Runde," *FZ* 2, no. 26 (29 June 1850): 7; "Briefe," *FZ* 1, no. 12 (7 July 1849): 7.

14. Anna, "Fruehlingsgruss deutscher Frauen," *FZ* 1, no. 6 (26 May 1849): 8.

15. Otto, "Programm," *FZ* 3, nos. 1 and 2 (5 Feb. 1851): 1–2; "Abschiedswort," *FZ* 2, no. 52 (31 Dec. 1850): 1–3; Helene Lange, "Louise Otto und die erste deutsche Frauenzeitung," *Die Frau* 34, no. 5 (Feb. 1927): 263, n. 1, quotes a letter of Otto's on the press law and her decision.

16. "Schwesterlicher Rath fuer Alle, welche sich in den weiblichen Kreisen beengt fuehlen, und gern mit den Maennern fuer das Wohl der Voelker kaempfen moechten," *FZ* 1, no. 12 (7 July 1849): 6–7.

17. Georgine, "Reform der Familie," ibid., no. 17 (11 Aug. 1849), pp. 5–7, no. 18 (18 Aug. 1849), pp. 2–3, quotation, p. 3.

18. Johannes Ronge, "Sendschreiben an alle deutschen Frauen und Frauen-Vereine," ibid., no. 29 (3 Nov. 1849), p. 1.

19. Ronge, "Sendschreiben," ibid., no. 30 (10 Nov. 1849), pp. 2–3, no. 31 (17 Nov. 1849), pp. 3–4; "Rundschreiben an saemmtliche Vereine deutscher Frauen," *FZ* 2, no. 3 (19 Jan. 1850): 1–2, "Johannes Ronge an die deutschen Frauen," ibid., no. 7 (16 Feb. 1850), pp. 5–6; final quotation, "Johannes Ronge an die deutschen Frauen," *FZ* 2, no. 7 (16 Feb. 1850): 6; "Grundstimmungen und Verfassung der Vereine deutscher Frauen" by Ronge is a draft of the same proposal, Nls EW, St Ar Hmbg.

20. Ronge was a delegate to the pre-parliament at Frankfurt; he identified himself with radical causes throughout the revolution. For his tour, *AKZ* 28 (1849): 487–88, 739–44, 849–56, 857–63; on Ronge's following among women, Otto, "Auch ein Wort ueber den 30. November in Dresden," *Der Wandelstern* 2, no. 52 (Dec. 1845): 1055.

21. Gerhard, ed., *"Dem Reich der Freiheit,"* for example, does not even mention Otto's *Roemisch und Deutsch* in the list of her works, pp. 31–32. Otto's "Die Teilnahme der weiblichen Welt am Staatsleben" of 1847, quoted in Twellmann, *Deutsche Frauenbewegung*, 2: 5. Blum was a major figure in the German-Catholic movement, Catherine M. [Holden] Prelinger, "A Decade of Dissent in Germany: The German-Catholic Church and the Society of Protestant Friends 1840–1850" (Ph.D. Dissertation, Yale University, 1954), pp. 130–34; in "The Religious Context of Mid-Nineteenth Century German Feminism," American Historical Association annual convention, Washington, D.C., 1976, and in "Diversity and Uniformity: Women and the Religious Awakening in Early Nineteenth-Century Germany," Fourth Berkshire Conference on the History of Women, August 1978, Mount Holyoke College, I discussed religious differences and similarities among feminists. Hans Adler, "On a Feminist Controversy: Louise Otto vs. Louise Aston," *German Women in the*

Eighteenth and Nineteenth Centuries, ed. Ruth-Ellen B. Joeres and Mary Jo Maynes (Bloomington: Indiana University Press, 1986), pp. 193–214, examines this particular controversy from a literary perspective.

22. Otto, "Programm," *FZ* 1, no. 1 (21 April 1849): 1; "Vortrag," ibid., no. 12 (7 July 1849): 4, no. 14 (21 July 1849): 3.

23. Otto Stern [Louise Otto], "Gegen Jesuiten und Jesuitismus," *Der Wandelstern* 2, no. 18 (April 1845): 385–86; "Gott im Himmel sieh darein," ibid., no. 21 (May 1845), pp. 437–38; "Roemisch und Deutsch," ibid., no. 9 (Feb. 1845), pp. 185–86; "Roemisch und Deutsch," *FZ* 1, no. 2 (28 April 1849): 7; Siegfried Sieber, *Ein Romantik wird Revolutionaer* (Dresden: L. Ehlermann, 1949), p. 73; Otto, *Roemisch und Deutsch. Roman*, 4 vols., (Leipzig: Wienbrack, 1847).

24. Otto, "Auch ein Wort," p. 1055.

25. In Claire von Gluemer, *Fata Morgana. Ein Roman aus dem Jahr 1848* (Leipzig: O. Wigand, 1851), two clerics try to prevent a marriage to gain control of some estates for their order. Von Gluemer's father was a political radical; the family was frequently uprooted. Von Gluemer's brother participated in the May 1849 uprising in Dresden, after which she tried to help him escape. I am grateful to Ruth-Ellen B. Joeres for this information. Von Gluemer's connection with the free religious movement is indirect through her intimate association with Auguste Scheibe, the writer. Scheibe lost her job as governess in a household when a German-Catholic book was found in her possession: Amalie Auguste Scheibe to Louise Otto, n.d., Aktenlagen und Aktenbogen gemein- und staatsgefaehrliche Personen betr., Ministerium des Innern Nr. 459, StAr D.

26. Fanny Lewald-Stahr, *Eine Lebensfrage. Roman*, rev. ed. *Gesammelte Werke*, vol. 10 (Berlin: Janke, 1872), p. 144, originally published in 1845. In this story a landed estate is inheritable only by Catholics. Clergy attached to the estate maneuver to preserve, then dissolve, a marriage, in order to retain control of the land.

27. Unsigned review of *Freischaerler*, *FZ* 1, no. 21 (8 Sept. 1849): 5–6; Luise Aston, *Meine Emancipation: Verweisung und Rechtfertigung* (Brussels: C. G. Vogler, 1846); Adler, "On a Feminist Controversy." Franz Jacob Schell, "#20. der Grundrechte: Die buergerliche Giltigkeit der Ehe ist nur von der Vollziehung des Civil-Actes abhaengig," *FZ* 1, nos. 22, 23 (15 and 22 Sept. 1849): 3–4, 2–4.

28. Von Gluemer, "Haben die Frauen eine Arbeit fuer das Allgemeine?" *FZ* 2, no. 52 (31 Dec. 1850): 3–5.

29. Ida Frick, *Der Frauen Sclaventhum und Freiheit. Ein Traum am Hans-Heiling Felsen. Allen deutschen Frauen und Jungfrauen gewidmet.* (Dresden and Leipzig: Arnoldische Buchhandlung, 1845). Louise Dittmar, *Das*

Wesen der Ehe (Leipzig: O.Wigand, 1850), is another highly critical view of marriage and the concomitant economic dependence of women.

30. The reality of German-Catholic membership in Saxony suggests an interesting variant on Otto's theme. In both Dresden and Leipzig significant numbers of married women enrolled in dissident congregations without their spouses. Without more information these figures cannot be interpreted. The presumption is either that religious integrity was of sufficient importance to these women to justify conversion even in the absence of marital support, or that these women were partners of mixed marriages; for them, as for the characters in Otto's novel, the new sect acted as a confessional bridge. Bedruckte Mitglieder-Verzeichnisse, Deutschkatholische Gemeinde Dresden Nr. 124, Acta der deutschkatholischen Gemeinde zu Dresden, StAr D; "Verzeichniss der stimmberechtigen Mitglieder vom 25. Februar 1845 bis 31. Mai 1860," Deutschkatholischer Landeskirchen Vorstand Nr. 176, Leipzig, StAr D. In Dresden in 1849 sixteen of a total of seventy-eight women were listed as married to non-members. In Leipzig in 1845 the figures were thirty-one out of ninety. Membership figures in general are hard to come by. Many congregations did not keep lists, for reasons of security. Elsewhere, for instance in Heidelberg and Darmstadt, irreconcilable discrepancies exist between archival sources and local histories.

31. Ida von Dueringsfeld, *Lieder meiner Kirche* (Breslau: Kern, 1845); Otto on Dueringsfeld in Twellmann, *Die Frauenbewegung*, 2: 5.

32. See my "The German-Catholic Church: From National Hope to Regional Reality," *The Consortium on Revolutionary Europe Proceedings 1976*, Athens, Ga.: The Consortium on Revolutionary Europe, 1978, pp. 88–101; *BAKZ* 7, no. 13 (14 Feb. 1846): 157.

33. *BAKZ* 7, no. 25 (26 March 1845): 249; J. Dominik C. Brugger, *Der Deutschkatholizismus . . . in der . . . Gemeinde Heidelberg*, 2 vols. (Heidelberg: Bangel und Schmitt, 1852) 2: 162; *BAKZ* 7, no. 52 (28 June 1845): 534.

34. *See* note 30 above. Anzeige wegen der sog. deutsch-katholischen Pfarrer Kerbler am Landungsplatze in Gernsheim widerfahrenen Beleidigung, 1845, Rept. Abt. Es, v. A. Evangelische Kirche, Konv. 45, Bensheimer Kreisamtsakten betr, StAr Dmst. Letters from Pirazzi, 11 Jan. 1848, Gulde, 21 Jan. 1848, and Zoebel, 11 Nov. 1847, Nls Kathinka Zitz, StAr Mainz.

35. Wolfgang Kloetzer, "Johannes Ronge an die Frauen von Worms, [1848]," *Wormsgau* 3 (1958): 479–80; *BAKZ* 7, no. 25 (26 March 1845): 255; "Bitte um Beitraege . . . 15. Januar 1847," Geldbeitraege zum Bau eines Gemeinde Hauses betr., Deutsch-katholische Gemeinde Dresden Nr. 105, StAr D, the signers indicate that they are Protestant; *BAKZ* 8,

no. 100 (16 Dec. 1846): 1004. Brugger, *Deutschkatholizismus in Heidelberg* 2: 158; "Adress-Kalender saemmtlicher Bewohner der Stadt Heidelberg fuer das Jahr 1848," p. 53, Amtsbucherei, StAr Hlbg; "Aus Hirschberg," *FCL* 1: 274–75; "Gehorsamste Bitte eines Frauen-Vereins...," Prof. Karl Roeder an der h. Ministerium des Innern den 31. Oktober 1845, Die kirchlichen Verhaeltnisse der d.k. Gemeinde in Heidelberg 1845–1865, GlAr Krlsr; *BAKZ* 7, no. 83 (15 Oct. 1845): 849.

36. Ronge's Ulm sermon in Georg Kaufmann, "Treitschkes Urtheil ueber Johannes Ronge," *Historische Zeitschrift* 99 (1907): 519; also "Kirchenchronik und Miscellen: Speier," *AKZ* 27, no. 188 (26 Nov. 1848): 1551. Otto's attitude is apparent in her novel.

37. Mary J. Lyschinska, *Henriette Schrader-Breymann. Ihr Leben aus Briefen und Tagebuechern*, 2 vols. (Berlin and Leipzig: Walter de Gruyter u. Co., 1922), 1: 107.

38. Hedwig und Eleanore, "Was heisst Frau?" *FZ* 3, no. 18 (10 May 1851): 119; Brugger, *Deutschkatholizismus in Heidelberg*, 2: 233 identifies them.

39. Ronge, *Maria, oder: die Stellung der Frauen der alten und neuen Zeit* (Hamburg: G. W. Niemeyer, 1849), pp. 8–13.

CHAPTER 6

The Challenge of Social Change

THE COLLEGE PROJECT AND ITS NETWORK

The college in Hamburg was certainly the most ambitious institutional venture undertaken by German women during the revolutionary era. Resolute in its sense of mission and confident of broad support, the *Hamburger Hochschule* opened to students in January 1850, "a national undertaking in origin and in goal," "a foundation of German women under the particular direction of the Hamburg Education Association."[1] The association was reasonably effective in translating the ideals promoted by the women's press into academic reality. The responsibilities as well as the personnel of the administration, the support network, the faculty, and the student body succeeded in reflecting the national aspirations and ecumenical scope of its sponsors. The college addressed a glaring deficiency in the area of women's education but as an institution directed to a necessarily restricted constituency, it drew more controversy than any other segment of the inter-confessional enterprise.

Karl Froebel was the administrative head or *Rektor* of the college; Johanna Kuestner Froebel directed the *pension* for boarding students. The executive committee, chaired by the *Rektor*, included the director of the *pension*, the treasurer, and a number of members elected to the administration by the Education Association. This committee required a two-thirds membership of women. The general committee for information included two non-residents among its male members, as well as a Protestant clergyman. The non-residents were Eduard Duller, the German-Catholic pastor in Darmstadt, and, ironically, Friedrich Froebel. Notwithstanding his initial reluctance to be associated with a nephew whose views on women and their future in the professions he did not share, the senior Froebel in the end lent his name to the project. Among the twenty stockholders, three were non-residents of Hamburg. The original membership of the association, sixty-eight people, included Jews and Christians.

The funding of the college suggests that the formal national network of women's clubs which Ronge had announced in his circular operated according to expectation. The three women's clubs designated as provincial centers: Hanau, Nuernberg, and Breslau, made substantial contributions, as did at least eight other women's clubs. The Hamburg Women's Club of 1847 was also a donor to the national coordinating association. Student tuition, at a steep 1000 marks annually, provided the major source of funding. Wuestenfeld hoped that by setting a high tuition, women who could afford the full fee would subsidize the cost of educating women who could not.[2]

Beyond the formal coalition of women's clubs allied to the Hamburg Education Association moreover, individual women were invited to support the college as corresponding members. Among themselves these women constructed a vigorous support system. The record, dispersed and fragmentary, requires persistence and imagination on the part of the historian to reconstruct. It documents the operation of a diffuse, informal network of progressive women, a network that mobilized to promote the cause of the new institution. The ingenuity its members displayed to overcome their geographic and political separation, not to speak of surveillance by the police, was a measure of their determination. Not every woman in the chain of houseguests, acquaintances, and correspondents greeted the birth of the college with equal enthusiasm, but in general the campaign succeeded.

A woman named Henriette Bock was apparently a particularly colorful link in this chain. A prominent figure in the Hanau women's club and an active German-Catholic, Bock visited Dresden and Leipzig in 1850 to make contact with Louise Otto and the widow of Robert Blum. With condescending tolerance, the police dismissed her as an eccentric who was not politically dangerous. The women's club in Hanau was among the most ambitious clubs conducted by inter-confessional women anywhere in Germany. With a membership of 300, it sponsored an elaborate program of poor and sick relief not unlike the Paulsen association in Hamburg, as well as a school of its own. Vocal in anticipation of the college project, the Hanau club offered financial support and served as host institution to Karl and Johanna Froebel when they were en route between Zurich and Hamburg.[3]

Emilie Wuestenfeld conducted an extensive correspondence designed to promote the women's college, to recruit students, and to raise funds. A donation from Schweinfurt reflected pressure she exercised. Wuestenfeld's correspondence reinforced the impact of Ronge's Bavarian trip the previous summer. The principal factory owner in Schweinfurt, a man named Sattler who was a friend of Julius Wuestenfeld's, had been so profoundly stirred by Ronge's religious insights that he became a German-Catholic himself, and brought his entire labor force with him.[4] The impact of these events apparently extended to the members of his family. Two Sattler daughters, Rosalie and Marianne, became students at the college, and they in turn tried to recruit Marie Schwarzenberg from Cassel.[5]

Louise Otto, for her part, was in contact not only with Henriette Bock; she was also a correspondent of Kathinka Zitz, the writer in Mainz. Zitz was involved in many of the radical causes of the period. She had personally visited the scenes of the Baden revolution, and the club, Humania, that she founded and chaired in Mainz dwarfed other similar projects. An active contributor to the *Frauen-Zeitung* and a correspondent of many religious and political radicals, female and male, Zitz may also have influenced the appointment of Eduard Duller as outside informant for the Hamburg college. Beyond their common commitment to German-Catholicism, Duller was plainly a close friend. He and his wife are represented in her personal guest book by autographed intimacies, and Zitz published a moving eulogy at the time of his premature death. Another house guest, represented by a drawing and a poem in the Zitz guest book, is Malwida von Meysenbug (1816–1903), the writer and memorialist. It is likely that the opportunity to publish in the Mainz democratic press was negotiated for Meysenbug through Zitz. In any event, they shared congenial values. Meysenbug wrote to Zitz for the express purpose of recruiting students for the college, soliciting Zitz's help in locating women who, like herself, might have reason to seek advanced education for independence and singlehood.[6]

Meysenbug herself was the greatest reward of the campaign to recruit students for the college beyond the confines of Hamburg. Later as a writer and mentor both to Wagner and to Nietzsche, she was to become the college's most notorious alumna. Her memoirs, long regarded as the only first-hand account of life at the college in Hamburg, are still without question the most complete. Some of her personal story bears repeating. A woman whose girlhood was not unlike that of Amalie Sieveking's and other contemporary women aristocrats, she responded very differently, and ultimately as a feminist, to the religious and political upheaval of her surroundings. Malwida was the daughter of a nobleman attached to the electoral Hessian court. As a child she was raised in the society of the small pre-revolutionary royal residence; her intellectual precosity led her increasingly to cultivate an independent, often lonely, existence. She found companionship in the pastor's household in Detmold where her family resided during the 1840s. She was an intimate friend of the pastor's daughter and enjoyed a relationship with the son, Theodor Althaus, which had the quality of a courtship. The possibility of marriage gradually faded as Malwida discovered that Theodor was what she called a Don Juan of the heart. Theodor shared with Malwida his repudiation of orthodoxy, which became the basis of his book, *The Future of Christianity (Die Zukunft des Christenthums)*. God, Althaus believed, "is not outside man. Our striving to know God is in the first instance a striving to become ever more certain in spirit of what is truly human. Our religion is to be understood..., as a power which pulsates through our heart and spirit,... bringing into reconciliation the forces of conflict."[7] Meysenbug nominally accepted the Althaus critique of orthodoxy although she found it unnecessarily abstract. To relinquish the belief in personal immortality she found particularly painful. As Althaus once wrote to her:

> You still resist a little in believing that everything mortal is mortal. If I found it in my heart to believe in immortality, then my reason would not let me do so.... If I wanted to speak of immortality, then every rose, every spring flower, the song of the nightingale and everything that ever charmed me would have to come with me and I know that the rose fades, that the flower falls apart, the eyes grow dim, the hair pales and the heart itself with its love turns to dust. Immortality is only in poetry.[8]

For a while Meysenbug joined Althaus at the Frankfurt Parliament where, as a journalist, he was attached to the circle of radicals that included Friedrich Hecker, Gustav Struve, and Julius Froebel. Her family situation demanded that she return to Detmold but ideologically her continued existence in that community was untenable. She found herself retreating into a life of scholarship and uncertainty about how, as a single woman, she might support herself. The foundation of the college in Hamburg prompted her immediate application.

THE ACADEMIC PROGRAM

In its purpose and in its conduct the college embodied much of what Karl and Johanna Froebel had originally proposed in their brochure. The promotional literature spoke ambitiously of a training that "comprised everything that practical, social and intellectual life could demand of an educated woman;" in Malwida's more considered words, "to make possible the economic independence of woman through her development as a being which is first and foremost an end in itself, to develop according to the needs and abilities of its own nature."[9] The term "*Hochschule*," however, was really a misnomer: the women's college did not resemble a contemporary *Hochschule*, or university. But as one of its contemporary advocates argued, "*Hochschule*" suggested something more serious and more comprehensive than existing institutes for girls—hence the name.[10]

The program was strenuous. Admission, by examination, was restricted to girls who had reached the age of sixteen. Amalie Sieveking, an inveterate opponent of the college, conceded "that the scientific instruction of the institute is good."[11] Emphasis in the curriculum during the first semester was on philosophy and educational theory, reinforced each day by observation and practice-teaching in the kindergarten. This discipline was supplemented by instruction in French, English, literature, history, and geography. The second semester curriculum added three hours a week of mathematics, two of chemistry, and one each of botany and astronomy. The faculty came from the boys' gymnasia and from the churches of Hamburg. Anton Rée of the Jewish school taught language, poetry, and physics; Georg Weigelt of the German-Catholic congregation taught astronomy and geography. Their ranks were swelled from the increasingly large population of refugees who appeared in the city: radical intellectuals forced to flee the states where they had participated in the revolution, among them Adolf Strodtmann (1829–1879), the poet and writer from Schleswig-Holstein, who offered courses in literature, Carl Volckhausen (1822–1899), teacher at the gymnasium in Detmold whom Malwida called "the Democrat," and Jakob Venedy (1805–1871), the Rhenish publicist who had participated in the Baden revolution. These men took advantage of the idiosyncratic course of events in Hamburg to pursue their own commitments, for the political climate in the city-republic continued favorable to radicalism for at least another year.

Adolf Diesterweg also was a ubiquitous figure at the college. He spent some time there in the spring of 1850 in order to compose an article about women's education for his newspaper, the *Rhenish Reports for Education and Instruction (Rheinische Blaetter fuer Erziehung und Unterricht)*. At first the professors were skeptical about the feasibility of the experiment, afraid that their courses might prove too rigorous for their students. Time vindicated the students. The college was not conducted according to contemporary German university practice; lectures were interrupted by discussion and always introduced a period of questioning, in which the students proved themselves adept. Occasionally three generations of women were represented in one lecture hall. Altogether the student body numbered about 100 women.[12]

THE COLLEGE IN ITS WIDER SETTING

Much of the life of the college evolved outside the formal setting of the lecture hall and classroom altogether. Students were actively encouraged to take advantage of the city and its wealth of facilities.[13] An effective supplement to the college curriculum was the *pension* administered by Johanna Froebel. Experience in communal living was Froebel's goal, frustrated at first by the divergent interests and backgrounds of the residents. Meysenbug ultimately came to the rescue. Her commitment to the spirit and practice of collective enterprise, particularly to manual labor, instilled the others with a sense of community: "the frivolous became serious, the lazy, diligent."[14] Evening readings, musicals, excursions, and debates exposed the students to the constant stimulus of public events, legitimating the expression of ideas and, as Meysenbug observed, compelling the most modest to formulate and articulate their opinions. Amalie Sieveking herself commented on the range of activities the college provided.[15]

The religious life of the college was scrupulously non-confessional. In this commitment even more than in its commitment to intellectual rigor lay its originality. As promoters of the college enthusiastically argued, only a few cities offered higher education of any kind to women, and what existed was controlled by Jesuits and Pietists. The college curriculum at Hamburg excluded religion as such; during the second semester there was an hour lecture once a week on religious history. There were no house devotions, prayer meetings, or Scripture readings.[16] What particularly horrified Amalie Sieveking was that "this lack of belief goes so far that, with few exceptions among teachers and pupils, belief in the personal immortality of the human being after death is counted in the category of pious fairy tales."[17] Both Jews and Christians alike were admitted to the college. Even Diesterweg, who was in most respects an enthusiast for the experiment, feared that the diversity of religious belief that the college condoned would indeed promote a destructive spirit of skepticism and religious indifference.[18]

For Malwida von Meysenbug, however, the college provided the opportunity for a religious awakening. All the students, according to her own account, participated in the life of the free congregation—the religious community that had evolved from the German-Catholic congregation. To her it offered the answer to an abiding need: it was, she wrote, "worship in the spirit and the truth for which I had yearned; religion, liberated from the limits of the church, became living, flourishing, presence, essence, content and not empty rigid form."[19] She welcomed the fellowship and the ethical concern of the free congregation with its heterogeneous membership, moral commitment and communal meal once a week. Baptism had been abolished in the free congregation to encourage Jewish membership; seating at the services was random to eliminate segregated seating of the poor and the rich. Meysenbug was particularly exhilarated by the immediate presence of the poor. At the same time, when she enrolled in the congregation, she forfeited her right to an endowment arranged by her father through the electoral Hessian court, one for which only Lutherans were eligible. There was consequently the genuine urgency of economic necessity in her involvement with the Hamburg college.[20]

SOURCES OF OPPOSITION

Meysenbug's written legacy is interesting not simply for its anecdotal account of college life and its narrative of a woman preparing herself for economic independence; it also captures the dilemma of a woman torn by the demands of two conflicting theories of womanhood. On the one hand there was the ideology of the woman's college; on the other, the traditionalism of her family. Malwida's enrollment in the college threatened what remained of an intimacy with her mother, to whom she defensively described her new circle of friends as "people who are honorable even if they are not princes and barons." Her sister chided her with the pejorative *"Emancipierte."*[21] To her brother, Malwida embodied the immorality he identified with the contemporary women's movement:

The true destiny of the woman [he wrote] is that of remaining in the place that God has assigned her; your duty resides with your mother, with your own. . . . You have falsified all questions of justice and morality because you have abandoned the only true basis, the laws of God, which he has revealed to us through his Son. . . . It is useless and destructive vanity on the side of women, to want to mix in this [public leadership], thereby stepping outside of the territory to which God and female humility assigns them.[22]

He urged his sister to throw herself on her knees and ask for forgiveness.

The women's college encountered opposition in unexpected quarters as well. At the third convention of northern German teachers, which met outside of Hamburg in the summer of 1850, Meysenbug introduced a resolution advocating the higher education of women in principle and its extension in practice. Notwithstanding the influence of Diesterweg in this circle and an eloquent defense of women's intellectual capability by faculty representatives from the college, the resolution failed in deference to a statement hedged with concerns for "safeguarding femininity."[23]

More puzzling was Louise Otto's ambivalence about opening the college, an apparent contradiction to the extensive and positive coverage provided by the *Frauen-Zeitung*. In March of 1850, she accepted a letter for publication from an anonymous male correspondent attacking the new institution from a misinformed, partisan—indeed misogynous—perspective. It charged the college with exacting tribute from educational associations in other cities for the purpose of educating the daughters of the Hamburg patriciate. Confessional differences and their power to obscure the common concerns of women had fueled the campaign for the college; in this writer's opinion, disagreements over religion were no longer a divisive force within the German people, nor did "they need to be buried belatedly by colleges for rich peoples' daughters." Couched in the language of class, the letter in reality singled out women as the target for attack—women who, however privileged, were certainly not members of the patriciate. Claiming religious neutrality, the writer was insensitive to the issues of gender that the confessions embraced. By reducing the higher education of women to self-indulgence and feminism to class privilege, he was able to ignore confessionalism as a political issue. This was a dramatic but not unique display of anti-feminism within the male radical camp. Viewed in this perspective, a feminist strategy rooted in the concept of woman's nature assumes real legitimacy. For the inter-confessional women of the college project, the construct of woman's nature served as a defense against both the divisiveness of confessionalism and the complacency of male politicians toward women's issues.

Louise Otto recognized the need to justify her decision to print the anonymous letter. Ignoring the class and gender bias of the correspondent, she articulated instead her own political priorities, which made it difficult for her to support the college. She believed that all efforts of the women's movement should defer to the demands of prisoner relief. At this moment in the revolution she refused to acknowledge, as she once had, that the needs of women and men within the radical movement might be different.[24]

Nevertheless, the *Frauen-Zeitung* increasingly examined the issues and aims of higher education for women. The patriotic appeal of Georgine's "Reform of the Family" in the summer of 1849 had justified the education of women in the interests of marital harmony and companionship, republican motherhood and citizenship.[25] In the spring of 1850, "Emmy," a seasoned correspondent on educational issues, began to write about higher education for women as an end in itself. In an essay called "Learned Women" *(Gelehrte Frauen)* she exploded many of the stereotypes connected with female scholars and concluded that to resist the education of women was, at the very least, to resist the inevitable.[26] In the December 31, 1850 issue of the *Frauen-Zeitung*, which Otto believed would be the last, she republished a section of Claire von Gluemer's novel about the revolution, *Fata Morgana*, under the title: "Is There Women's Work for the General Good?" *(Haben die Frauen eine Arbeit fuer das Allgemeine?)* Here quite a different rationale appears. The protagonist contended that women must seek the kind of education that would equip them for an active role in the world of affairs alongside of men, not simply one that would permit them to participate vicariously through their male associates. Otto's own interest in education deepened with her concern for women dependents who were suddenly compelled by the death, exile, or imprisonment of male radicals to support themselves.[27]

THE WIDER AGENDA FOR INTER-CONFESSIONAL WOMEN'S CLUBS

Generally Johannes Ronge's letter on behalf of the Hamburg Education Association was not perceived as a solicitation for the college. It was read rather as the statement of an agenda for women's clubs, part of a general initiative to stimulate their spread and to widen their focus from charity to education and self-improvement. The club in Hamburg itself donated contributions to a number of these clubs to help fund new enterprises, and consequently enjoyed a relationship with them that was reciprocal.

ELEMENTARY EDUCATION

The foundation of primary schools by the new women's associations represented a particularly effective arena of development, one that exploited the concurrent involvement of both church and state in German education. As an extension of the free religious movement, the network of these schools took advantage of the duality of German-Catholicism as both a religious confession and a champion of religious neutrality. Religious confessions were permitted to conduct schools and select teachers by criteria different from those of the public schools (*Volksschule*) in Germany. Women, for instance, were not hired in the public schools although by law they could teach in confessional schools. Women came to assume a high posture in the inter-confessional schools because as schools they were legally confessional although in practice they were studiously secular. Students were admitted from any confessional background, Jewish, Christian, or independent, and no formal religion was taught within the curriculum. Such schools existed not only in Hamburg, Breslau, and Hanau, but also in the Silesian towns of Liegnitz and Stiegau, in the Bavarian town of Schweinfurt, and elsewhere.

Theodor Hofferichter, a German-Catholic educator in Breslau, defended the ethical training offered in these schools as opposed to the mandatory confessional instruction the state schools required. This, coupled with a generally broader curriculum than the prematurely specialized education of the traditional system, resonated with the democratic values that Hofferichter himself represented. The Breslau inter-confessional primary school whose curriculum he designed was one of the institutions that received financial aid from the Women's Club of 1847 in Hamburg.[28]

Henriette Breymann taught in such a school in Schweinfurt where to honor the commitment of the parents required a special brand of courage. The law required children to attend confirmation classes in either the Roman Catholic or the Evangelical confession, a law the parents, as members of the free congregation at Schweinfurt, resisted. Breymann's class was subjected to forceable entry by the police, who threatened the children with physical coercion if they failed to leave the class voluntarily for the mandatory instruction. Breymann interceded by quite literally injecting herself between the police and the terrified children. In Hanau, the primary school, next to a visitation program for the invalid poor, became the primary commitment of the inter-confessional women's club. The school numbered 133 pupils in the spring of 1850 and 168 in the fall of 1851. The consistent demand for additional places led to plans for immediate expansion. The women of the club also exerted pressure on the employers of women servants to give them two days leave a week to attend classes.[29]

Malwida von Meysenbug was elected to the executive committee that organized the primary school for the free congregation in Hamburg. Two female and four male teachers constituted the faculty at this school. The school was designed to be self-supporting; tuition was scaled according to the ability to pay. The school in Hamburg, reputedly the very first public non-sectarian school in Germany, emphasized the assimilation of all social classes as well as the integration of girls with boys. The curriculum for both sexes was identical throughout the school. At the elementary level girls and boys shared classes; in the upper grades the sexes were segregated but they continued to study the same disciplines. The school did not pretend to equip its pupils for all occupations, but instruction was understood to be a "means to make people independent and free." Religious instruction was prohibited. The school was committed to furthering the moral consciousness of its pupils through example and instruction in the arts and sciences. Three hundred children applied for admission, of whom 200 matriculated from various social classes and confessions.[30]

The removal of education from the control of the state churches, an issue debated but not resolved by the Frankfurt Parliament, was one of particularly intense concern to progressive women. The only issue of Mathilde Franziska Anneke's *Frauen-Zeitung* ever published was devoted to the problem of the separation of school and church. The topic recurred as a theme in the correspondence of Johanna Kinkel, exiled in England, and the writer Fanny Lewald. Kinkel, wife of the Bonn democrat Gottfried Kinkel, was herself intellectually and musically gifted. The choice of a free religious school for her child was of sufficient importance to her to justify the "second exile" of mutual separation.[31]

THE KINDERGARTEN MOVEMENT

Kindergartens organized in accordance with the Froebel system multiplied during these years, particularly within the network of women and women's clubs supporting free religion. According to Johanna Goldschmidt, the movement for public, as opposed to confessional or free religious, kindergartens favored by Froebel himself failed on a national scale largely because Froebel's own flawed manner of presentation made it impossible for him to attract a following. His sojourn in Hamburg was a disappointment. Froebel delivered the six-month demonstration seminar; twenty-two women, some of them also students at the college, completed the course.[32] But the early-childhood project on which Goldschmidt and the coalition to combat religious prejudice had staked their hopes, the initiative that had very nearly threatened their solidarity and jeopardized the founding of the college, did not really materialize. If their commitment to early childhood training superceded confessional commitments for this particular circle of Jewish and Christian women, their own determination rather than Froebel's presence was responsible. Failure resided not in the rivalry of uncle and nephew, although the college certainly eclipsed the seminar as a center for professional training. Rather, as Henriette Breymann had insisted, "Uncle is totally unsuited to public life.... such lectures as he has actually held here [in Dresden] for the educational association ...[do] serious damage to the kindergarten cause.... Froebel should not go to Hamburg."[33] Her advice was ignored. Goldschmidt concluded Froebel accomplished very little in Hamburg, but for one important legacy: the public kindergarten. A group of artisans had attended Froebel's demonstrations and on their initiative with their own children as subjects, created this facility, the first of its kind in Germany.

The public kindergarten in Hamburg provided Goldschmidt with an occasion to address the class implications of the Froebel system. The Young German journalist Karl Ferdinand Gutzkow (1811–1878) had publically disparaged the Froebel movement as a class enterprise, addressing the needs of privileged children. He argued that priority should be assigned to day-care centers for the children of laborers who required supervision while their parents worked. Goldschmidt cited the Hamburg kindergarten as a case study in worker adaptation of the Froebel method to class needs. Froebel himself believed that his was a universal system; he specifically objected to the equation of the kindergarten with the charitable day-care or protective institution whose purpose was to manage improvident children. One reason he originally welcomed the overture from Goldschmidt was that the women of the Social Club intended to introduce the kindergarten method into their own circle. Goldschmidt shared the optimism of the mid-century with a middle class whose ranks were conceived to be infinitely expandable from recruits of the educated and aspiring working class. The Froebel system eliminated passivity from the learning process and thereby prepared the child for a life of practicality and enterprise, one that set entrepreneurs and laborers alike apart from the traditional—and in Goldschmidt's view, degenerate—ruling class whom she identified with a surfeit of abstract learning.[34]

The energy of the free religious movement provided an impetus that the kindergarten movement by itself could not generate. Reports in Otto's *Frauen-Zeitung* suggest that by 1851 approximately thirty kindergartens were in operation. The majority were located in Prussia and Saxony; others included those in Cassel and in Schweinfurt where the Hamburg Women's Club of 1847 had extended financial aid to clubs for the express purpose of promoting educational goals. Interest was also reported in Baden and in the cities of Darmstadt, Frankfurt, Goettingen, and Lunen.[35] Only a few of the clubs and their kindergartens can be documented. The so-called Christian-Catholic—originally German-Catholic—women's club in Breslau, for instance, adopted the Hamburg model. They created an independent education association, inclusive both as to gender and confession, to administer the kindergarten. Female control was assured in the composition of the executive committee. A Froebel trainee was hired and a stipulated annual donation from the women in Hamburg enabled the Christian-Catholic women of Breslau to select ten of the children each year for kindergarten admission. By this device they hoped to preserve the working-class composition of their project and distinguish their social and confessional priorities from those of the local orthodox Evangelical women's club.[36]

The Hamburg example was also a source of inspiration to Adolf Diesterweg, who made a number of attempts to promote the training of kindergarten teachers. After his summer at Bad Liebenstein he proposed the foundation of a national Goethe Institute for the education of women and children in the Froebel method, a plan that never materialized. He was more effective in Berlin, where he sponsored an educational association in conscious imitation of the one in Hamburg. His association apparently owed its origin to a visit from two of the Hamburg Meyer sisters to their Berlin friend, identified only as Frau Toberanz. The Berlin educational association tried to encompass within a single society the breadth of activity that the Hamburg women conducted under a variety of organizational sponsorships: a domestic institute modeled after the institute for servant girls in Hamburg, a systematic program of lectures for women interested in self-improvement, a Pestalozzi program dedicated to the care of abandoned children, and the administrative machinery for implementing a Froebel kindergarten. The manifesto published by the association blamed men for the absence of training opportunities for women, arguing that "many of them desire a wife who will allow herself to be dominated and who will concern herself about nothing but the household and the children."[37] The club in Berlin permitted only those women to attend the lecture course who were enrolled in some community facet of the club's program. This provision was designed to discourage self-indulgent learning and offers a clue to Diesterweg's own priorities. In his correspondence with Johanna Goldschmidt he complained about the "blasé" attitude of Berlin women and an intoxication with the evening scholarly program that compromised their sense of social engagement.[38] Apparently the Berlin project fell considerably short of expectations. Evidence is fragmentary but it is reasonable to conjecture that Diesterweg's excessive intervention was at fault. Diesterweg had applauded the uniquely female initiative of the Hamburg Education Association but he apparently failed to draw the appropriate conclusion. German progressive women were as much committed to the process of implementing their agenda as they were to the substance of the agenda itself.[39]

THE DRESDEN KINDERGARTENER

Beyond the Hamburg circle, Auguste Herz, a resident of Dresden, emerged as the outstanding practitioner of women's vocational training in Froebel methods. Her institute was already entering its fourth session during the summer the kindergarten of Berlin was struggling to organize. The Herz course represented a particularly poignant example of the successful program designed by a woman to meet contemporary women's needs. In March 1848 when the first stages of revolution established a liberal government in Saxony, Herz opened a kindergarten for needy children in Dresden. She was guaranteed state protection by Minister of the Interior Martin Oberlander (1801–1868), himself a political moderate. Her husband's financial support allowed her to work without a salary.[40] Herz was a woman for whom Friedrich Froebel himself had predicted a "lofty educational calling."[41] Henriette Breymann was a member of the Herz household in the winter of 1849. Auguste Herz had long supported free religious causes: she was one of the Protestant women engaged in the fund-raising campaign for the construction of a German-Catholic church in Dresden. Heinrich Herz was a member of the extreme left, editor of the *Dresden News (Dresdener Zeitung)* and also an educator. Froebel, in his correspondence with the Social Club in Hamburg, referred to Auguste Herz as "a simple but highly respected prosperous citizen;" her father had been a mechanic and a violin maker. She was, Froebel believed, a disciple who demonstrated with particular sensitivity what could be accomplished through his method.[42] Opponents and supporters alike marvelled at Herz's talent with children. The police dossier on her observed: "Herz is there all by herself for hours on end in the room occupied with playing and teaching and I don't know what-all."[43] And "Georgine," correspondent for the *Frauen-Zeitung*, wrote of the "special pleasure to see her in the circle of children with genuine enthusiasm and geniality teaching and playing with them simultaneously."[44]

The kindergarten Herz conducted was not affiliated with a free congregation as so many were, but a critical, immanent religion permeated her thinking and writing. "On the Ethical Training of Children and Their First Religious Instruction in Kindergarten" *(Ueber die sittliche Bildung der Kinder und deren ersten Religionsunterricht in dem Kindergarten)* argued that the nursery years were optimal to cultivate religious sensibility in children. The little child still asked the fundamental questions of why and how, uncontaminated by the later compulsion to imitate. Literal-mindedness in early childhood could be enlisted to discover and respect the workings of God in nature.[45] The similarities in outlook between Auguste Herz and the women of the women's college circle in Hamburg are compelling. Habituated to a religious mode of thought, these women found the kind of sustenance and direction in critical religion that the orthodox faiths could no longer provide them; while the content of their thought was new, its structure remained essentially religious.

When the failure of the May 1849 uprising in Saxony condemned Herz's husband to life imprisonment, she found herself responsible not only for her own livelihood but for that of four children and a mother-in-law as well. She converted what she originally believed was simply a vocation into a profession, expanding her kindergarten classes to include children whose families paid tuition.[46] At the same time she started a program in teacher training. There was an entire constituency of women in Saxony and in some of the other German states as well who were suddenly confronted with the unfamiliar task of self-support because their husbands or fathers were political prisoners. It was for this desperate contingent—women made single by circumstance—that Herz designed her institute. The essential teachings of her program were brought together for publication in the volume *Domestic Education and Kindergarten: Lectures for Women and Young Women Wishing to Prepare Themselves as Educators either for Family or for Kindergarten (Hauserziehung und Kindergarten: Vortraege fuer Frauen und Jungfrauen, welche fuer die Familie oder den Kindergaerten sich zu Erzieherinnen bilden werden).*[47] Herz's lectures assume the existence of the mother-centered bourgeois family and a constituency of women who recognized the need to train themselves in the appropriate moral and educative tasks that the vanishing patriarchal household relinquished to women. The erosion of traditional paternal functions was accelerated in Saxony by the circumstantial absence of men who were politically condemned, but the process was already well advanced there as in Hamburg by the inroads of capitalist production. Herz's book, like Goldschmidt's *Delights and Cares of Motherhood*, reflected the experience of a particular economic and social environment, one more familiar to German women of the next generation. Books like these punctuated the loss of the patriarchal household and served to make the ideals and process of the new maternalism intelligible to those most immediately affected.

FREEDOM AND SERVICE

The manifesto that Johannes Ronge published in the name of the Education Association in Hamburg articulated the needs of the same constituency. Correspondents to the *Frauen-Zeitung* welcomed the statement with a spontaneity and appreciation that suggest how well he had gauged their sentiments. They interpreted the statement both as an agenda and as an invitation to share their experiences. Their comments are confident and self-conscious. Ronge's appeal resonated with the need progressive women felt for a release from domesticity, for action, and for a national sense of solidarity. One woman who wrote from Breslau particularly welcomed Ronge's metaphor of the diamond girdle. In a thoughtful analysis she ascribed the domestic isolation of women to the combined forces of modern individualism and the priesthood. She challenged women, using Ronge's words, to encircle the fatherland with a living band of women's clubs; she proclaimed: "The visionary passive life is over!"[48]

The constancy of themes from the various individual clubs is striking. There was an evident pride in the extent and solidarity of the network of women that the clubs represented: "We women are now everywhere bound together in clubs and the clubs are allied once more among themselves." At the same time there was an insistence that domesticity was intensified, not threatened, by the new direction: "We wish only to extend our own families as we make ourselves sisters to all humanity and particularly to the suffering."[49] Ronge's appeal, particularly his reassuring dissociation from theories of political emancipation for women, resonated with the doctrine of extended domesticity. The ideology of domesticity uniquely legitimated philanthropy in the public sphere to the contingent of German women who could neither identify with the rationale of orthodox Christianity nor with that of political activism. This position is very clearly captured in a dispatch to the *Frauen-Zeitung* from a cochairwoman of the German-Catholic women's club in Leipzig:

We also acknowledge in freedom one of the highest goods. We also acknowledge not only the complete competence of women to work and struggle for it—indeed even their obligation to do so—and we would like to recruit women citizens everywhere for the empire of freedom [here, of course, the writer is echoing Otto's words and the slogan of the *Frauen-Zeitung*]. But not for political freedom, at least not for the struggle for liberty in the sense of state constitutions. The struggle for that kind of freedom belongs only to men. ... [Political freedom does not comprise the entire structure of freedom. Sensuality, vanity, religious indifference as well as religious orthodoxy are also obstacles to the full enjoyment of freedom]. We mean to help the present generation liberate itself from these bonds. This is the foremost task of women.

...But the stage is not public life, rather it is the domestic circle and its immediate environs.[50]

Friedericke Koschuetzki, one of the most incisive and consistently feminist journalists on the *Frauen-Zeitung*, offered an interesting twist to the doctrine of domesticity insofar as domesticity translated to motherhood. Her article, "The Right of Women" *(Das Recht der Frauen)*, argued that motherhood itself could liberate women if they would only reject the interpretations developed by men and permit themselves to experience motherhood in their own terms.[51]

Ronge's open letter provoked a flood of response from clubs eager to record how their own activities corresponded with the proposed agenda. A particularly illuminating account came from Danzig, where Ronge himself had participated in founding a women's club devoted to charitable work among German-Catholic children. As the correspondent put it, the club had been on the way to becoming a "lifeless foddering station, to which creatures were being sent simply to fill their stomachs." Then a new pastor appeared and helped the women to reorganize in the spirit of the times. Home visits to the sick, regular instruction for the children, and a reading-lecture-discussion group replaced former activities. "Bitterness and alienation must disappear where so great an effort brings everyone together!"[52] The very active Danzig affiliate of the Sieveking association may also have challenged these women.

The Hanau inter-confessional association of women justified its designation as a provincial center in the national network by an ambitious program of service. In addition to the large primary school, these women sponsored an elaborate program of benevolent visitation accomplished by dividing the city into geographic districts of responsibility, a program similar to, if not modeled after, the Paulsen program. Fifty-six invalid poor were supported with the essentials of medicine, food, clothing, fuel, and household assistance in 1851. A relief service for families made homeless by a major fire in that year succeeded in sheltering twelve families with upwards of twelve children each. The association created an additional auxiliary to support indigent pregnant women. As the annual report indicated, the club had established sufficiently reliable communications with the city poor relief administration to preclude any conflict or duplication with the "women's club in existence here a long time,"[53] very likely an affiliate of the Sieveking coalition. In Chemnitz a club of free religious women was organized in April 1850, "a guardian angel to our suffering sisters," but only, it was reported, after "we endured bitter experiences, having to expose ourselves to persecution."[54] Not every initiative succeeded. "Ida" wrote to the *Frauen-Zeitung* from Freiberg that a number of attempts to organize associations on the model of those in Dresden and Altenburg had failed, that "the women's club which had already existed here for a number of years is worse than pre-revolutionary [*vormaerzlich*]; it belongs to those who make the souls of poor sinners mellow for the after-life!"[55]

RADICAL MISOGYNY

The success of the women's coalition exposed it to an attack from within the free religious movement itself, uncovering a core of anti-feminist sentiment in the ranks of the male leadership. Early in January 1850 a provincial synod of free-Christian, or German-Catholic, congregations in Nuernberg issued a resolution on women's clubs. Concealed in an effusive statement proclaiming "the annihilation of chains which woman has born in the past . . . [precluding the exercise] of moral and educative functions for which she is naturally endowed," the resolution attacked the inclusive membership and agenda of the women's clubs. Autonomy from the free congregations and lack of selectivity allowed the women's coalition to pursue goals insufficiently differentiated from those of traditional charity. The resolution proposed to integrate the women's clubs into the structure of the congregations even at the price of a reduced membership. The goals of the women's clubs—the development of opportunities for women's and children's education—would be assumed by the entire movement.[56] The tactic was an undisguised bid for male control of the membership selection and agenda of the women's associations.

The maneuver drew vehement protest from the women's club in Hamburg, which called the Nuernberg statement intolerant

and unworkable. The Hamburg and Breslau clubs jointly endorsed a report that ascribed both the rapid growth and the
successful alliance of the independent women's clubs to their
inclusive membership and their commitment to humane activities, of whatever confessional origin. The debate reached the
national administrative council of free religious congregations
in May 1850. The women's clubs were defended on two grounds:
first, for their role in introducing women to the responsibilities
of leadership; second, for their success in formulating the concept of extended domesticity in terms that recommended community activity to women. As single-sex, separatist organizations,
they were attacked for perpetuating traditional sex roles.[57]
"Emmy," a regular correspondent of the *Frauen-Zeitung* who was
probably Emily LeCerf, educator and social activist in Dresden,
insisted that the debate was artificial. On the one hand, the separatism of the women's clubs was separatist in the most restricted
sense since their existence derived from the financial support of
men; on the other, however conventional the activities of women
in their clubs, the institutionalization of female roles reflected
the general social ethos, not the unique ethos of the clubs. Emmy
supported the continuation of women's associations on grounds
that the experience women gained from the conduct of their
own affairs would promote the self-assurance necessary for subsequent public roles. The controversy, in fact, voiced many of
the unresolved themes of modern feminist history, turning as it
did on the issue of separatism versus integration. The council
of religious radicals, however, was in a particularly vulnerable
position. There was not a single woman credentialed as a delegate; the only women in attendance had appeared on their own
as lobbyists.[58] The ostensible egalitarianism of the free religious
movement was consequently suspect; separatism was validated
as a strategy against discrimination.

One quality came to distinguish progressive and free religious
women from their male peers: their commitment to ecumenism
seemed to increase while many of their male colleagues moved
in the direction of greater partisanship. Many of the prominent
males among the religious separatists served in radical political
capacities during the revolution. In the wake of political re-
trenchment the conviction hardened among them that, short of

a comprehensive religious reeducation that would dismantle the customs and institutions of orthodoxy in Germany, political change was unattainable. Confirmed in this belief, they refused to recognize the legitimacy of any other agenda. The women's agenda embraced a different set of priorities, one which valued female solidarity over other loyalties, among them confessional loyalty. Friedericke Koschuetzki believed that radical men had betrayed the cause of women's freedom in the revolution; her disillusionment expressed itself in an increasing preference for sisterhood over a position of coherence within the spectrum of male political alignments. In one of the late issues of the *Frauen-Zeitung*, she contributed an essay on the deaconess institution Bethanien in Berlin; an anonymous essay praised the life of the English Quaker Elizabeth Fry, friend of Amalie Sieveking and Theodor Fliedner.[59] These articles might be dismissed as strategies for survival under the political reaction, as indeed they were, but they were part of a larger trend as well.

There was an increasing recourse to the equation of religion with woman's nature, a kind of undifferentiated association of all religious sentiment with women and a generalized piety lacking in any confessional specificity whatever. Progressive women—those in Hamburg, for example—invoked woman's nature as a concept to signify the assimilation of values shared by Jewish and Gentile women as distinct from the values of Christian orthodoxy. The article "Democracy, the Religion of Women" *(Demokratie, die Religion der Frauen)* in the *Frauen-Zeitung* expressed the sense of supra-confessionalism that animated the independent women's club network. Recognizing women's special capacity for religion, "Martha," the author, distinguished the religion of democracy from the politics of democracy. Removed from legislative concerns and grounded in the spirit of love, the religion of democracy should inform the conduct of women in the public sphere. The partisanship that governed the choice of decisions and commitments in the male sphere should not be replicated by women. "Martha's" posture reduced confessionalism to a necessity of the male world and equated genuine religion and genuine Christianity with an embracing and egalitarian sisterhood.[60] The socialist Hermann Semmig, a frequent contributor to the *Frauen-Zeitung*, articulated the substitution of woman's nature for religion particularly vividly when he wrote: "The chill wind of critical thought has disrobed the Virgin of her holiness and blown her halo away, yet the fact remains that humanity has inextricably connected the concept of the godly and the redeeming with pure femininity."[61]

The ways in which women were able to make use of the potentialities of critical religion for their own ends we have seen evolve out of the original circle of progressive women in Hamburg. In the city-republic the reconciliation of Jews and Christians was a particularly urgent priority and the circumstance of a German-Catholic congregation reinforced by the personal involvement of Johannes Ronge produced a particularly vibrant women's community. Women committed to religious change found in the very process of commitment a means for identifying their concerns as a gender. Charlotte Paulsen's enlightened charity was the institutional starting point; closely connected associations dedicated to early childhood education and the training and vocational advance of women followed. When the women of Hamburg took their message to the rest of the nation the response was positive. Progressive women who either shied away from political engagement or who believed their aspirations would not be addressed by male radicals found an acceptable public role; women whose political aspirations failed with the failure of the revolution discovered a viable alternative. The new network threatened the earlier conservative coalition. Amalie Sieveking fought heterodox women with tenacity every step of the way. She denounced their philanthropic style in Hamburg, she insulted the pastor of the local German-Catholic church, she disparaged the women's college, and finally, like her rivals, she took her message to the national arena, adding her voice to the growing crescendo of reaction. Whatever difference she may once have harbored against Theodor Fliedner, she sacrificed it to the larger cause. In their distinctive styles, Sieveking and Fliedner each mobilized the particular resources at their command to discredit the work of inter-confessional women. Their strategies included both confrontation and cooptation. From their vantage point as innovators and women's leaders, they were able to extend the prevailing anti-feminism of reaction in its religious dimension. To this very effective campaign of abuse and appropriation we must turn our attention.

NOTES

1. "Die Hochschule fuer das weibliche Geschlecht in Hamburg," *FZ* 2, no. 5 (5 Feb. 1850): 2; "Plan der Hochschule fuer das weibliche Geschlecht in Hamburg," ibid., no. 10 (9 March 1850): 3.

2. "Plan der Hochschule," ibid., 2, no. 10 (9 March 1850): 3–5; Vorstand der Frauen-Vereins von 1847, Bericht, [1851] Nls EW, StAr Hmbg; Marie Kortmann, *Emilie Wuestenfeld. Eine Hamburger Buergerin* (Hamburg: Georg Westermann, 1927), pp. 37–38. In the Wuestenfeld Nachlass see also "Statuten der Hochschule fuer das weibliche Geschlecht in Hamburg," Hamburg, 1850.

3. Henriette Bock, Aktenlagen und Aktenbogen gemein- und staatsgefaehrliche Personen betr., Ministerium des Innern Nr. 455, StAr D; "Der Frauenverein in Hanau," *Deutsch-Katholisches Sonntagsblatt*, no. 18 (30 Nov. 1851): 71–72; "Briefe: Hanau, Ende November," *FZ* 1, no. 34 (8 Dec. 1849): 6. There was a notice in ibid., 2, no. 27 (26 July 1850): 8 that Blum's widow was accepting girls into her home for education in French, English, music, and practical feminine skills.

4. Kortmann, *Emilie Wuestenfeld*, p. 34; "Kirchenchronik und Miscellen: Bayern," *AKZ* 28 (15 April 1849): 488. The Sattler daughter became a student at the college; undated letter, tentatively dated early 1851, from Johanna Froebel to the executive board of the college, Nls EW, StAr Hmbg.

5. I am grateful to Stanley Zucker for this information which he located in a letter of Marie Schwarzenberg to Julius Schwarzenberg, 13 October 1850, in the Nachlass Ludwig Schwarzenberg (of Cassel), at the Bundesarchiv Ausstelle Frankfurt.

6. Nachlass Kathinka Zitz, StAr Mainz; Nachlass Zitz, H HstAr W. Zitz's correspondence from Louise Otto, from Malwida von Meysenbug, the records of Humania, and the various letters indicating her contributions to German-Catholic congregations are in Mainz. Her unpublished autobiography and the guestbook are in Wiesbaden. Meysenbug's piece was entitled "Ein Frauenschwur" and appeared in *Mainzer Tageblatt*, no. 260 (22 Sept. 1850).

7. Quoted in my "Religious Dissent, Women's Rights and the *Hamburger Hochschule fuer das weibliche Geschlecht* in Mid-Nineteenth-Century Germany," *Church History* 45 (1976): 11.

8. Ibid.

9. Marie Kortmann, "Aus den Anfaengen socialer Frauenarbeit," *Frau. Monatschrift fuer das gesammte Frauenleben unserer Zeit* 20 (1931): 428; Malwida von Meysenbug, *Memoiren einer Idealistin*, Volksausgabe, 3 vols. in 2 (Berlin and Leipzig: Schuster und Loeffler, 1907) 1: 298. By 1927 Meysenbug's *Memoiren* had gone through forty-three editions.

10. "Briefe: Hamburg, Ende April," *FZ* 2, no. 19 (11 May 1850): 7.

11. Sieveking to Princess von Hohenlohe-Schillingsfuerst, Sept. 1850, Nls AWS, StAr Hmbg.

12. Eduard Spranger, *Die Idee einer Hochschule fuer Frauen und die Frauenbewegung* (Leipzig: Duerrsche Buchhandlung, 1916), p. 32; Rudolf Kayser, "Malwida von Meysenbugs Hamburger Lehrjahre," *ZVHG* 28 (1927): 122–23; Kortmann, *Emilie Wuestenfeld*, p. 37; Friedrich Adolf Wilhelm Diesterweg, "Der Frauen-Bildungsverein in Hamburg," *Saemtliche Werke*, ed. Heinrich Deiters and others, 15 vols. to date (Berlin: Volk und Wissen Volkseigener Verlag, 1956–) 9: 143–64.

13. "Anzeige," *FZ* 2, no. 34 (24 Aug. 1850): 7.

14. Undated letter, tentatively dated early 1851, from Johanna Froebel to the executive board of the college, Nls EW, StAr Hmbg; Meysenbug, *Memoiren* 1: 315. The names of the students in the pension are mentioned in J. Froebel's letter; an additional list appears in Kortmann, *Emilie Wuestenfeld*, p. 38.

15. Meysenbug, *Memoiren*, 1: 316; Sieveking to Princess von Hohenlohe-Schillingsfuerst, Sept. 1850, Nls AWS, StAr Hmbg.

16. Johannes Ronge, "Sendschreiben," *FZ* 1, no. 29 (3 Nov. 1849): 1; "Lehrplan," in Karl Froebel and Johanna Froebel geb. Kuestner, *Hochschulen fuer Maedchen und Kindergaerten als Glieder einer vollstaedigen Bildungsanstalt... nebst Briefen...* (Hamburg: G. W. Niemeyer, 1849), p. 60.

17. Sieveking to Princess von Hohenlohe-Schillingsfuerst, Sept. 1850, Nls AWS, StAr Hmbg.

18. Diesterweg, "Der Frauen-Bildungsverein in Hamburg," pp. 154–55.

19. Meysenbug, *Memoiren*, 1: 305.

20. Ibid., 308–9.

21. Gabriel Monod, "Briefe von Malwida von Meysenbug an ihre Mutter 1850–52," *Deutsche Revue* 30, no. 3 (July-Sept. 1905): 226; ibid., 31, no. 1 (Jan.-March 1906): 368.

22. Quoted in Meysenbug, *Memoiren*, 1: 373.

23. Wichard Lange, "Bemerkungen ueber die dritte Versammlung norddeutscher Volksschullehrer," *Rheinische Blaetter fuer Erziehung und Unterricht* N. F. 42 (Nov.-Dec. 1850): 369–70; Monod, "Briefe," *Deutsche Revue* 30, no. 4 (Oct.-Dec. 1905): 235–36; Meysenbug mentions that

the Sattlers, the family from Schweinfurt, attended this meeting on their way to American emigration.

24. No author, the letter is date-lined Hamburg, Ende Maerz, *FZ* 2, no. 17 (27 April 1850): 7–8, (Otto's note, p. 7), no. 18 (4 May 1850): 5–6. One correspondent pointed out that club donations were designated for the support of non-tuition-paying students at the college who might be residents anywhere, ibid., no. 19 (11 May 1850): 7. Another, suggesting the latent conservativism of much of the *Frauen-Zeitung* constituency, repeated the belief some held that women's clubs should be devoted exclusively to charity, ibid., no. 27 (6 July 1850): 6.

25. Georgine, "Reform der Familie," *FZ* 1, no. 17 (11 Aug. 1849): 5–7, no. 18 (18 Aug. 1849): 2–3, the title notwithstanding, a modest proposal and one similar to the sentiments expressed in the radical press generally, such as "Zuruf an alle patriotischen Frauen und Jungfrauen," *Heidelberger Journal*, no. 32 (8 Feb. 1849), where the writer deplores the exclusion of women from an education that would permit them to educate the children of the future in the interests of the fatherland.

26. Emmy, "Gelehrte Frauen," ibid., 2, no. 15 (13 April 1850): 4–5, no. 16 (20 April 1850): 4–5.

27. "Haben die Frauen eine Arbeit fuer das Allgemeine?" *FZ* 2, no. 52 (31 Dec. 1850): 3–5; Otto, "Eine Mahnung," ibid., 4, no. 2 (18 Jan. 1852): 15–16, no. 3 (25 Jan. 1852): 23–24; "Des Weibes Beruf," ibid., no. 14 (14 April 1852): 109–10, no. 15 (21 April 1852), pp. 113–15; emphasizing the reality of male emigration carried a covert message for women, Friedericke von Koschuetzki, "Der Sohn der Freiheit," *FZ* 3, no. 19 (17 May 1851): 113–18, no. 20 (19 May 1851): 121–25.

28. Theodor Hofferichter, "Gedanken ueber das Schulwesen in der christkatholischen Gemeinde," *FCL* 1: 222–24; Vorstand des Frauen-Vereins von 1847, "Bericht," [1850], "Bericht," [1851], Nls EW, StAr Hmbg.

29. Mary J. Lyschinska, *Henriette Schrader-Breymann: Ihr Leben aus Briefen und Tagebuechern*, 2 vols. (Berlin and Leipzig: Walter de Gruyter u. Co., 1922), 1: 157; "Der Frauenverein in Hanau," *Deutsch-katholisches Sonntagsblatt*, no. 18 (30 Nov. 1851): 71–72.

30. '+', "Hamburg im Oktober 1851," *FZ* 3, no. 43 (9 Nov. 1851): 309–10; Rudolf Kayser, "Die deutsch-katholische Bewegung in Hamburg" *ZVHG* 25 (1925): 153–54 for quotation; Meysenbug, *Memoiren*, 1: 317–19.

31. Mathilde Franziska Anneke, ed. *Frauen-Zeitung*, no. 1 (27 Sept. 1848), Fritz and Mathilde Anneke Papers, State Historical Society of Wisconsin Archives; Fanny Lewald-Stahr, *Zwoelf Bilder nach dem Leben*.

Erinnerungen (Berlin: Janke, 1888): 19–27. Male radicals led the fight for church-school separation at Frankfurt. The radical press, like the women's press, was full of the issue; see, for example, Pastor L. in M., "Herzenergiessung ueber die beabsichtige Trennung der Volksschule von der Kirche," and K.F.W. Wander, "Des Lehrers Beruf in der Gegenwart," *Schlesische Provinzialblaetter* 128, no. 9 (Sept. 1848): 200–208, 208–14. Wander was himself a teacher and a German-Catholic; he occasionally wrote to or about the *Frauen-Zeitung, FZ* 2, no. 21 (25 May 1850): 7, no. 22 (1 June 1850): 4–5; "Ein Urtheil Wanders ueber unsere Frauen Zeitung," ibid., 1, no. 25 (6 Oct. 1849): 4–6; also, Diesterweg, "Brochueren ueber die Schulfrage," *S. W.* 8: 22–40.

32. Von einer Frau [Goldschmidt], "Zur Sache Froebel's. Herr Dr. Gutzkow und die Froebel'schen Kindergaerten," *Rheinische Blaetter fuer Erziehung und Unterricht* N. F. 47, no. 3 (May-June 1853): 326; we know this is Goldschmidt from a reference of Diesterweg's in a letter to her of 6 November 1852, Karl Mueller, *Kulturreaktion in Preussen im 19. Jahrhundert. Mit einem Anhang: Briefe Froebels und Diesterwegs* (Berlin: Verlag fuer Kulturpolitik, 1929), p. 142; Elfriede Strnad, *Hamburgs paedagogisches Leben in seiner Beziehung zu Friedrich Froebel* (Hamburg: Verlag der Gesellschaft d. Freunde d. vaterlaend. Schul- und Erziehungswesen, 1951), p. 13.

33. Lyschinska, *Henriette Schrader-Breymann*, 1: 112–13.

34. [Goldschmidt], "Zur Sache Froebel's," pp. 325–44; Friedrich Froebel to Johanna Goldschmidt, 17 March 1849, PFVAr.

35. "Briefe: Dresden," *FZ* 3, no. 15 (19 April 1851): 86, where a list is given; other mentions in *FZ* 3, no. 12 (29 March 1851): 62, no. 19 (17 May 1851): 120, no. 30 (2 August 1851): 208, no. 41 (26 Oct. 1851): 293, see also Mueller, *Kulturreaktion*, p. 57. On contributions from Hamburg, see Vorstand des Frauen-Vereins von 1847, "Bericht," [1851], Nls EW, StAr Hmbg. The esteem in which Froebel was held by the free religious movement is additionally substantiated in the continuing interest of leading male leaders; see K. Th. Bayrhoffer, "Friedrich Froebels 'Kommt, lasst uns unsern Kinder leben!' Ein Sonntagsblatt," *Hallische Jahrbuecher* 3 (1839): 447–55; Bayrhoffer founded the German-Catholic, later independent, congregation at Marburg; Rudolf Benfey, "Friedrich Froebels Kindergarten Briefe, hrsg. Hermann Poesche," *Rheinische Blaetter* N. F. 62 (Jan.-Feb. 1888): 54–66; Benfey was originally Jewish and became a major activist in the free religious movement at Halle.

36. "Briefe: Breslau," *FZ* 2, no. 49 (7 Dec. 1850): 7–8; Vorstand des Frauen-Vereins von 1847, "Bericht," [1850], "Bericht," [1851], Nls EW, StAr Hmbg; "Briefe: Breslau im Juni," *FZ* 2, no. 27 (6 July 1850): 6.

The correspondent claimed that the sole interest of the *evangelische Verein* in the education of the cholera orphans was to prevent their becoming a hostile proletariat that would turn against the property of people like themselves!

37. The plan was first published in *Rheinische Blaetter fuer Erziehung und Unterricht* in the end of 1849, *see* Diesterweg, "Friedrich Froebel und die Goethe-Stiftung," *S. W.* 8: 157–74; it was then taken up in "Aufruf an die deutschen Frauen von einer Frau," *FZ* 1, no. 35 (15 Dec. 1849): 3–5; see also his letter to Johanna Goldschmidt of 3 Sept. 1849 in Mueller, *Kulturreaktion*, pp. 117–18; Bertha Traun and Amalie Westendarp, "Der Berliner Frauen-Verein zur Bildung tuechtiger Dienstboten," *FZ* 2, no. 16 (20 April 1850): 6–7; "Der Berliner Frauen-Bildungsverein," *FZ* 3, no. 46 (30 Nov. 1851): 333.

38. Diesterweg, "Der Berliner Frauen-Bildungsverein," *S. W.* 9: 211–16, and statutes in ibid., pp. 562–63, n. 423; also "Der erste Kindergarten in Berlin," ibid., pp. 285–92; Mueller, *Kulturreaktion*, pp. 126–27.

39. Diesterweg sent his plan for Louise Otto's appraisal via Auguste Herz, the Dresden educator. Although the statement appeared to come from the association as a whole, Diesterweg himself was the author, note 35 above and Diesterweg's letter to Herz, *S. W.* 9: 563–64; idem, "Der Frauen-Bildungsverein in Hamburg," ibid., p. 144.

40. Kurt Emil Riedel, "Die Dresdener Kindergaertnerin Auguste Herz geb. Kachler," Karl Krause Schriftkreis, Sondersende 3 (Dresden, 1941): mimeographed, p. 11; Louise Otto, commentary without a title, *FZ* 3, no. 47 (7 Dec. 1851): 339–40.

41. Friedrich Froebel to Johanna Goldschmidt, 17 March 1849, PFVAr.

42. Lyschinska, *Henriette Schrader-Breymann*, 1: 110. "Bitte um Beitraege...15. Januar 1847," Geldbeitraege zum Bau eines Gemeinde Hauses betr., Deutschkatholische Gemeinde Dresden Nr. 105, StAr D, where Herz's name appears as one of the Protestant women raising money for the German-Catholic church building; Friedrich Froebel to Johanna Goldschmidt, 17 March 1849, PFVAr, for quotation.

43. Die demokratischen Kindergaerten 1851, Ministerium des Innern Nr. 73, StAr D.

44. Georgine, in a letter, *FZ* 1, no. 32 (24 Nov. 1849): 7.

45. Auguste Herz, "Ueber die sittliche Bildung der Kinder und deren ersten Religionsunterricht in dem Kindergarten," *Friedrich Froebels Wochenschrift* no. 13 (1 April 1850): 97–101.

46. Riedel, "Die Dresdener Kindergaertnerin," p. 14.

47. Auguste Herz, *Hauserziehung und Kindergarten. Vortraege fuer*

Frauen und Jungfrauen welche fuer die Familie oder den Kindergaerten sich zu Erzieherinnen bilden wollen (Leipzig: Ernst Keil, 1851); the volume is reviewed in *FZ* 3, no. 32 (16 Aug. 1851): 221–22.

48. 'a', "Briefe: Breslau," *FZ* 2, no. 9 (2 March 1850): 6–7.

49. "Briefe: Hanau Mitte Jan.," *FZ* 2, no. 6 (9 Feb. 1850): 4.

50. Eine Mitvorsteherin des deutsch-katholischen Frauen-Vereins Leipzig, "Briefe: Leipzig, Anfang August," *FZ* 1, no. 19 (25 Aug. 1849): 5.

51. Friedericke, "Das Recht der Frauen," *FZ* 2, no. 21 (25 May 1850): 3–4.

52. "Briefe: Danzig im Mai 1851," *FZ* 3, no. 20 (24 May 1851): 126.

53. "Briefe: Hanau Mitte Jan.," *FZ* 2, no. 6 (9 Feb. 1850): 4; "Hanau," *FZ* 3, no. 50 (31 Dec. 1851): 363–64.

54. Viola, "Chemnitz 16. April 1850," *FZ* 2, no. 18 (4 May 1850): 7; she had written earlier, ibid., no. 9 (2 March 1850): 4–5.

55. Ida, "Briefe: Freiberg Ende Maerz," *FZ* 2, no. 13 (30 March 1850): 6.

56. Vorstand des fraenkischen Kreises der freien christlichen Gemeinden, den 31. Maerz 1850, Deutsch-katholischer Landeskirchenvorstand No. 23, StAr D.

57. Vorstand des Frauen-Vereins von 1847, "Bericht," [1850] Nls EW, StAr Hmbg; "Sind Frauen-Vereine zweckmaessig oder nicht?" *FZ* 2, no. 27 (6 July 1850): 3–4.

58. Emmy, "Gemeinsam zu einem Ziel," *FZ* 2, no. 38 (21 Sept. 1850): 6–7; "Kirchenchronik und Miscellen," *AKZ* 29, no. 89 (6 June 1850): 735–36, Guenter Kolbe, "Demokratische Opposition in religioesem Gewande" (Dissertation, Karl Marx Universitaet Leipzig, 1964), p. 150, claims that one of the women observers was Louise Otto.

59. Johannes Ronge, *Religion und Politik* (Frankfurt a.M.: Literarische Anstalt, 1850), especially as summarized on pp. 5–7, was a major treatment of the connections between religious symbol and polity, and political practice; for many individuals active in politics, my "The German-Catholic Church: From National Hope to Regional Reality," *The Consortium on Revolutionary Europe Proceedings 1976* (Athens, Ga.: The Consortium on Revolutionary Europe, 1978) pp. 93, 100–101. Friedericke von Koschuetzki was acutely aware of what she perceived as the failure of radical men to acknowledge women's autonomy; she expresses with no ambivalence the growing tension between the sexes: "You fight for the freedom of peoples; [but] for your mothers, wives, and daughters you speak not a word of love or of justice. Will women never find an advocate? Each living creature struggles for independence. Should this be denied only to women?" Friedericke, "Die Ehe," *FZ* 2, no. 24 (15

June 1850): 2; idem, "Die Diaconissen-Anstalt Bethanien in Berlin," *FZ* 3, no. 18 (10 May 1851): 106–7; "Ernste Mahnung zur Abhilfe der drueckenden Zeitverhaeltnisse," *FZ* 2, no. 3 (19 Jan. 1850): 4–6.
60. Martha, "Demokratie, die Religion der Frauen," *FZ* 2, no. 25 (22 June 1850): 2–3.
61. Hermann Semmig, "An die Frauen," *FZ* 1, no. 28 (27 Oct. 1849): 3.

Conclusion: Reaction, Repression, Cooptation

The political and religious reaction of the 1850s adopted two strategies with respect to women. Women and women's associations uncongenial to the restored order were systematically persecuted and suppressed. At the same time, women's organizations that could be shaped to the purposes of the reaction received financial aid, official support, and recognition. The legitimacy of religious ecumenism and confessional pluralism, principles that women in inter-confessional clubs upheld, was denied by the state. The events of the revolution thoroughly politicized religious difference and engaged the state in a much more unequivocal relationship with the church than that of the pre-revolutionary era *(Vormaerz)*. Liberal politicans habitually expressed their goals in the language of ethics; Leonard Krieger attributes their failure in the revolution to their inability to convert metaphysics into the mechanisms of politics.[1] By contrast the moral rhetoric of reaction readily translated into an even more complete institutional integration of throne and altar.

LEGAL MEASURES: MIRROR OF THE MODEL FAMILY

The first indication that women would constitute a special target of persecution during the reaction was the Prussian Law of Association of February 1850, imposed as one of the earliest acts of the restored absolutism. Under the pretext of protecting the right of political parties to organize, the law prescribed the limits within which parties could recruit membership and the circumstances under which they could meet and organize. Two categories of persons were summarily excluded from the possibility of membership: women and minors or dependents. The *Frauen-Zeitung* challenged both the intention and the language of the new law: "we protest against the impolite expression '*Frauenperson*'; we protest against...being coupled with minors."[2] Women were particularly vulnerable to the reprisals of the religious reaction. Progressive women found themselves at risk whether they were members of independent religious congregations or members of coalitions to support such congregations. Froebel's kindergartens were suspect under whatever sponsorship they operated. The incidence of the reaction varied as to time and place, but it was surprisingly uniform in its impact on women, and it implied a uniform consensus about woman's place.

The law of association illustrated one of the principal tactics adopted by the reaction with respect to women, that of misrepresentation and distortion. Their numerical presence in the galleries of constituent parliaments was exaggerated to imply misplaced ambition by contemporary observers such as Wilhelm Heinrich Riehl, the principal ideologue of reactionary sociology.[3] Riehl's treatise *The Family (Die Familie)*, center piece of his "natural history of peoples as a foundation of German policy," went through no fewer than seventeen editions between 1855 and 1935 and served as the standard reference of lay sociologists. Central to his theory of society was the belief that the family was the germ cell of the state and the source of civic stability. The family in turn encapsulated the natural differences of the sexes. In what Riehl called the "great dual empire of society and state,"

Custom, the moving power of society, is cherished by the woman. Woman exists in the natural life of custom; man then creates law from the consciousness of right, the moving power of the state....In that God created man and woman, he established inequality and dependence as the basic condition of all human development. The woman is principally the family-oriented sex.[4]

Riehl spoke of the sanctuary of the domestic circle. This was not the kind of domestic circle, however, that had fueled discussions in the *Frauen-Zeitung* and provided a model for interconfessional activism. Nor was it a circle of domesticity in which women exercised control and autonomy. On the contrary, Riehl specifically emphasized that in the domestic sanctuary as well as in public, the social and political power of the father prevailed. Consistent with this position he opposed the higher education of women.[5]

The same ideology promoted a move to revise the legal code governing marriage and divorce in Prussia. It proposed to eliminate the possibility of divorce for childless couples, to forbid remarriage, to seek out and punish a guilty party in instances of divorce, and, should the guilty party prove to be a woman, to establish a penalty doubly severe as that exacted against a male. The dual standard was justified on grounds that the "great moral position of the female sex . . . [is the grounds] on which . . . rests the future of generations."[6] Public outcry against these proposals when they first surfaced in 1842 precluded their implementation, but in the climate of the reaction they were gradually incorporated into the body of private law. The *Frauen-Zeitung* construed the proposed revisions in religious terms as a reversion to the kind of Pietism which had condoned the marriage lot.[7]

The impact of the law of association on women was in actuality at first relatively slight; women were not usually participants in the political clubs that were its major target. The Prussian order against Froebel kindergartens for the immediate future was far more devastating. The order, issued August 7, 1851, announced that "schools which are organized along Froebel or similar principles cannot be tolerated."[8] The prohibition was based on the assumption that the kindergarten was part of an atheistic scheme. Both Karl Froebel and Friedrich Froebel protested against the decree. The younger Froebel claimed that, far from an atheist, he was a "living member of Christendom" and a "member of the free Christian congregation . . . of Hamburg."[9] Friedrich Froebel, for his part, dissociated himself once again from the ideas of his nephew and argued that the decree had confused the two educators one with the other.[10] To Prussian

Minister of Education Karl von Raumer, the differences were inconsequential since both men believed that children could be educated without reference to Christian dogmatics. In a marginal note, Raumer observed that what "Karl Froebel said was at least clear and consistent, whereas his uncle expressed himself 'mysteriously' and 'confusedly' and probably did not know himself what he wanted."[11] Although at first Prussian local officers acted inconsistently, it was idle to assume, as did many correspondents to the *Frauen-Zeitung*, that the order would not be enforced.[12] In an unusually perceptive comment from Breslau, one woman recognized the double penalty embedded in the anti-Froebel legislation:

Apart from the general loss incurred here to children's education, the situation of the female kindergarten teachers is also regrettable. They now find themselves without any sphere of effective action or means of existence. ... But who inquires about it when girls and women are suddenly confronted with such a fate? Wasn't it already an unseemly departure from their proper sphere *[aus ihrem Kreis]* both to work for the general good and to wish to be self-supporting? The political state which men govern *[Maennerstaat]* has the right to punish this behavior and to repudiate those who encroach on its privileges without further concern.[13]

The reaction in Saxony adopted a somewhat different tactic. Rather than enacting inclusive legislation, the Saxon government singled out a number of individual women to harass, and succeeded by this means in destroying the influence of their philanthropic and educational initiative. One case which attracted wide attention was that of Adele Erbe. During the summer of 1851 Erbe enrolled in Auguste Herz's institute for training in the Froebel method. Like most of the other women in the course including Herz herself she belonged to a family whose men had taken an active part in the Dresden uprising during the spring of 1849. These women were suddenly confronted with the necessity of supporting themselves: their husbands and fathers were political prisoners or exiles. Erbe was not directly interested in politics, but she had conducted a lottery for the independent women's club in Altenburg to raise money for families victimized by the revolution. She was declared a person dangerous to the state and threatened with imprisonment. To satisfy these charges, she had paid a fine, resigned from the club at Altenburg and moved to Dresden. When the government threatened to reopen her case in Dresden, she and her father hurriedly fled the country.[14] The persecution of Erbe precipitated a chain reaction among Dresden's progressive women; many of them withdrew from Herz's institute. When Herz reported to the government that her own capacity to earn a living was in jeopardy, the government responded by closing her kindergarten.[15]

Elsewhere the persecution of women was less explicit but no less effective. In the Rhineland, for example, the government encouraged the development of Catholic women's clubs but systematically withheld licenses for lotteries and denied permits for meeting halls to such clubs as Humania.[16] Virtually every German state censured the independent congregations either as illegal political associations or as religious sects barred from legal recognition. The incidence of this campaign fell with particular severity on women. In Schweinfurt Henriette Breymann lost both her kindergarten and her primary school when the free congregation was designated in violation of the Bavarian law of association. Johanna Herbert in Nuernberg hoped that her involuntary return to the "mother church" would protect the kindergarten where she taught.[17] In Hamburg the independent congregation was dissolved after the prosecution demonstrated that its statutes no longer conformed to those originally submitted to the Senate. The proscription of the congregation condemned the school as well, the program with which Malwida von Meysenbug was so deeply involved. Malwida herself fled to England when, during a sojourn in Berlin to visit friends from the college, her brother reported her to the police.[18] The school conducted by Charlotte Paulsen's benevolent society was also disbanded on the charge that it was linked to the German-Catholic (or independent) congregation. The executive committee argued to no avail that the school was in fact inter-confessional.[19]

The college in Hamburg closed its own doors without waiting for government intervention. A campaign of abuse in which Amalie Sieveking played a significant role destroyed the sources of its financial support in the community. Sieveking made it clear in her correspondence that by her standards the divorce proceedings against Wuestenfeld and Traun reflected poorly on the college. The Inner Mission issued a brochure that denounced the curriculum at the college as a scientific disguise for revolutionary propaganda.[20]

SIEVEKING'S CAMPAIGN

Sieveking tried to conform the reaction to her own goals. With characteristic aggressivity and direction, she attacked every manifestation of the inter-confessional enterprise both privately and in public, and she carried her campaign beyond the city republic to the national arena. She presented herself as the champion of "a certain emancipation" that encouraged women "to aim at a higher cultivation of their intellectual powers, without the danger of being marked as blue stockings. I wish to see them admitted to a larger share of activity in philanthropic interests." But she condemned the Hamburg college because of ostensible associations with Judaism, German-Catholicism, and the promotion of a "spirit of irreligion."[21]

In 1849, for the first time, Sieveking's association lost more members than it gained in new applicants.[22] The sense of imminent danger lent a quality of urgency to Sieveking's campaign. As she recognized, the sponsors of the college were "those very people . . . who had taken on the assignment to introduce our poor to viewpoints in diametric opposition to my own form of instruction."[23] She feared the competitive potential of the inter-confessional coalition in its own right; she also realized that it could be used to discredit the entrance of women into public life, notably into charity, where the work of women continued to be considered novel and slightly suspect.

In the spring of 1849 Sieveking took her campaign to Berlin, where she delivered a public address as guest of the court preacher Snethlage (1780–1861). Her talk was a skillful maneuver aimed at winning recruits by appropriating phrases from the rhetoric of contemporary feminism while at the same time invoking the sentiments of the establishment with respect to woman's place. "I want an emancipation of our sex," she announced, "but not, to be sure, in the sense of many contemporaries who, pushing aside all godly and human order, would like to abrogate even that subordination of the weaker sex to the stronger established by God." She made a striking concession—and for her, new—to the reality of the bourgeois world when she spoke of the increasing division of contemporary society, one in which men, "overwhelmed by business" and "the powerful drives and pressures of the present," should relinquish the responsibility for philanthropy to women.[24] But she assiduously avoided any suggestion that in charitable or any other domains, women might require a sphere of autonomy. Sieveking believed that she had secured the recognition of "thinking men" to her "reasonable demands;"[25] what she underestimated was the prevailing mistrust of women. In the aftermath of the revolution, Johann Hinrich Wichern emerged to reclaim philanthropy for male direction in the interests of inner mission.

THE INNER MISSION

Johann Hinrich Wichern, founder of the Rauhe Haus for abandoned boys, emerged as the chief architect of post-revolutionary philanthropy in Germany and a major spokesman of the reaction. During the summer of 1848 when Protestant leaders assembled in Wittenberg to confer on strategies to deal with the upheaval, Wichern proclaimed the need for an inner mission, an aggressive Pietist crusade to meet the social crisis of the day. He compared the revolution to the coming of the Antichrist, which

suddenly revealed itself as the organizing principle, opposing the eternal truth with scorn, contempt and sacrilege. This spirit no longer remains the secret conviction of a few, but quickly became a widely expressed opinion that the church had to disappear and be destroyed, that God's words were outworn fallacy, that Christ was like anybody, that heaven was an empty dream, and the Last Judgment was but the monster of excited Oriental fantasy and that the hope for resurrection was but the conviction of a despicable sect.[26]

The revolution revealed the "sin and moral corruption which had become epidemic and which had spread throughout the German nation."[27]

To reverse this course Wichern advanced the concept of inner mission; for him only the Inner Mission could recreate the church as a national institution rather than a conglomerate of state churches and thereby inspire national rebirth. Wichern was an enormously charismatic person: his Wittenberg speech has been likened to the Communist Manifesto, and when royal power was fully restored in Germany his movement assumed massive proportions. His vision of a regenerate society embraced charitable work in all German states and endeavored to save the church by enlisting the spirit of practical Christianity against the forces of subversion and fragmentation. Wichern strove to restore the traditions of society: the family, the corporation, and the state as well as the church, to their organic interconnectedness. When the Inner Mission was in place, the organization stimulated the establishment of countless new charities and the federation of those already in existence. Wichern's scheme was so immense that even a fellow believer observed that an enterprise of such proportion might at some point use its control over the population for "dangerous purposes." Correspondents of the *Frauen-Zeitung* considered Wichern's alliance with the Prussian court sinister and called his famous children's shelter the *graue Haus* or grey house.[28]

Wichern accepted the inclusion but not the leadership of Christian women in the field of charity. He spoke of the increase of women's public activity as a sign of social renewal and he systematically assembled the reports of women's benevolent societies in Sieveking's coalition and publicized their accomplishments in the *Fliegende Blaetter* or *Fly Leaves* from the Rauhe Haus, the journal of the Inner Mission.[29] For this reason Sieveking herself was compelled to come to public terms with Wichern. With reference to what she clearly considered Wichern's grandiosity, she pointed out during her speech in Berlin that she herself had been engaged in the work of inner mission for twenty years. She applauded Wichern's spirit but announced her determination to defend the organizational independence of her own society.[30]

While Wichern welcomed the work of women, his goals were very different from Sieveking's. He was unsympathetic to the principle of autonomy and occasionally chided her affiliates as well as those of the Inner Mission for insufficient attention to order and uniformity. He was not in the least interested in the potentiality of women's charity for its own sake nor as an instrument to develop women's skills and liberate them from useless lives.[31] On the contrary, a general congress of 1854 made this revealing comparison: it likened the relationship between Sieveking and the Inner Mission to that of John the Baptist and Jesus Christ![32] Sieveking succeeded in preserving the independence of the Hamburg society; elsewhere women's clubs were increasingly incorporated into the Inner Mission. After 1850 direct inquiries to Sieveking dropped off severely; at the same time many women's clubs came into existence with male—often clerical—leadership under the umbrella of the Inner Mission.[33] To this degree Sieveking's organization, like those of her opponents, fell victim to the anti-feminism of the reaction.

FROM ANTI-CATHOLICISM TO ANTI-RADICALISM: THE FEMALE DIACONATE COOPTS THE WOMEN'S MOVEMENT

Next to Wichern, Theodor Fliedner of the deaconess institute at Kaiserswerth was the most prominent spokesman of the reaction on issues pertaining to women's philanthropy. During the twenty-year span of his nursing order, opposition to Fliedner in Protestant circles had all but vanished. A network of motherhouses affiliated with Kaiserswerth extended over Germany—indeed over the world—and Fliedner's model shaped not only the king's plans for Bethanien in Berlin but the work of the new generation of Protestant leaders as well, among them Wilhelm Loehe (1808–1872) and Friedrich von Bodelschwingh (1831–1910). The revolution replaced Catholicism as the target of Fliedner's militancy, particularly those aspects of revolutionary rhetoric relating to women. The institution at Kaiserswerth offered its full collaboration to the Inner Mission and to the Prussian monarchy itself in the campaign to contain the religious implications of the revolution. The women's movement, particularly the inter-confessional experiments in early childhood teaching, assumed particular importance for Fliedner.

There had always been a modest teaching program at Kaiserswerth; it had simply been eclipsed by the centrality of nursing at the institution. Fliedner launched a vigorous campaign for the recruitment of teachers to stem the "uncontrolled rebellion against godly and human laws." He advocated a system of education which would penetrate every village of the realm and, instead of starting with five- or six-year-olds, would admit children at ages two or three. By 1854, 638 women had received some kind of teacher training at Kaiserswerth. Seminars of one- and two-year duration trained teachers for the several levels of schooling; the recruitment effort was designed expressly to attract lay women with no necessary interest in the deaconess office.[34]

What is interesting in the promotional literature is not the curriculum but the rationale of the program, which clearly betrays the impact of contemporary events. Fliedner defended the introduction of women teachers in girls' schools, a practice so far exceedingly limited, on the grounds that "womanly modesty, morality and discipline, love of cleanliness, a sense of order and sensitivity" could be more effectively instilled by female than male teachers—precisely the ideology of woman's nature favored by the *Frauen-Zeitung*. Focusing on the professional aspirations of unmarried women, Fliedner invited single women and widows to apply to the program at Kaiserswerth "to make themselves into useful members of society." Appeals to patriotism, to vocational and social utility, even to domesticity were something altogether new to the literature of the diaconate. Fliedner adopted the use of a concept, *christlich-muetterlicher Sinn*, or Christian maternal instinct, which was in fact very close to the language of Froebel.[35] There was justice to the claims and the warnings lodged by Louise Otto's *Frauen-Zeitung* in 1850 that the deaconess movement was usurping their rhetoric for the purpose of detracting from the appeal of the women's movement.[36]

Fliedner's tactic was one of both cooptation and confrontation. In a prospectus on nursery teaching he directly attacked Friedrich Froebel and challenged the belief that Bible stories and fairy tales were unsuitable fare for little children. "According to [Froebel's] opinion," Fliedner observed, "children's hearts are all pure and guiltless and have no need for a Savior....[I find it] impossible to come to any kind of reconciliation with such enemies of godly revelation."[37] In sarcastic allusion to the hallmarks of

Froebel pedagogy, Fliedner announced that since so many children were destined to die between the ages of two and seven, "it was better to prepare them for eternity in the knowledge of their Creator and Savior than with songs of blocks, balls, and cubes on their lips."[38] In disdainful reference to the women engaged in teaching under the auspices of the new movement, Fliedner assured employers that they could expect women trained at the deaconess institute to be "exempt from any urge to be in vogue."[39] The concerted push into teaching was a success in attracting a broader constituency to Kaiserswerth. Fliedner, like his inter-confessional competitors, saw a close affinity between women's philanthropy and the rudimentary women's professions. In the final decade of his life he grafted the language of women's professions onto the existing imagery of the surrogate family at the motherhouse. Similarly he adopted the concept of bourgeois motherhood from the rhetoric of the women's movement and deprived it of moral hegemony. The new maternity was incorporated into the secure structure and context of the traditional household. In sum, the institute at Kaiserswerth usurped and neutralized many of the goals articulated by the women's movement during the revolution.

LINKS TO LATER GERMAN BOURGEOIS FEMINISM

It has been customary to speak of the feudalization of liberal movements in the Bismarckian period, the bourgeois women's movement among them. But what really was feudalized? "Feudalization" makes certain assumptions about the earlier phase of the movement that surely are erroneous. The later women's movement can only be understood within the context of its own epoch but every evidence from the mid-century suggests continuity with the past.

This study has documented the development of a religiously inspired movement of women, one committed to inter-confessional collaboration on several levels of community and self-service in the name of woman's nature. Its origins lay in a response to charitable enterprises of women serving orthodox Protestantism who themselves were innovators in their effort to create a female presence in the realm of philanthropy. The aims and rhetoric of the mid-nineteenth-century movement were heavily influenced by the religious context out of which it evolved. In the freer climate of the revolution it was possible for inter-confessional women to create an institutional structure for their activity, a structure that was also attractive to women whose feelings about political conduct were ambivalent. As the political vitality of the revolution ebbed, women with political commitments also welcomed the opportunity to engage in more conventional public activities under congenial auspices. For most women the women's movement of the mid-century was never exclusively nor even primarily political. The contemporary religious upheaval offered women a means to conceptualize issues of particular relevance to them, both personal and public.

The ideology of the General German Women's Association *(Allgemeiner Deutscher Frauenverein)*, with its commitment to women's education and professionalization as well as its emphasis on charitable service, perpetuated a legacy from the past. The *Frauenverein* embodied another legacy from the revolution: a mistrust of male leadership coupled with the conviction that women should identify goals and strategies of their own, distinct from those of political liberalism. The ADF was the organization through which Louise Otto launched—or relaunched—the bourgeois women's movement in 1865. One analysis of the later movement suggests that the ADF accommodated official morality and the ideology of the "true German woman."

Their enthusiastic acceptance of the role created for them and their attempt to use this acceptance to gain more privileges for themselves within the social and moral system which the Junkers had created was a classic example of the 'feudalisation' of the German bourgeoisie in the later 19th century.[40]

The Junkers, however, had not manufactured the concept of woman's nature. The term was current in the wake of the Enlightenment. As this study has documented, progressive women of the mid-century embraced a belief in their distinctive nature with the hope of establishing a precarious autonomy for themselves outside the demands of patriarchal subordination and beyond the reach of orthodox Christianity. The limitations of this concept were already apparent in the controversy between Friedrich and Karl Froebel, and in the efforts of women like Doris Luetkens to dilute the Froebel system by conforming it to Christianity. In the years immediately after the revolution there was an aggressive effort on the part of the reaction, particularly its philanthropists, to deprive the concept of any distinctive meaning apart from Christian orthodoxy. By 1865 the rhetoric of the early women's movement as well as the national-liberal rhetoric of the revolution as a whole had been thoroughly assimilated by the state and its various agents, for self-serving ends.

The religious climate of the Bismarckian and Wilhelmian periods differed altogether from that of the mid-century. Protestantism was more pliant with respect to the state; secular ideology corroded religious dogma and the polity of the church was subject to the secular bureaucracy. Contradictions between the Christian spirit and woman's nature which had provided a basis for partisan controversy in the 1840s and 1850s were no longer relevant to the religious dialogue. The dismantling of religious separatism destroyed the one consistent ally of moderate feminism and with it, the climate of religious contention that had sustained the combative stance of the women involved. Feminism had no institutional allies in 1865.

There was a consistently utopian character to late-nineteenth-century–early-twentieth-century German feminism. Equality of rights was never understood simply in terms of political progress but rather as a means to an end, that of implementing the higher ethical order associated with the qualities residing in woman's nature. Emancipation was justified in terms of liberating women to perform their cultural destiny, the moral improvement of humanity. The bourgeois women's movement encompassed several phases. Until the repeal of the association law in 1908, the possibilities for political activity were circumscribed. When the ADF first surfaced in the 1860s, educational and occupational opportunities for women preempted attention. In subsequent decades, and in response to the changing social and political climate, other issues took precedence, most conspicuously those arising from the double standard. Radicals in the ranks campaigned to protect single mothers and to destroy the regulatory system that made legalized prostitution possible. Moderates focused on the inequities imposed on women in marriage and divorce. Some women were willing to take enormous risks in the service of these goals. But political suffrage itself was never an exclusive or even a primary target. It is important not to exaggerate the differences between German women and their British and American sisters in this respect. Women's suffrage in both England and the United States was widely believed to offer the means of moral and social betterment.

The appearance of the German Society for Ethical Culture in the 1890s[41] performed a function not unlike the role of religious sectarianism in the 1840s and 1850s: it stimulated and valorized feminist objectives. Ethical Culture stood outside the existing structure of confessions and political parties. In the sphere of morality where women felt most competent, the society, for a brief period, provided a radical impetus to bourgeois feminism without exacting political commitments. The bourgeois women's movement cannot be equated with dominant turn-of-the-century political structures and concerns in Germany any more than the mid-nineteenth-century women's movement can be understood as a product of the revolutionary ideology of 1848. Mid-nineteenth-century feminism developed in a religious environment and embraced an ethical agenda; bourgeois feminism was heir to this legacy.

NOTES

1. Leonard Krieger, *The German Idea of Freedom: History of a Political Tradition* (Boston: Beacon Press, 1957), pp. 300–303.

2. W. Lueders, "Die Frauen und das preussische Vereinsgesetz," *FZ* 2, no. 20 (18 May 1850): 3–5, where Lueders quotes "Hermine" in an article for the 9 March 1850 *Abendpost*, a Berlin democratic newspaper no longer extant.

3. R., "Die Frauen. Eine social-politische Studie," *Deutsche Vierteljahrs-Schrift* 15, no. 3, (1852): 239–40; *FZ* 3, no. 47 (7 Dec. 1851): 341.

4. Quoted in Ute Gerhard, *Verhaeltnisse und Verhinderungen. Frauenarbeit, Familie und Recht der Frauen im 19. Jahrhundert. Mit Dokumenten* (Frankfurt a.M.: Suhrkamp Verlag, 1978), p. 150. See also, among others, Bogumil Goltz, *Zur Charakteristik und Naturgeschichte der Frauen* (Berlin: Janke, 1863) which makes an identical argument.

5. R., "Die Frauen," pp. 296, 259; "Wider die hoeheren Toechter-anstalten. Ein Beitrag zur " 'Emancipation von den Frauen,' " *Deutsche Vierteljahrs-Schrift* 18 (1855) 4: 257.

6. Quoted in Gerhard, *Verhaeltnisse*, p. 170.

7. "Die Liebe und der Pietismus," *FZ* 4, no. 8 (21 March 1852): 58–60.

8. Quoted in Karl Mueller, *Kulturreaktion in Preussen im 19. Jahrhundert. Mit einem Anhang: Briefe Froebels und Diesterwegs* (Berlin: Verlag fuer Kulturpolitik, 1929), p. 66.

9. Ibid., p. 60.

10. *FZ* 3, no. 46 (30 Nov. 1851): 335.

11. Mueller, *Kulturreaktion*, p. 61.

12. *FZ* 3, no. 46 (30 Nov. 1851): 335.

13. Ibid., 4, no. 1 (11 Jan. 1852): 6.

14. *FZ* 3, no. 47 (7 Dec. 1851): 341; ibid., no. 22 (7 June 1851): 143; also "Bericht des Oberbuergermeisters und Polizeidirektors," Die Frauen-vereine betr. 1851, Ministerium des Innern Nr. 309, and Charlotte Erbe, Aktenlagen und Aktenbogen gemein- und staatsgefaehrliche Personen betr, Ministerium des Innern Nr. 456, StAr D.

15. *FZ* 3, no. 47 (7 Dec. 1851): 339–40; ibid., 2, no. 30 (27 July 1850): 5.

16. Ibid., no. 48 (17 Dec. 1851): 350–51; "Satzungen des Vereines von der h. Elisabeth in Mainz," *Katholische Sonntagsblaetter zur Belehrung und Erbauung*, no. 50 (10 Dec. 1848): 397–98; "Die zehnte oeffentliche generale Versammlung des Vincenz- und Elisabethvereines zu Mainz," ibid., no. 10 (6 March 1859): 74–77.

17. Members of the congregation at Altenburg thought at first they would be considered under the law of associations and hence in violation of the law because of their female constituents; the congregation was recognized as a religious society, but its members believed they were living under the sword of Damocles, *FZ* 3, nos. 5 and 6 (22 Feb. 1851): 23; Mary J. Lyschinska, *Henriette Schrader-Breymann. Ihr Leben aus Briefen und Tagebuechern*, 2 vols. (Berlin and Leipzig: Walter de Gruyter u. Co., 1922), 1: 157; F. Froebel to Johanna Hebert 22 Nov. 1851 in Hermann Poesche, ed., *Friedrich Froebels Kindergarten-Briefe* (Vienna and Leipzig: Pichlers Wwe. und Sohn, 1887), pp. 236–38.

18. Rudolf Kayser, "Die deutsch-katholische Bewegung in Hamburg," *ZVHG* 26 (1925): 164; Malwida von Meysenbug, *Memoiren einer Idealistin*, Volksausgabe, 3 vols. in 2 (Berlin and Leipzig: Schuster und Loeffler, 1907), 1: 332–33.

19. "Die Schliessung des Unterrichts-Cursus des Frauen-Vereins zur Unterstuetzung des Armenpflege. Aktenstuecke," Hamburg, June

1854, p. 12, Polizeiliche Untersuchungsakten Serie VI, Unterrichtsan-stalten des sog. Frauen-Vereins, StAr Hmbg.

20. Kayser, "Die deutsch-katholische Bewegung," p. 159; Sieveking to Princess von Hohenlohe-Schillingsfuerst, Sept. 1850, Nls AWS, StAr Hmbg.

21. Ibid.

22. Elisabeth Haupt, *Amalie Sieveking als Gruenderin des weiblichen Vereins fuer Armen- und Krankenpflege in Hamburg* (Berlin-Spandau: Wichern Verlag, 1933), p. 27.

23. Sieveking to Princess Hohenlohe-Schillingsfuerst Sept. 1850, Nls AWS, StAr Hmbg.

24. *WVAK, 17. Bericht*, p. 55.

25. [Emma Poel], *Denkwuerdigkeiten aus dem Leben von Amalie Sieveking in deren Auftrage von einer Freundin derselben verfasst* (Hamburg: Agentur des Rauhen Hauses, 1860), pp. 310–11.

26. Quoted in Hartmut Lehmann, "Pietism and Nationalism: The Relationship between Protestant Revivalism and National Renewal in Nineteenth-Century Germany," *Church History* 51 (1982): 48.

27. Ibid.

28. William O. Shanahan, *German Protestants Face the Social Question* (Notre Dame: University of Notre Dame Press, 1954), pp. 208–9, 223–26; *The Missionary: A Monthly Periodical devoted to the Work of Inner, Home and Foreign Missions in the American Lutheran Church*, ed. Rev. W. A. Passavant, 4 (Jan. 1851): 2; "Das graue Haus und die innere Mission," *FZ* 2, no. 25 (22 June 1850): 3.

29. For example, *Fliegende Blaetter* 4 (1847): 228–33; 8 (1851): 347–51, 379–85; 9 (1852): 26–31, 239–51.

30. *WVAK, 17. Bericht*, pp. 76–79.

31. Haupt, *Amalie Sieveking*, pp. 12, 31–32 and note 303 in which Haupt offers personal knowledge as well as a letter from Wichern to document the antagonism between them. Also *Fliegende Blaetter* 4 (1847): 228, 295; 10 (1853): 263.

32. Martin von Gerhardt, *Johann Hinrich Wichern. Ein Lebensbild*, 3 vols. (Hamburg: Buchhandlung des Rauhen Hauses, 1927–31), 2: 348.

33. "Nach dem Muster des Hamburger Vereins an anderen Orten gegruendete Frauenvereine," Verzeichnis, pp. 60–63, Nls AWS, StAr Hmbg; for examples of the expansion of women's clubs sponsored by males, *Fliegende Blaetter* 9 (1852): 196, 287; 10 (1853); 24, 262; and 13 (1856): 107–9, where Wichern wrote that whereas before 1848, Sieveking was considered the mother of visiting societies, thereafter the clergy and "friends of the church" tried to convert the congregation itself, under clerical administration, into a caretaking station for the poor.

34. Catherine M. Prelinger, "The Nineteenth Century Deaconessate in Germany: The Efficacy of a Family Model," *German Women in the Eighteenth and Nineteenth Centuries: A Social and Literary History*, ed. Ruth-Ellen B. Joeres and Mary Jo Maynes (Bloomington: Indiana University Press, 1986), p. 221–22; [Theodor Fliedner], *17. Jahresbericht ueber die Diakonissen-Anstalt zu Kaiserswerth am Rhein* (1848), p. 181.

35. [T. Fliedner], "Wirksamkeit und Werth der christlichen Elementar- und Industrie-Lehrerinnen, und Einrichtung des Seminars fuer dieselben," *AuKF* 2 (June 1850): 2, 13, 3.

36. *FZ* 2, no. 43 (26 Oct. 1850): 8.

37. [T. Fliedner], "Nothwendigkeit der Kleinkinderschulen, und Einrichtung des Seminars fuer Kleinkinder-Lehrerinnen zu Kaiserswerth," *AuKF* 1, no. 1 (1849): 25.

38. Fliedner's *Lieder-Buch fuer Kleinkinder-Schulen*, quoted in Martin Gerhardt, *Theodor Fliedner. Ein Lebensbild*, 2 vols. (Duesseldorf-Kaiserswerth: Buchhandlung der Diakonissenanstalt, 1933–37), 2: 336.

39. [T. Fliedner], *Das zweite Jahr-Zehnt der Diakonissen-Anstalt* (Kaiserswerth: Buchhandlung der Diakonissenanstalt, 1857), p. 197.

40. Richard J. Evans, *The Feminist Movement in Germany 1894–1939* (London and Beverly Hills: SAGE Publications, 1976), p. 26.

41. Barbara Greven-Aschoff, *Die buergerliche Frauenbewegung in Deutschland 1894–1933* (Goettingen: Vandenhoeck und Rupprecht, 1981), p. 67.

Selected Bibliography

ARCHIVAL RESOURCES

STAATSARCHIV DARMSTADT

Repertorien Abt E S V. A. Evangelische Kirche Konv. 45 Fasc. 13, 14
Bensheimer Kreisamtsakten betr. die am 6. Okt. 1845 zu Gernsheim erfolgte Ankunft des Predigers Ronge
Bensheimer Kreisamtsakten betr. Anzeige wegen der dem sog. deutsch-katholischen Pfarrer Kerbler am Landungsplatze in Gernsheim widerfahrenen Beleidigung 1845

STAATSARCHIV DRESDEN, DDR (Formerly The LANDESHAUPTARCHIV)

Ministerium des Innern
Nrs. 455–459: Aktenlagen und Aktenbogen Gemein- und staatsge-faehrliche Personen (Bock, Erbe, Gluemer, Herz, Kuschmann, Meysenbug, Otto, Scheibe)
Nr. 426: Papiere ueber politisch-verdaechtige Persoenlichkeiten und Zustaende, Drohbriefe etc. 1840'ger–1860'ger Jahre
Nr. 11038: Demokratenverzeichniss
Nr. 309: Die Frauenvereine betr. 1851
Nrs. 72, 73: Die demokratischen Kindergaerten 1851
Nr. 10962: Politische Polizeiangelegenheiten
Nr. 11021: Die politisch-revolutionaeren Verbindungen in den Jah-ren 1814 bis 1852 und deren Revolutionen; von L. Noes, Gross. hess. Polizei Commissaer

Deutschkatholische Gemeinde Dresden
Nr. 24: Acta der deutschkatholischen Gemeinde zu Dresden Bedruckte Mitglieder-Verzeichnisse
Deutschkatholischer Landeskirchenvorstand
Nr. 176: Leipzig. "Verzeichniss der stimmberechtigen Mitglieder vom 25. Februar 1845 bis 31. Mai 1860"
Dissertation: Guenter Kolbe, "Demokratische Opposition in religoesem Gewande und antikirchliche Bewegung im Koenigreich Sachsen," Karl Marx Universitaet Leipzig, 1964

FACHBUECHEREI FUER FRAUENDIAKONIE UND FLIEDNERARCHIV, KAISERSWERTH

Briefe an Theodor Fliedner
Briefe der Schwestern, Pfarrer usw. betr. Aufnahme
Theodor Fliedner an verschiedene Empfaenger

STAATSARCHIV HAMBURG

Familienarchive
Archiv: Emilie Wuestenfeld Nachlass
Familie Sieveking III: Schriftlicher Nachlass von Amalie Wilhelmine Sieveking
Archiv des weiblichen (Sieveking'schen) Vereins fuer Armen- und Krankenpflege, Nr. 42
Archivalien des Frauenvereins zur Unterstuetzung der Armenpflege von 1849
Hamburgisches Adress Buch fuer 1847
Niedergericht B 1226 Acta in Sachen Herrn Dr. juris Carl Petersen mandati nomine C.J.F. Traun
Niedergericht B 1301 Acta in Sachen Marie Emilie Wuestenfeld Paulsenstiftschule 27, 51
Polizeiliche Untersuchungsakten Serie VI Lit Z No. 2873: Unterrichtsanstalten des sog. Frauen-Vereins
Polizei Behoerde–Kriminalwesen C Serie VI Lit Y No. 1856 Bd. 1: Designatio Actorum No 11 Acta betr. C. Volckhausen
Schule des Paulsenstifts A 558
Dissertation: Ingrid Lahrsen, "Beitraege zum kirchlichen und religioesen Leben Hamburgs zur Zeit der Erweckungsbewegung," Philosophische Fakultaet der Universitaet Hamburg, 1957

STADTARCHIV HEIDELBERG

Stadtarchiv Amtsbuecherei AF: Adress-Kalender saemtlicher Bewohner der Stadt Heidelberg fuer das Jahr 1848

Stadtgemeinde Heidelberg Archiv Nr. 155 Fasc 2: Stadtraths-Acten XV.
Kirchen Sachen. Eine Deutschkatholische Kirchen–Gesellschaft
1848–1855

GENERALLANDESARCHIV KARLSRUHE

Stadtamt Mannheim. Verwaltungs-Sachen Mannheim. X: Kirchen und
Religionsgemeinschaften
362/1341 Die Gruendung einer Deutsch-katholischen Gemeinde
dahier
362/1342 Die Anhaenger des Leipziger Glaubensbekenntnisses
Staatsministerium Generalia: Religion
233/32305 Uebertritte zur sog. "freikatholischen Kirche" insbesondere in Mannheim und Freiburg 1845
233/32307 Gesuch der sog. Alt- oder Christkatholiken in Mannhein,
Verfuegungen ueber katholische Dissidenten 1845–1867
233/31444 Vortrag des Geheimrats Bekk betr. die Verhaeltnisse der
Deutschkatholiken 1846
Grossherzogl. katholischer Ober-kirchenrath. Acta Generalia
235/41 Kirchl.-religioese Wirren, insbesondere die sog. deutsch-
katholische Kirche 1845–1852
Grossherzogl. Badisches Oberamt Heidelberg. Verwaltungs-Sachen
Ort Heidelberg. Rubrik X: Kirchensachen
356/566 Die Kirchl. Verhaeltnisse der deutsch-kath. Gemeinde in
Heidelberg, 1845–1865

STADTARCHIV MAINZ

Nachlass Kathinka Zitz

PESTALOZZI-FROEBEL VERBAND (BERLIN)
ARCHIV

Friedrich Froebel an Johanna Goldschmidt 17 March 1849 (typescript
copy)
Froebel Worte (typescript copy)
"Johanna Goldschmidt," *Frauen-Zeitung* 27 December 1884 (typescript
copy)
Doris Luetkens, "Lehrerinnen-Bildung durch Friedrich Froebel," *Ham-
burger Nachrichten*, No. 55 (1852), Sonderdruck
Allwine Middendorff an Friedrich Froebel 18 April 1848–13 Feb. 1849
(typescript copies)
Anna Wartburg. Vortrag: Friedrich Froebel und Hamburg (aus alten

Berichten, Briefen und Buechern zusammengestellt) gehalten
am 18 April 1932 (typescript)
Emilie Wuestenfeld an Johanna Goldschmidt [1851?] (typescript copy)

HESSISCHES HAUPTSTAATSARCHIV WIESBADEN

Nachlass Kathinka Zitz

THE STATE HISTORICAL SOCIETY OF WISCONSIN

Fritz and Mathilde Franziska Anneke Papers

NEWSPAPERS

Allgemeine Kirchen-Zeitung 23 (1844)–34 (1855).

Der Armen- und Krankenfreund. Eine Zeitschrift fuer die Diakonie der evangelischen Kirche 1849–1864. Edited by Theodor Fliedner.

Berliner Allgemeine Kirchenzeitung 6 (1844)–10 (1848).

Breslauer Volksspiegel. Eine unterhaltende und belehrende Monatsschrift zur Beleuchtung.... Edited by Ferdinand Berend, 1 (1846); continued as *Volksspiegel. Monatschrift fuer politisches u. soziales Leben* 2 (1847).

Der Demokrat (Mainz) 1 (1848)–2 (1849).

Deutsche Vierteljahrs Schrift 15 (1852)–18 (1855).

Deutschkatholisches Sonntags-Blatt (Aug.-Dec.1851). Edited by Predigern und Vorstehern sueddeutscher Gemeinden.

Fliegende Blaetter aus dem Rauhen Haus zu Horn (Sept. 1844–1856). Edited by Johann Hinrich Wichern.

Frauen-Zeitung, no. 1 (27 Sept. 1848). Edited by Mathilde Franziska Anneke.

Frauen-Zeitung 1 (1849), 2 (1850). Edited by Louise Otto; continued as *Frauen-Zeitung fuer die hoeheren weiblichen Interessen* 3 (1851)–4 (1852).

Der Freischuetz 25, nos. 69–79 (28 Aug.–2 Oct. 1849).

Fuer christkatholisches Leben. Materialien zur Geschichte der christkatholischen Kirchen 6 vols. (1845–48). Edited by Ottomar Behnsch.

Heidelberger Journal 1 (1848)–2 (1849).

Koelnische Zeitung 28 (1845)–33 (1850).

Mannheimer Abendzeitung (1845).

Paedagogische Mittheilungen fuer Eltern und Lehrer aus Literatur und Leben. ...Edited by Doris Luetkens. 2 vols. (1846–47); continued as

Unsere Kinder. Vereins-Schrift oder literarischer Sprechsaal fuer Eltern, Lehrer, Lehrerinnen. . . . 2 vols. (1849–50).

Schlesische Provinzialblaetter. Vols. 125–26 (1847)–129–30 (1849).

Schlesische Zeitung. Vol. 2 (1850).

PRIMARY SOURCES

Aston, Luise. *Meine Emancipation: Verweisung und Rechtfertigung.* Brussels: C. G. Vogler, 1846.

Benfey, Rudolf. "Friedrich Froebels Kindergartenbriefe, Herausg. Hermann Poesche." *Rheinische Blaetter fuer Erziehung und Unterricht* N.F. 62 (Jan.-Feb. 1888): 54–66.

Bergmann, Alfred, ed. "Fuenfzehn Briefe Carl Volkhausens an Malwida von Meysenbug a.d.J. 1849–52." *Mittheilungen aus der Lippischen Geschichte und Landeskunde* 23 (1954): 159–243.

Brugger, J. Dominik C. *Der Deutschkatholizismus in seiner Entwicklung dargestellt in der Geschichte der deutschkatholischen Gemeinde zu Heidelberg.* 2 vols. Heidelberg: Bangel und Schmitt, 1852.

Campe, Joachim Heinrich. *Vaeterlicher Rath fuer meine Tochter. Ein Gegenstueck zum Theophon.* Der erwachsenen weiblichen Jugend gewidmet. Brunswick: Schulbuchhandlung, 1791.

Diesterweg, Friedrich Adolf Wilhelm. *Saemtliche Werke.* Edited by Heinrich Deiters et al. 15 vols. to date. Berlin: Volk und Wissen Volkseigener Verlag, 1956– .

Dittmar, Louise. *Das Wesen der Ehe.* Leipzig: O. Wigand, 1850.

Dueringsfeld, Ida von. *Lieder meiner Kirche.* Breslau: Kern, 1845.

Feuerbach, Ludwig. *The Essence of Christianity.* Translated by George Eliot. Harper Torchbooks, 1957.

[Fliedner, Theodor]. *Das erste Jahr-Zehnt der Diakonissen-Anstalt.* Kaiserswerth: Buchhandlung der Diakonissenanstalt, 1847.

——— *Das zweite Jahr-Zehnt der Diakonissen-Anstalt.* Kaiserswerth: Buchhandlung der Diakonissenanstalt, 1857.

Frick, Ida. *Der Frauen Sclaventhum und Freiheit. Ein Traum am Hans-Heiling-Felsen.* Allen deutschen Frauen und Jungfrauen gewidmet. Dresden and Leipzig: Arnoldische Buchhandlung, 1845.

Froebel, Friedrich. *Mottoes and Commentaries of Friedrich Froebel's Mother Play.* Edited and translated by Henrietta R. Eliot and Susan E. Blow. New York: D. Appleton & Co., 1899.

Froebel, Friedrich et al. "Einladung zu einer Versammlung von Volkslehrern und Freunden deutscher Volkserziehung, besonders von Kindergaerten, zu Rudolstadt, am 17.–19. August 1848." *Allgemeine Schulzeitung,* no. 120 (30 July 1848): 969.

Froebel, Johanna geb. Kuestner. "Schule und Familie." *Rheinische Blaetter fuer Erziehung und Unterricht* N.F. 44 (July-Aug.): 71–76.

Froebel, Karl and Johanna Kuestner. *Hochschulen fuer Maedchen und Kindergaerten als Glieder einer vollstaendigen Bildungsanstalt welche Erziehung fuer Familie und Unterricht der Schule verbindet, nebst Briefen ueber diesen Gegenstand als Programm zu den Plaenen der Hochschule fuer das weibliche Geschlecht in Hamburg.* Hamburg: G. W. Niemeyer, 1849.

Geffcken, Dr. J. (Prediger zu St. Michaelis). *Statistische Tabellen ueber die kirchlichen Verhaeltnisse Hamburgs in den letzten fuenfundzwanzig Jahren 1818–1842.* Mit Anmerkungen begleitet. Hamburg: Perthes-Besser und Mauke, 1843.

Gervinus, Georg. *Die Mission der Deutsch-Katholiken.* Heidelberg: C. F. Winter, 1845.

Gluemer, Claire von. *Fata Morgana. Ein Roman aus dem Jahr 1848.* Leipzig: Otto Wigand, 1851.

[Goldschmidt, Johanna]. "Zur Sache Friedrich Froebels. Herr Dr. Gutzkow und die Froebelschen Kindergaerten." *Rheinische Blaetter fuer Erziehung und Unterricht* N.F. 47 (May-June 1853): 325–46.

Goltz, Bogumil. *Zur Charakteristik und Naturgeschichte der Frauen.* Berlin: Janke, 1863.

Herz, Auguste. "Ueber die sittliche Bildung der Kinder und deren ersten Religionsunterricht in dem Kindergarten." *Friedrich Froebels Wochenschrift. Ein Einigungsblatt fuer alle Freunde der Menschenbildung,* no. 13 (1 April 1850): 97–101.

Hudtwalcker, Martin Hieronymus. *Ein halbes Jahrhundert aus meiner Lebensgeschichte.* Hamburg: Agentur des Rauhen Hauses, 1862–64.

Jahresberichte des Frauen-Vereins zur Unterstuetzung der Armenpflege 1 (1849)–13 (1862). Hamburg: Druck von Kniesch und W. Gente, Kniesch Nachf., 1850–63.

"Die Lehrerversammlung in Rudolstadt am 17., 18., 19. Aug. 1848." *Allgemeine Schulzeitung,* no. 166 (19. Oct. 1848): 1337–40.

Leppla, Rupprecht, ed. "Johanna und Gottfried Kinkels Briefe an Kathinka Zitz 1849–1861." *Bonner Geschichtsblaetter* 12 (1958): 7–61.

Lewald-Stahr, Fanny. *Clementine. Auf rother Erde . . . Gesammelte Werke.* Vol. 8. Berlin: Janke, 1872.

———. *Eine Lebensfrage. Roman.* Rev. ed. *Gesammelte Werke.* Vol. 10. Berlin: Janke, 1872.

Luetkens, Doris. geb. von Cossel. "Friedrich Froebel und sein Erziehungsprincip." *Hamburger Nachrichten,* no. 38 (13 Feb. 1852): 3.

———. *Froebel'sche Kindergaerten. Eine Beantwortung der kleinen Schrift von J. Foelsing: "Froebel'sche Kindergaerten."* Hamburg: Perthes-Besser & Mauke, 1849.

———— "Kindergarten des Instituts Luetkens in Hamburg." *Rheinische Blaetter fuer Erziehung und Unterricht* N.F. 47 (May-June 1853): 348–51.

Meysenbug, Malwida von. *Memoiren einer Idealistin.* Volksausgabe. 3 vols in 2. Berlin: Schuster und Loeffler, 1907.

———— "Frauenschwur zur Demokratie." *Sonntagsblaetter. Beiblatt zum Mainzer Tagblatt,* no. 1 (22 Sept. 1850).

Monod, Gabriel, ed. "Briefe von Malwida von Meysenbug an ihre Mutter 1850–52." *Deutsche Revue. Eine Monatsschrift* 30, no. 3 (July-Sept. 1905): 217–26; no. 4 (Oct.-Dec. 1905): 229–41, 344–53; 31, no. 1 (Jan.-March 1906): 359–70.

Otto, Louise. "Auch ein Wort ueber den 30. November in Dresden." *Der Wandelstern. Blaetter fuer Unterhaltung, Literatur, Kunst, und Theater,* no. 52 (1845): 1054–58.

———— *Das erste Vierteljahrhundert des Allgemeinen deutschen Frauenvereins gegruendet am 18. Oktober 1865 in Leipzig.* Leipzig: Kommissions-Verlag von Moritz Schaefer, 1890.

———— *Roemisch und Deutsch. Roman.* 4 vols. Leipzig: Adolph Wienbrack, 1847.

———— "Roemisch und Deutsch." *Der Wandelstern. Blaetter fuer Unterhaltung, Literatur, Kunst und Theater,* no. 9 (1845): 185–87.

———— [Otto Stern]. "Gegen Jesuiten und Jesuitismus." *Der Wandelstern. Blaetter fuer Unterhaltung, Literatur, Kunst und Theater,* no. 18 (1845): 388–89.

———— [Otto Stern]. "Gott im Himmel sieh darein." *Der Wandelstern. Blaetter fuer Unterhaltung, Literatur, Kunst und Theater,* no. 21 (1845): 437–38.

Passavant, Rev. W. A., ed. "Inner Mission." *The Missionary. A Monthly Periodical Devoted to the Work of Inner, Home and Foreign Missions in the American Lutheran Church* 4 (Jan. 1851): 2.

[Poel, Emma]. *Denkwuerdigkeiten aus dem Leben von Amalie Sieveking* in deren Auftrage von einer Freundin derselben verfasst mit einem Vorwort von Dr. Wichern. Hamburg: Agentur des Rauhen Hauses, 1860.

[Poel, Emma and Sophie Wattenbach]. *Arbeit der Frauen in Vereinen fuer Armen- und Krankenpflege. Ein Briefwechsel zweier Freundinnen.* Eingefuehrt durch Amalie Sieveking. Berlin: Verlag von Wilhelm Hertz, 1854.

Poesche, Hermann, ed. *Friedrich Froebels Kindergartenbriefe.* Vienna and Leipzig: Pichlers Wwe. und Sohn, 1887.

R. "Die Frauen. Eine social-politische Studie." *Deutsche Vierteljahrs-Schrift* 15, no. 3 (1852): 236–96.

Riehl, Wilhelm Heinrich. *Die Naturgeschichte des Volkes als Grundlage einer deutschen Sozial-Politik.* 3 vols. Vol. 3, *Die Familie.* Stuttgart: Cotta'sche Buchhandlung, 1855.

Ronge, Johannes. *Aufruf an die deutschen Maenner und Frauen nebst Grundstimmungen der freien Kirche.* Hamburg: G. W. Niemeyer, 1850.

——— *Maria, oder: Die Stellung der Frauen in der alten und neuen Zeit. Eine Erwiderung auf das Rundschreiben des Papstes wegen dringender Verehrung der Maria.* Hamburg: G. W. Niemeyer, 1849.

——— *Religion und Politik.* Frankfurt a.M.: Literarische Anstalt, 1850.

Ronge, Johannes and Bertha. *A Practical Guide to the English Kindergarten [Children's Garden]; for the Use of Mothers, Nursery Governesses and Infant Teachers....* accompanied by a great variety of ... songs set to music and arranged for the exercises. London: A. L. Myers & Co., 1871.

Schleiermacher, Friedrich Daniel. *Katechismus der Vernunft fuer Edle Frauen* mit einem Nachwort von Herbert Thiele. Neustadt an der Haardt: Musen-Verlag, 1947.

——— *Werke: Auswahl.* Edited by Otto Braun and D. Joh. Bauer. 4 vols. Leipzig: Felix Meiner, [1910]. Vol 3, *Predigten ueber den christlichen Hausstand: Ueber die Ehe* (1818).

"Schriften ueber die Reform des preuss. Eherechts," *Allgemeine Literatur Zeitung* 135, nos. 129–34 (July 1843): 417–22, 425–64.

Schuselka, Franz. *Das deutsch-katholische Priestertum, mit einer Erinnerung....* Weimar: Wilhelm, 1846.

——— *Deutsche Worte eines Oesterreichers.* Hamburg: Hoffmann und Campe, 1845.

——— *Die freie Kirche und die alte Politik.* Leipzig: Weidmann'sche Buchhandlung, 1845.

Seele, Ida. "Meine Erinnerungen an Friedrich Froebel." *Kindergarten* 27 (1886): 132–35.

[Sieveking, Amalie W.] *Berichte ueber die Leistungen des weiblichen Vereins fuer Armen- und Krankenpflege* 1 (1832)–25 (1856). Hamburg: Langhoff'sche Buchdruckerei, 1833–57.

Voght, Caspar Freiherr von. *Account of the Management of the Poor in Hamburg since the Year 1788.* London: reprinted by G. Davidson, 1817.

"Wider die hoeheren Toechteranstalten. Ein Beitrag zur 'Emancipation von den Frauen.'" *Deutsche Vierteljahrs-Schrift* 18, no. 4 (1855): 223–73.

Wiener-Pappenheim, Anna. "Froebels Idee der Muetterbildung in ihrer geschichtlichen Entwicklung." *Kindergarten* 68 (1927): 241–46.

SECONDARY SOURCES

Ahlstrom, Sydney E. "The Romantic Religious Revolution and the Dilemmas of Religious History." *Church History* 46 (1977): 149–70.

Albisetti, James, C. "Could Separate be Equal? Helene Lange and Women's Education in Imperial Germany." *History of Education Quarterly* 22 (1982): 301–18.

Alexander, Edgar. "Church and Society in Germany: Social and Political Movements and Ideas in German and Austrian Catholicism 1789–1950." *Church and Society: Catholic Social and Political Thought and Movement 1789–1950.* Edited by Joseph N. Moody. New York: Arts Inc., 1953.

Allen, Ann Taylor. "Spiritual Motherhood: German Feminists and the Kindergarten Movement, 1848–1911." *History of Education Quarterly* 22 (1982): 319–39.

Baasch, Ernst. *Geschichte Hamburgs 1814–1918.* 2 vols. Gotha-Stuttgart: Friedrich A. Perthes, 1924.

Baeumer, Gertrud. *Gestalt und Wandel: Frauenbildnisse.* Berlin: F. A. Herbig, 1939.

Baumeister, H. *Das Privatrecht der freien und Hansestadt Hamburg.* 2 vols. Hamburg: Hoffmann und Campe, 1856.

Bavendamm, Dirk. *Von der Revolution zur Reform: Die Verfassungspolitik des hamburgischen Senats 1849–50.* Schriften zur Verfassungsgeschichte, vol. 10. Berlin: Duncker und Humblot, 1969.

Beckmann, Hanna. *Evangelische Frauen in bahnbrechender Liebestaetigkeit im 19. Jahrhundert.* Quellenheft 20 zum Frauenleben in der Geschichte. Berlin: F. A. Herbig, [1927].

Bergemann, Hans Georg. *Staat und Kirche in Hamburg waehrend des 19. Jahrhunderts.* Arbeiten zur Kirchengeschichte Hamburgs, vol. 1. Hamburg: Friedrich Wittig Verlag, 1958.

Berkner, Lutz K. "The Stem Family and the Developmental Cycle of the Peasant Household: An Eighteenth-Century Austrian Example." *American Historical Review* 77 (1972): 398–418.

Beuys, Barbara. *Familienleben in Deutschland: Neue Bilder aus der deutschen Vergangenheit.* Reinbeck bei Hamburg: Rowohlt Verlag, 1980.

Beyreuther, Erich. *Die Erweckungsbewegung.* Die Kirche in ihrer Geschichte. Ein Handbuch, edited by K. D. Schmidt and Ernst Wolf. Vol. 4, "R," part 1. Goettingen: Vandenhoeck und Rupprecht, 1963.

Bigler, Robert M. *The Politics of German Protestantism: The Rise of the*

Protestant Church Elite in Prussia 1815–1848. Berkeley, Los Angeles, London: University of California Press, 1972.

Blos, Anna. *Die Frauen der Revolution von 1848: Zehn Lebensbilder und ein Vorwort.* Dresden: Kaden, 1928.

Brunner, Otto. "Das ganze Haus und die alteuropaeische Oekonomik." *Neue Wege der Verfassungs- und Sozialgeschichte.* Goettingen: Vandenhoeck und Rupprecht, 1956.

Conze, Werner, ed. *Sozialgeschichte der Familie in der Neuzeit Europas.* Stuttgart: Klett-Cotta Verlag, 1976.

Cott, Nancy F. *The Bonds of Womanhood: "Women's Sphere" in New England, 1780–1835.* New Haven and London: Yale University Press, 1977.

Dalton, Hermann. *Johannes Gossner: Ein Lebensbild aus der Kirche des neunzehnten Jahrhunderts.* Berlin: Gossner, 1874.

Derwein, Herbert. "Heidelberg im Vormaerz und in der Revolution 1848–49. Ein Stueck Badischer Buergergeschichte." *Neue Heidelberger Jahrbuecher 1955–56,* edited by the Universitaetsgesellschaft Heidelberg.

Douglas, Ann. *The Feminization of American Culture.* New York: Alfred A. Knopf, 1977.

Droz, Jacques. "Die religioesen Sekten und die Revolution von 1848." *Archiv fuer Sozialgeschichte* 3 (1963): 109–18.

Duden, Barbara. "Das schoene Eigentum. Zur Herausbildung des buergerlichen Frauenbildes an der Wende vom 18. zum 19. Jahrhundert." *Kursbuch 47,* edited by Karl Markus Michel and Harald Wieser (March 1977): 125–42.

Engelsing, Rolf. *Zur Sozialgeschichte deutscher Mittel- und Unterschichten.* 2d ed. Goettingen: Vandenhoeck und Rupprecht, 1978.

Esselborn, Karl. *Der Deutschkatholizismus in Darmstadt.* Schriften zur Hessischen Geschichte, Landes- und Volkskunde 1. Darmstadt: Verlag der Litera, 1923.

Evans, Richard J. "Feminism and Female Emancipation in Germany 1870–1945: Sources, Methods and Problems of Research." *Central European History* 9 (1976): 323–51.

————— *The Feminist Movement in Germany 1894–1933.* SAGE Studies in Twentieth Century History 6. London and Beverly Hills: SAGE Publications, 1976.

————— *The Feminists: Women's Emancipation Movements in Europe, America and Australasia 1840–1920.* London: Croom Helm; New York: Barnes and Noble, 1977.

————— "Liberalism and Society: The Feminist Movement and Social Change." *Society and Politics in Wilhelmine Germany.* Edited by R. J. Evans. London: Croom Helm, 1978.

───── "Women's History: The Limits of Reclamation." *Social History* 5 (1980): 273–81.

Evans, Richard J. and W. R. Lee, eds. *The German Family: Essays on the Social History of the Family in Nineteenth- and Twentieth-Century Germany.* London: Croom Helm; Totowa, N.J.: Barnes and Noble, 1980.

Feiner, Josef. *Anton Rée: Ein Kaempfer fuer Fortschritt und Recht.* Hamburg: A. Janssen, 1916.

Fischer, Fritz. "Der deutsche Protestantismus und die Politik im 19. Jahrhundert." *Historische Zeitschrift* 171 (1951): 473–518.

Fliedner, Georg. *Theodor Fliedner. Durch Gottes Gnade Erneurer des apostolischen Diakonissenamtes in der evangelischen Kirche: Sein Leben und Wirken.* 3 vols. Kaiserswerth: Buchhandlung der Diakonissenanstalt, 1908–12.

Fout, John C., ed. *German Women in the Nineteenth Century: A Social History.* New York and London: Holmes and Meier, 1984.

Freudenthal, Herbert. *Vereine in Hamburg: Ein Beitrag zur Geschichte und Volkskunde der Geselligkeit.* Hamburg: Museum fuer Hamburgische Geschichte, 1968.

Gehrmann, Max. *Geschichte der freireligioesen Gemeinde in Offenbach am Main.* Offenbacher Geschichtsblaetter no. 18. Offenbach Geschichtsverein, 1968.

Gerhard, Ute. *Verhaeltnisse und Verhinderungen: Frauenarbeit, Familie und Rechte der Frauen im 19. Jahrhundert. Mit Dokumenten.* Frankfurt a.M.: Suhrkamp Verlag, 1978.

Gerhardt, Martin von. *Theodor Fliedner: Ein Lebensbild.* 2 vols. Duesseldorf-Kaiserswerth: Verlag der Buchhandlung der Diakonissenanstalt Kaiserswerth, 1933–37.

───── *Johann Hinrich Wichern: Ein Lebensbild.* 3 vols. Hamburg: Buchhandlung des Rauhen Hauses, 1927–31.

Gerhard, Ute, Elisabeth Hannover-Drueck, and Romina Schmitter, eds. *"Dem Reich der Freiheit werb' ich Buergerinnen." Die Frauen-Zeitung von Louise Otto.* Frankfurt a.M.: Syndikat, 1979.

Gillis, John R. *The Prussian Bureaucracy in Crisis 1840–1860: Origins of an Administrative Ethos.* Stanford, Calif.: Stanford University Press, 1971.

Goltz, Eduard Freiherr von der. *Deutsche Frauenarbeit der Kriegszeit.* 2d ed. Leipzig: J. C. Hinrichs'sche Buchhandlung, 1915.

Greven-Aschoff, Barbara. *Die buergerliche Frauenbewegung in Deutschland 1894–1933.* Kritische Studien zur Geschichtswissenschaft 46. Goettingen: Vandenhoeck und Rupprecht, 1981.

Hackett, Amy. "The German Women's Movement and Suffrage, 1890–

1914: A Study of National Feminism." *Modern European Social History*. Edited by Robert J. Bezucha. Lexington, Mass., Toronto, London: D. C. Heath, 1971.

———— The Politics of Feminism in Wilhelmine Germany 1899–1918. Ph.D. dissertation, Columbia University, 1976.

Hamerow, Theodor S. *Restoration, Revolution, Reaction: Economics and Politics in Germany 1815–1871*. Princeton: Princeton University Press, 1958.

Haupt, Elisabeth. *Amalie Sieveking als Gruenderin des weiblichen Vereins fuer Armen- und Krankenpflege in Hamburg*. Berlin-Spandau: Wichern Verlag, 1933.

Hausen, Karin. "Family and Role-Division: The Polarisation of Sexual Stereotypes in the Nineteenth Century—An Aspect of the Dissociation of Work and Family Life." *The German Family*. Edited by R. J. Evans and W. R. Lee. London: Croom Helm, 1980.

Heiland, Helmut. *Literatur und Trends in der Froebel Forschung. Ein kritischer Literatur-Bericht*. Literatur und Forschungsberichte zur Paedagogik, 1. Weinheim: Beltz Verlag, 1972.

Holborn, Hajo. "Der deutsche Idealismus in sozial-geschichtlicher Beleuchtung." *Historische Zeitschrift* 174 (1952): 359–84.

———— *A History of Modern Germany: The Reformation*. New York: Alfred A. Knopf, 1959.

———— *A History of Modern Germany: 1648–1840*. New York: Alfred A. Knopf, 1964.

Huber, Ernst Rudolf. *Deutsche Verfassungsgeschichte seit 1789*. 2 vols. Stuttgart, Berlin, Cologne, Mainz: W. Kohlhammer Verlag, 1960.

Hummel-Haasis, Gerlinde, ed. *Schwestern, zerreisst eure Ketten. Zeugnisse zur Geschichte der Frauen in der Revolution von 1848–49*. Munich: Deutscher Taschenbuch Verlag, 1982.

Joeres, Ruth-Ellen Boetcher. *Die Anfaenge der deutschen Frauenbewegung: Louise Otto-Peters*. Die Frau in der Gesellschaft. Texte und Lebensgeschichten, edited by Gisela Brinker-Gabler. Frankfurt a.M.: Fischer Taschenbuch Verlag, 1983.

———— "Louise Otto and Her Journals: A Chapter in Nineteenth-Century German Feminism." *Internationales Archiv fuer Sozialgeschichte der deutschen Literatur* 4 (1979): 100–129.

Joeres, Ruth-Ellen B. and Mary Jo Maynes, eds. *German Women in the Eighteenth and Nineteenth Century: A Social and Literary History*. Bloomington: Indiana University Press, 1986.

Joerg, Joseph Edmund. *Geschichte des Protestantismus in seiner neuesten Entwicklung*. Freiburg i.B.: Herder'scher Verlag, 1858.

Kaplan, Marion A. *The Jewish Feminist Movement in Germany: The Campaigns of the Juedischer Frauenbund, 1904–1938.* Contributions in Women's Studies, no. 8, Westport, Conn. and London: Greenwood Press, 1979.

Karstaedt, Otto. "Das preussische Kindergartenverbot 1851. Eine Uebersicht bisher nicht beruecksichtigter Urkunden." *Kindergarten* 70 (1929): 25–34.

Katzenbach, Friedrich Wilhelm. *Geschichte des Protestantismus von 1789–1848.* Guetersloh: Guetersloher Verlagshaus, 1969.

Kaufmann, Georg. "Treitschkes Urtheil ueber Johannes Ronge." *Historische Zeitschrift* 99 (1907): 515–30.

Kayser, Rudolf. "Charlotte Paulsen." *Hamburgische Geschichts- und Heimatsblaetter* 2 (1926): 33–43.

———— "Die deutsch-katholische Bewegung in Hamburg." *Zeitschrift des Vereins fuer Hamburgische Geschichte* 26 (1925): 147–68.

———— "Friedrich Perthes und das religioese Leben seiner Zeit." *Zeitschrift des Vereins fuer Hamburgische Geschichte* 25 (1924): 89–109.

———— "Friedrich Perthes und seine katholischen Freunde." *Zeitschrift des Vereins fuer Hamburgische Geschichte* 34 (1934): 1–24.

———— "Henri Merle d'Aubigné und die Anfaenge der Erweckung in Hamburg." *Zeitschrift des Vereins fuer Hamburgische Geschichte* 30 (1929): 106–35.

———— "Malwida von Meysenbugs Hamburger Lehrjahre." *Zeitschrift des Vereins fuer Hamburgische Geschichte* 28 (1927): 116–28.

Kissling, Johannes Baptist. *Der deutsche Protestantismus 1817–1917: Eine geschichtliche Darstellung.* 2 vols. Muenster in Westf.: Aschendorff, 1917–18.

Kloetzer, Wolfgang. "Johannes Ronge an die Frauen von Worms [1846]. Zur Geschichte der deutschkatholischen Bewegung." *Der Wormsgau* 3, no. 7 (1958): 479–80.

Kolbe, Guenter. "Demokratische Opposition in religioesem Gewande: Zur Geschichte der deutsch-katholischen Bewegung in Sachsen am Vorabend der Revolution von 1848–49." *Zeitschrift fuer Geschichtswissenschaft* 20 (1972): 1102–12.

Koellmann, Wolfgang and Peter Marschalck. *Bevoelkerungsgeschichte.* Cologne: Kiepenheuer und Witsch, 1972.

Kollmann, Paul. *Die Wirksamkeit der Allgemeinen Armenanstalt der Stadt Hamburg von 1788 bis 1870.* Hamburg: O. Meissner, 1871.

Kortmann, Marie. "Aus den Anfaengen sozialer Frauenarbeit." *Frau. Monatschrift fuer das gesammte Frauenleben unserer Zeit* 20 (1913): 425–34, 467–72.

———— *Emilie Wuestenfeld: Eine Hamburger Buergerin.* Hamburgische Hausbibliothek. Hamburg: Georg Westermann, 1927.

Koselleck, Reinhard. *Preussen zwischen Reform und Revolution: Allgemeines Landrecht, Verwaltung und soziale Bewegung von 1791 bis 1848.* Industrielle Welt. Schriftreihe des Arbeitskreises fuer moderne Sozialgeschichte, edited by Werner Conze, vol. 7. Stuttgart: Ernst Klett Verlag, 1967.

Kraus, Antje. *Die Unterschichten Hamburgs in der ersten Haelfte des 19. Jahrhunderts: Entstehung, Struktur und Lebensverhaeltnisse: Eine historisch-kritische Untersuchung.* Sozialwissenschaftliche Studien: Schriftreihe de Seminars fuer Sozialwissenschaft der Universitaet Hamburg 9. Stuttgart: Gustav Fischer Verlag, 1965.

Krieger, Leonard. *The German Idea of Freedom: History of a Political Tradition.* Boston: Beacon Press, 1957.

Krohn, Helga. *Die Juden in Hamburg. Die politische, soziale und kulturelle Entwicklung einer juedischen Grosstadtgemeinde nach der Emanzipation 1848–1918.* Hamburger Beitraege zur Geschichte der deutschen Juden 4. Hamburg: Hans Christians Verlag, 1974.

——— *Die Juden in Hamburg 1800–1850: Ihre soziale, kulturelle und politische Entwicklung waehrend der Emanzipationszeit.* Hamburger Studien zur neueren Geschichte 9.

Kuhn, Annette and Ruth-Ellen B. Joeres, eds. *Frauen in der Geschichte VI: Frauenbilder und Frauenwirklichkeiten: Interdisziplinaere Studien zur Frauengeschichte in Deutschland im 18. und 19. Jahrhundert.* Studienmaterialien Band 26: Geschichtsdidaktik. Duesseldorf: Paedagogischer Verlag Schwann-Bagel, 1985.

LaVolpa, Anthony J. *Prussian Schoolteachers: Profession and Office, 1763–1848.* Chapel Hill: University of North Carolina Press, 1980.

Lee, W. R. "Bastardy and the Socioeconomic Structure of South Germany." *Journal of Interdisciplinary History* 7 (1977): 403–25.

Lehmann, Hartmut. "Pietism and Nationalism: The Relationship between Protestant Revivalism and National Renewal in Nineteenth-Century Germany." *Church History* 51 (1982): 39–53.

Liese, Wilhelm. *Geschichte der Caritas.* 2 vols. Freiburg i.B.: Caritasverlag, 1922.

Lyschinska, Mary J. *Henriette Schrader-Breymann: Ihr Leben aus Briefen und Tagebuechern.* 2 vols. Berlin and Leipzig: Walter de Gruyter u. Co., 1922.

Magnus-Hausen, Frances. "Ziel und Weg in der deutschen Frauenbewegung des XIX. Jahrhunderts." *Deutscher Staat und deutsche Parteien . . . Friedrich Meinecke zum 60. Geburtstag dargebracht.* Edited by Paul Wentscke. Munich and Berlin: R. Oldenbourg, 1922.

Medick, Hans. "The Proto-industrial Family Economy: The Structural Function of Household and Family during the Transition from

Peasant Society to Industrial Capitalism." *Social History* 1 (1976): 291–315.

Meyer, Heinrich Ad. *Erinnerungen an Heinrich Christian Meyer: Stockmeyer.* Introduction by Victor Bohmert. Hamburgische Liebhaberbibliothek, edited by Alfred Lichtwark. Hamburg: Printed by Lutcke und Wulff, 1900.

Moehrmann, Renate. *Die andere Frau: Emanzipationsansaetze deutscher Schriftstellerinnen im Vorfeld der Achtundvierziger-Revolution.* Stuttgart: J. B. Metzler, 1977.

———, ed. *Frauenemanzipation im deutschen Vormaerz. Texte und Dokumente.* Stuttgart: Philipp Reclam Jun., 1978.

Moeller, Kurt Detlev. "Beitraege zur Geschichte des kirchlichen und religioesen Lebens in Hamburg in den ersten Jahrzehnten des 19. Jahrhunderts." *Zeitschrift des Vereins fuer Hamburgische Geschichte* 27 (1926): 1–129.

Morgenstern, Lina. "Die ersten Pionierinnen der Lehre Friedrich Froebels." *Kindergarten* 43 (1902): 200–203.

——— "Johanna Goldschmidt." *Kindergarten* 26 (1888): 6–9.

Mueller, Karl. *Kulturreaktion in Preussen im 19. Jahrhundert.* Mit einem Anhang: Briefe Froebels und Diesterwegs. Berlin: Verlag fuer Kulturpolitik Berlin, 1929.

Mueller, Maria. *Frauen im Dienste Froebels. Wilhelmine Hoffmeister, Bertha von Marienholtz-Buelow, Henriette Schrader-Breymann, Henriette Goldschmidt.* Forschungen zur Geschichte der Philosophie und der Paedagogik, 11. Leipzig: Felix Meiner, 1928.

Noyes, P. H. *Organization and Revolution: Working Class Associations in the German Revolutions of 1848–49.* Princeton: Princeton University Press, 1966.

O'Boyle, Leonore. "The Problem of an Excess of Educated Men in Western Europe 1800–1850." *Journal of Modern History* 42 (1970): 471–95.

Pataky, Sophie. *Lexikon deutscher Frauen der Feder. Eine Zusammenstellung der seit dem Jahre 1840 erschienenen Werke weiblicher Autoren,* nebst Biographieen der Lebenden und einem Verzeichnis der Pseudonyme. 2 vols. Berlin: C. Pataky, 1898.

Perthes, Klemens Theodor. *Friedrich Perthes Leben.* Nach dessen schriftlichen und muendlichen Mittheilungen aufgezeichnet. 3 vols. Gotha: F. A. Perthes, 1855.

Plothau, Anna. *Die Begruenderinnen der deutschen Frauenbewegung.* Leipzig: Friedrich Rothbarth, 1907.

[Prelinger], Catherine M. Holden. "A Decade of Dissent in Germany: An historical study of the German-Catholic Church and the Society of Protestant Friends." Ph.D. dissertation, Yale University, 1954.

Prelinger, Catherine M. "Diversity and Uniformity: Women and the Religious Awakening in Early Nineteenth Century Germany." Paper read at the Fourth Berkshire Conference on the History of Women, Mount Holyoke College, August 23–5, 1978.

——— "The German-Catholic Church: From National Hope to Regional Reality." *The Consortium on Revolutionary Europe Proceedings 1976*. Athens, Ga.: The Consortium on Revolutionary Europe, 1978.

——— "The Religious Context of Mid-Nineteenth Century German Feminism." Paper read at the Annual Convention of the American Historical Association, 1976.

——— "Religious Dissent, Women's Rights, and the Hamburger Hochschule fuer das weibliche Geschlecht in Mid-Nineteenth-Century Germany." *Church History* 45 (1976): 42–55.

Prochaska, F. K. "Women in English Philanthropy 1790–1830." *International Review of Social History* 19 (1970): 426–45.

Quartaert, Jean H. *Reluctant Feminists in German Social Democracy 1885–1917*. Princeton: Princeton University Press, 1979.

Remé, Richard. *Amalie Sieveking: Eine Vorkampferin der christlichen Frauenbewegung*. Hamburg: Agentur des Rauhen Hauses, 1911.

Riedl, Kurt Emil. "Die Dresdener Kindergaertnerin Auguste Herz geb. Kachler." Karl Krause Schriftkreis. Sondersende 3. Dresden: n.p., 1941 (mimeographed).

Ritter, Gustav. *Kirchlich-Statistische Zusammenstellungen ueber die christlichen Stadt- und Land-Gemeinden Hamburgs*, Vierzehnter Jahrgang 1878. Hamburg: Graefe, 1879.

Roesche, Hugo and Auguste Schmidt. *Louise Otto-Peters: Ein Lebensbild*. Leipzig: I. Voigtlaender, [1898].

Rohr, Donald G. *The Origins of Social Liberalism in Germany*. Chicago and London: University of Chicago Press, 1963.

Ruether, Rosemary R. and Eleanor McLaughlin, eds. *Women of Spirit: Female Leadership in the Jewish and Christian Traditions*. New York: Simon and Schuster, 1979.

Ryan, Mary P. *The Empire of the Mother: American Writing about Domesticity 1830–1860*. Women and History nos. 2/3. New York: The Institute for Historical Research and The Haworth Press, 1982.

Sachsse, Christoph and Florian Tennstedt. *Geschichte der Armenfuersorge in Deutschland vom Spaetmittelalter bis zum Ersten Weltkrieg*. Stuttgart, Berlin, Cologne, Mainz: W. Kohlhammer, 1980.

Schaffenorth, Gerda. "Freunde in Christus. Die Beziehung von Mann

und Frau bei Luther im Rahmen seines Kirchenverstaendnisses."
'*Freunde in Christus werden . . .' Die Beziehung von Mann und Frau als Frage an Theologie und Kirche,* by Gerda Schaffenorth and Klaus Traede. Gelnhauser, Berlin: Burckhardthaus-Verlag; Stein/Mfr: Laetare Verlag, 1977.

Schieder, Wolfgang. "Kirche und Revolution: Sozialgeschichtliche Aspekte der Trierer Wallfahrt von 1844." *Archiv fuer Sozialgeschichte* 4 (1974): 419–54.

——— "Religionsgeschichte als Sozialgeschichte: Einleitende Bemerkungen zur Forschungsproblematik." *Geschichte und Gesellschaft. Zeitschrift fuer Historische Sozialwissenschaft* 3 (1977): 291–98.

Schleicher, Berta. *Malwida von Meysenbug.* Die Grossen Vorbilder 9. Wedel in Holstein, Alsterverlag, 1947.

Schnabel, Franz. *Deutsche Geschichte im neunzehnten Jahrhundert.* 4 vols., 3d. ed. Freiburg i.B.: Verlag Herder, 1948–55.

Schramm, Percy Ernst. *Hamburg, Deutschland und die Welt. Leistung und Grenzen hanseatischen Buergertums in der Zeit zwischen Napoleon und Bismarck.* Munich: Universitaetsverlag Georg D. W. Callwey, 1943.

Semmig, Jeanne Berta. *Louise Otto Peters: Lebensbild einer deutschen Kaempferin.* Berlin: Union Verlag, [1957].

Sengelmann, H. *Die Gegenwart der evangelisch-Lutherischen Kirche Hamburgs dargestellet, aus ihrer Vergangeheit erklaert, und nach ihren Forderungen fuer die Zukunft gedeutet.* Beilage II: Vereine, Stiftungen und Untersuchungen zur Abhuelfe leiblicher und geistiger Noth und zur Foerderung der sittlichen Wohlfahrt, ohne Zuthun des Staates und der Kirche gestiftet in den letzten 50 Jahren (1811–1861). Hamburg: Oncken, 1862.

Shanahan, William O. *German Protestants Face the Social Question. Vol. I: The Conservative Phase, 1815–1871.* Notre Dame: University of Notre Dame Press, 1978.

Sheehan, James J. *German Liberalism in the Nineteenth Century.* Chicago and London: University of Chicago Press, 1978.

Shorter, Edward. *The Making of the Modern Family.* New York: Basic Books, 1975.

Sieber, Siegfried. *Ein Romantiker wird Revolutionaer. Lebensgeschichte des Freiheitskaempfers August Peters und seiner Gemahlin Louise Otto-Peters, der Vorkaempferin deutscher Frauenrechte.* Dresden: L. Ehlermann, 1949.

Sieveking, Heinrich. "Zur Geschichte der geistigen Bewegung in Hamburg nach den Freiheitskriegen." *Zeitschrift des Vereins fuer Hamburgische Geschichte* 28 (1927): 129–54.

Snell, John L. *The Democratic Movement in Germany, 1789–1914.* Edited and completed by Hans A. Schmitt. The James Sprunt Studies in History and Political Science, vol. 55. Chapel Hill: University of North Carolina Press, 1980.

Spranger, Eduard. *Die Idee einer Hochschule fuer Frauen und die Frauenbewegung.* Leipzig: Duerrsche Buchhandlung, 1916.

Stadelmann, Rudolph. *Social and Political History of the German 1848 Revolution.* Translated by James G. Chastain. Athens, Ohio: Ohio University Press, 1948.

Sticker, Anna. *Die Entstehung der neuzeitlichen Krankenpflege.* Kaiserswerth-Stuttgart: W. Kohlhammer, 1960.

────── *Friedricke Fliedner und die Anfaenge der Frauendiakonie. Ein Quellenbuch.* 2d ed. Neukirchen-Vluyn: Buchhandlung des Erziehungsvereins, 1963.

Stoeffler, F. Ernst. *German Pietism during the Eighteenth Century.* Studies in the History of Religion, 24. Leiden: E. J. Brill, 1973.

Strnad, Elfriede. *Hamburgs paedagogisches Leben in seiner Beziehung zu Friedrich Froebel.* Zur Hamburg Schulreform 6. Hamburg: Verlag der Gesellschaft d. Freunde d. vaterlaend. Schul- und Erziehungswesens, 1951.

Tiesmeyer, Ludwig. *Die Erweckungsbewegung in Deutschland waehrend des XIX. Jahrhunderts.* 16 vols. Kassel: E. Roettger, 1901–12.

Tilly, Louise A. and Joan W. Scott. "Women's Work and the Family in Nineteenth Century Europe." *The Family in History.* Edited by Charles Rosenberg. Philadelphia: University of Pennsylvania Press, 1976.

Tilly, Louise A., Joan W. Scott, and Miriam Cohen. "Women's Work and European Fertility Patterns." *Journal of Interdisciplinary History* 6 (1976): 447–76.

Tischhauser, Christian. *Geschichte der evangelischen Kirche in der ersten Haelfte des 19. Jahrhunderts.* Basel: R. Reich, 1900.

Twellmann, Margrit. *Die deutsche Frauenbewegung. Ihre Anfaenge und erste Entwicklung.* Marburger Abhandlungen zur politischen Wissenschaft, vol. 17, 1/2, edited by Wolfgang Abendrot. Meisenheim am Glan: Anton Hain, 1972.

Uhlhorn, Gerhard. *Die christliche Liebestaetigkeit.* 2d rev. ed. Stuttgart: Verlag von D. Gundert, 1895.

Valentin, Veit. *Geschichte der deutschen Revolution.* 2 vols. Berlin: Verlag Ullstein, 1930–31.

Voss, Jo. *Geschichte der Berliner Froebel-Bewegung.* Weimar: Boehlau, 1937.

Wagner, Maria. *Mathilde Franziska Anneke in Selbstzeugnissen und Dokumenten.* Frankfurt a.M.: Fischer Taschenbuch Verlag, 1980.

Walker, Mack. *German Home Towns: Community, State and General Estate 1648–1871*. Ithaca, N.Y. and London: Cornell University Press, 1971.

———— *Germany and the Emigration 1816–1885*. Cambridge, Mass.: Harvard University Press, 1964.

Wangemann, Hermann. *Sieben Buecher preussischer Kirchengeschichte: Eine aktenmaessige Darstellung des Kampfes um die Lutherische Kirche im XIX. Jahrhundert*. 3 vols. Berlin: W. Schultze, 1860.

Weber-Kellermann, Ingeborg. *Die deutsche Familie: Versuch einer Sozialgeschichte*. Frankfurt a.M.: Suhrkamp Taschenbuch Verlag, 1974.

Wegele, Dora. "Malwida von Meysenbug und Theodor Althaus. Ein Beitrag zur Geschichte der vormaerzlichen Demokratie." *Deutscher Staat und deutsche Parteien . . . Friedrich Meinecke zum 60. Geburtstag dargebracht*. Edited by Paul Wentscke. Munich and Berlin: R. Oldenburg, 1922.

Wehler, Hans-Ulrich, ed. *Historische Familienforschung und Demographie: Geschichte und Gesellschaft. Zeitschrift fuer Historische Sozialwissenschaft* 1 (1975): nos 2/3.

Weigelt, Georg. *Christliche und humane Menschenliebe: Zur Erinnerung an Frau Emilie Wuestenfeld*. Hamburg: Otto Meissner, 1875.

Werdemann, Hermann. *Die evangelische Pfarrfrau: Ihre Geschichte in vier Jahrhunderten*. Witten: Westdeutscher Lutherverlag, 1935.

Wuppermann, Carl Wilhelm. *Kurhessen seit dem Freiheitskriege*. Cassel: Theodor Fischer, 1850.

Index

About the Author

CATHERINE M. PRELINGER is Associate Editor of *The Papers of Benjamin Franklin* at Yale University. A former president of the Berkshire Conference of Women Historians, her articles have appeared in books and journals including *German Women in the Eighteenth and Nineteenth Centuries, German Women in the Nineteenth Century, Women and Religion in America: Vol. II: The Eighteenth Century, Women in New Worlds Vol. II,* and *Church History.*